MW01712484

Speed keys used in the Edit screen (continued)

Ctrl-U	Underline the current word
Ctrl-V	Check spelling of the rest of the document
Ctrl-W	Delete the current word
Ctrl-X	Center the current line
Ctrl-Y	Turn drawing on/off
Ctrl-Z	Move cursor to end of current tabs or margins section
Ctrl-[	Select new left and right margins
Ctrl-PrtSc	Enter the Preview mode
Alt-0	Begin working with macros
Del	Delete current block and copy it to the clipboard

Speed keys used in the Preview mode

Alt-A	List currently available fonts
Alt-D	List the fonts used in the working copy
Alt-F	Change a font
Alt-P	Change the paper size
Alt-S	Set new print styles
Alt-V	Change the view
Alt-X	Return to previous position in the working copy

UNDERSTANDING PROFESSIONAL WRITE™

GERRY LITTON

SYBEX®

San Francisco • Paris • Düsseldorf • Soest

Acquisitions Editor: Dianne King
Editor: Alan Hislop
Technical Editor: Aziz Khatri
Word Processors: Scott Campbell and Chris Mockel
Layout and Chapter Art: Suzanne Albertson
Technical Art: Jeffrey James Giese
Typesetter: Robert Myren
Proofreader: Ed Lin
Indexer: Julie Kawabata
Cover Designer: Thomas Ingalls + Associates
Cover Photographer: Mark Johnson

Library of Congress Card Number: 89-63173
ISBN 0-89588-656-1

Manufactured in the United States of America
10 9 8 7 6 5 4 3 2

To my friends Ellen and Paul

ACKNOWLEDGMENTS

This book is the result of a good deal of energy generated by many people. Special thanks to Alan Hislop, whose editing skills kept the text orderly and coherent.

As always, the staff at Sybex has been helpful, supportive, and uplifting: Dianne King, for her ever-present encouragement and good humor; Barbara Gordon, for helping the team function; Ed Lin, proofreading; Scott Campbell and Chris Mockel, word processing; Aziz Khatri, technical editing; Suzanne Albertson, layout and chapter art; Jeff Giese, technical art; and Julie Kawabata, indexing.

My thanks also to the staff of Software Publishing Corporation for their assistance with this project. In particular, Bill Dawson, Brian Fordyce, and Angelica Bruno generously gave their time to make sure that my ignorance was properly enlightened.

I would also like to express appreciation to Joe Marenin and Terry Mitchell of the Hewlett-Packard Corporation for their support and assistance.

Contents at a Glance

Table of Contents

INTRODUCTION

Recent years have seen a competitive trend among many word processing packages to include more and more features. Not only are many of these features of little use to the average user, but—worse yet—they have contributed to a general increase in the complexity of these packages.

As a result, many of the popular word processors are both expensive and difficult to learn. The number of books and training courses available on any of these packages pays tribute to the difficulty of learning how to use them.

Professional Write is an outstanding exception.

This modestly-priced word processor is extremely easy to use, yet it contains many sophisticated features often associated with the more costly packages. Professional Write treads the "middle road": It doesn't contain every single feature that you could possibly imagine, yet it offers more than enough power to satisfy the needs of all but the most demanding users.

For the novice, Professional Write can be run as a completely menu-driven system. The pull-down menus are very well organized, so that even a beginner can easily perform all of the basic word processing operations without having to memorize any commands.

More experienced users can take advantage of Professional Write's large array of commands (called *speed keys* by Professional Write). These can be utilized instead of the menus for performing the more common operations, and they greatly enhance the speed with which documents can be created and edited.

Professional Write contains many desktop-publishing features that can be used for producing professional-looking documents. One of the most important of these features is that a wide assortment of printers can be used. In particular, laser printers are extremely well-supported by the software.

In addition, Professional Write's Preview mode displays on the screen how a document will appear when printed. This feature can be used for making design changes to a document while you are in the process of creating it.

Other desktop-publishing features include the ability to incorporate into a document lines and boxes, as well as graphs from a variety of software packages such as PFS:First Choice, PFS:First Graphics, Harvard Presentation Graphics, and others.

Professional Write contains many other features that are often associated with high-priced word processors, such as an easy-to-use spelling checker and thesaurus; the capability of creating your own personal dictionaries; a built-in calculator; and the ability to import files from other types of software packages, including spreadsheet and database programs, as well as other word processors.

The software contains an independent module that can be used for creating and maintaining one or more name and address files, a convenient way to easily access personal information that's used on a daily basis. In addition, a mail-merging feature allows you to create customized form letters and other standard forms, using the data from these name and address files.

Professional Write also enables you to create macros, which can be used for simplifying your work by automating tasks performed on a routine basis. Like the other features of this software package, macros are easy to use, and they can greatly enhance the efficiency of working with documents.

Why do you need a book to learn to use this program, when you have the manual that comes with the software? The manual is first-rate, and this book isn't intended to replace it, but *Understanding Professional Write* does have several features that the manual doesn't offer. To begin with, this book is designed to be used in either of two ways. First, you can use it as an online tutorial and follow along with the many useful examples as you learn about each feature.

You can also use this book as a reference guide. It contains descriptions of all of Professional Write's features, and the table of contents and index will help you find the section you need. After you have read the general description of a topic, you can study the associated examples to learn more about that particular subject. And, as an additional reference aid, tables and summaries that serve as quick guides to frequently used keystrokes and commands can be found inside the front and back covers.

This book also alerts you to some pitfalls that you might encounter when using the software. I can't guarantee to keep you completely out of trouble, but the margin notes draw your attention to particularly important or confusing items to help you avoid problems whenever possible. In addition, Appendix B contains a list of many commonly encountered problems, as well as their solutions.

HOW TO USE THIS BOOK

If you haven't yet installed Professional Write, you'll probably want to turn to Appendix A first. It gives step-by-step instructions for installing the software and customizing it for your system.

After you have installed Professional Write, read the first two chapters, which describe how to get started using the package. The more elementary editing features are covered in these chapters, and this information will allow you to begin to use Professional Write effectively.

Chapters 3 through 6 cover all of the basic features used when creating and editing documents. These include block operations, setting page layout features such as tabs and margins, and many others.

Chapters 7 through 10 can be read after you have mastered the basics of the software. These chapters cover the more intricate topics dealing with file management, printing, and fonts. If you're planning to use a laser printer with Professional Write, Chapter 8 will be of particular interest because it presents an orderly explanation to the confusing issue of laser printers and fonts.

Chapters 11 through 16 cover the advanced features to be found within Professional Write. These include page previewing, generating form letters, and using macros.

Appendix B is a compilation of the problems most likely to be encountered when using Professional Write. Each problem is described, and then the most likely causes are indicated, as well as the way to eliminate the problem.

1 PROFESSIONAL WRITE BASICS

STARTING PROFESSIONAL WRITE

Before reading this chapter, you must make sure that Professional Write is correctly installed for your computer. If you are installing the software for the first time, follow the instructions given in Appendix A, which covers installation both for hard-disk and floppy-disk computers. Also, make sure that you have a blank, formatted data disk that you can use for saving practice documents. Instructions for creating a data disk are also given in Appendix A.

The following sections describe how to start up Professional Write on hard-disk and floppy-disk computers. If your computer does not have a hard disk, you can skip the next section and go directly to the following one, "Floppy-Disk Computers."

HARD-DISK COMPUTERS

You should already have installed Professional Write in its own directory on the hard disk. If you haven't done so, go through the instructions in Appendix A before reading any further.

Starting Professional Write from a hard disk is easy. First, you select the directory in which the Professional Write program is stored; then you enter a command to run the program. For example, if you followed the installation procedure described in Appendix A, Professional Write will be on a directory named \PW. To run Professional Write, type in the following two DOS commands:

```
CD \PW
PW
```

(Remember to press the Enter key (↵) after each command. In this book, the ↵ symbol is used to indicate the Enter key.) The first of these commands selects the directory \PW, and the second command tells DOS to begin running Professional Write. After a brief pause, the Main menu will appear (Figure 1.1).

FLOPPY-DISK COMPUTERS

You can also run Professional Write from a computer that doesn't have a hard disk. Without a hard disk, your computer must have at least two floppy disk drives in order to run the software.

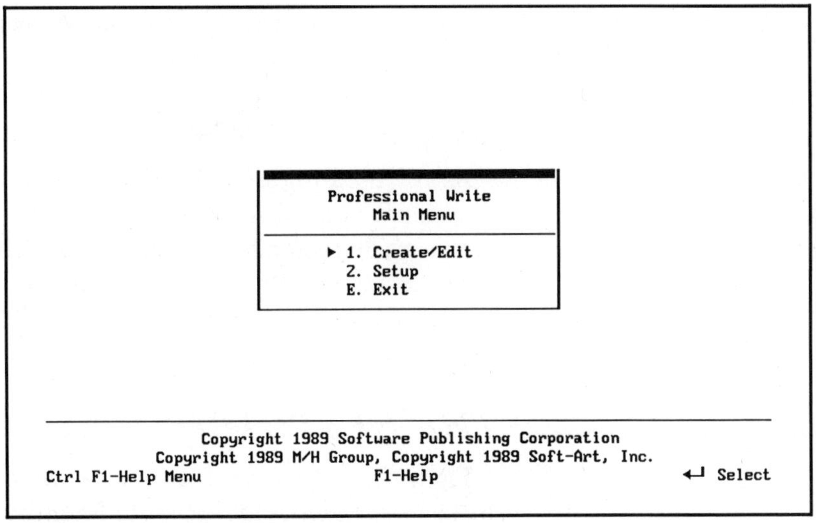

Figure 1.1: Professional Write's Main menu

See Appendix A for the procedure on making backup disks.

Before going on, make sure that you're using a backup copy of Professional Write rather than the original software disks. Your originals should be stored in a safe place and should be used only if you need to create a new backup copy.

If your computer uses 5¼-inch floppies:

1. Insert the disk labeled "Start Up Disk, Disk 1" into drive A.
2. Type **PW**, then press ↵.
3. Wait until you see a screen message telling you to insert the program disk.
4. Remove the Start Up disk from drive A and place it in drive B.
5. Insert the disk labeled "Program Disk, Disk 2" into drive A.
6. Press ↵ to begin the program.

If your computer uses 3½-inch floppies:

1. Insert the disk labeled "Start Up and Program Disk, Disk 1" into drive A.
2. Type **PW**, then press ↵.

After a brief pause, Professional Write's Main menu will appear (Figure 1.1), and you're ready to begin.

A Note on Using Floppies

As you use Professional Write, from time to time you'll see a message appear on the screen, asking you to replace one floppy with another. The reason for the message is that Professional Write needs to access a file that's not currently in a disk drive. Follow the directions given by these prompts.

THE KEYBOARD

Figure 1.2 shows some common keyboard layouts. As you can see, the keyboard layout for letters and numbers is the same as the layout on a standard typewriter. In one respect, the Shift keys also function like the ones on a typewriter: You press them to get uppercase letters, and to get some of the special characters—such as @ and # paired with the numbers 2 and 3 at the top of the keyboard.

KEYS TO KNOW ABOUT

Shift This key functions pretty much like the equivalent typewriter key, in that you use it to enter uppercase letters. You also use it to enter alternate values on the various keys.

Num Lock This key controls the keys on the numeric keypad—the 11 keys on the right-hand side of the keyboard. Normally, Num Lock is off and the keys are used for cursor control. (The IBM enhanced keyboard has a separate set of cursor-control keys.) When Num Lock is on, the keys are used for the digits 0 through 9 and the decimal point. The Num Lock key is a toggle: Press it once to turn Num Lock on; press it again to turn Num Lock off.

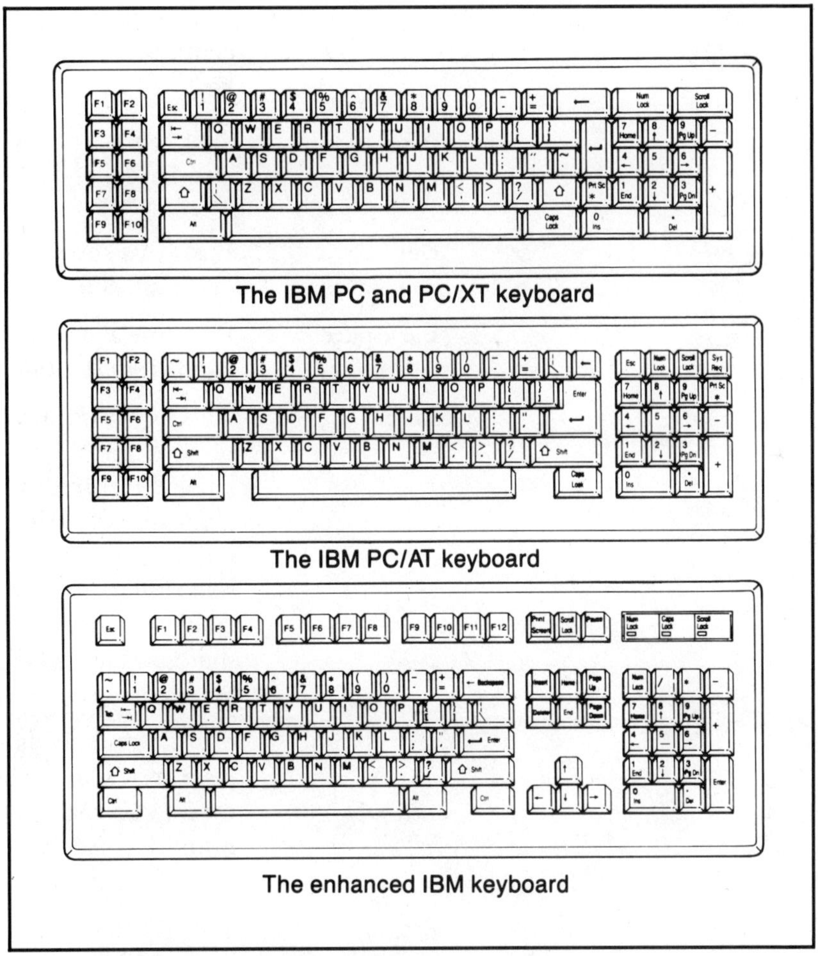

Figure 1.2: The IBM PC, PC/AT, and enhanced keyboards

Caps Lock This is another toggle key: Press it once and the letter keys are locked into uppercase; press it again to unlock the letters back to lowercase. Only the letter keys are affected by the Caps Lock key; none of the other keys is shifted.

Ctrl Like the Shift key, this key is used together with other keys. To use the Ctrl key, hold it down and then press another key. For special purposes, Professional Write uses several combinations of the Ctrl key plus another key.

Alt This key is also used in combination with other keys: Hold it down and then press another key.

Del Press this key and the character *directly over the cursor* is deleted.

Backspace Press the Backspace (⟵) key and the character *to the left of the cursor* is deleted.

Enter This key is usually labeled Enter, ↵, or both. On some older keyboards the key is labeled Return. It has a variety of uses in Professional Write. For example, in pull-down menus the Enter key is used to select the item that's currently highlighted. In dialog boxes, you press ↵ to indicate that you have finished making choices.

Cursor keys Four keys are used for moving the cursor up, down, left, and right within a menu. These keys are usually labelled ↑, ↓, ←, and →. On most keyboards, these keys will also have numerical labels (8, 2, 4, 6) because they are part of the numeric keypad.

Esc This is the Escape key. It is used mainly to back out of whatever you're doing at the moment. When you press Esc, Professional Write usually returns to what you were previously doing.

PgUp & PgDn These two keys, located on the right-hand side of the keyboard, are used for moving up and down the screen one entire page of text at a time rather than line by line.

Function Keys The ten (or twelve) keys labeled F1 through F10 are called function keys. Each is used for

	a special purpose by Professional Write, and you'll learn what these purposes are as you progress through the book.
Help	This is the F1 key, which calls up Professional Write's extensive Help system. You'll find out more about the Help system later in this chapter.

WORKING WITH MENUS

Professional Write's Main menu (Figure 1.1) is typical of many menus that you'll see as you work with the program: a series of items is presented on the screen, from which you select one. When a menu appears, usually the top item is highlighted. For example, in the Main menu the cursor is initially positioned at *1. Create/Edit*.

HOW TO SELECT A MENU ITEM

The easiest way to select an item is simply to press the number or letter of the item you want. For example, if the Main menu is displayed on the screen and you want to create a new document or edit an existing one, press the key labeled "1" at the top of the keyboard. (You can also use the numeric keypad at the right-hand side of the keyboard, but only if you first press the Num Lock key.)

You can also select a menu item with the following two steps:

1. Use the ↑ and ↓ keys to highlight the item you want.
2. Press the ↵ key to select that item.

THE MAIN MENU

Figure 1.1 shows the Main menu that appears after the software begins to run. This menu contains the following items:

- **1. Create/Edit:** Use this selection to create a new document or edit an existing one.

- **2. Setup:** Use this selection to customize the program for your particular hardware. The first time you run Professional Write on your computer, you'll probably want to select *Setup* so that you can tailor the software to your own computer system. You can also use this menu item at any time to change any of the current installation values (for example, if you change printers).
- **E. Exit:** Select this item to exit from Professional Write back to DOS.

You can use the Help key, F1, to display information about any of the items on the Main menu. For information about the Help system, see "Getting On-Line Help" later in this chapter.

EXPLORING THE EDIT SCREEN

If you select *Create/Edit* from the Main menu, the Edit screen will appear, as shown in Figure 1.3. This is where you'll create new documents or edit existing ones. Some of the elements in this display provide you with information, while others are used for specific purposes. These elements are explored below.

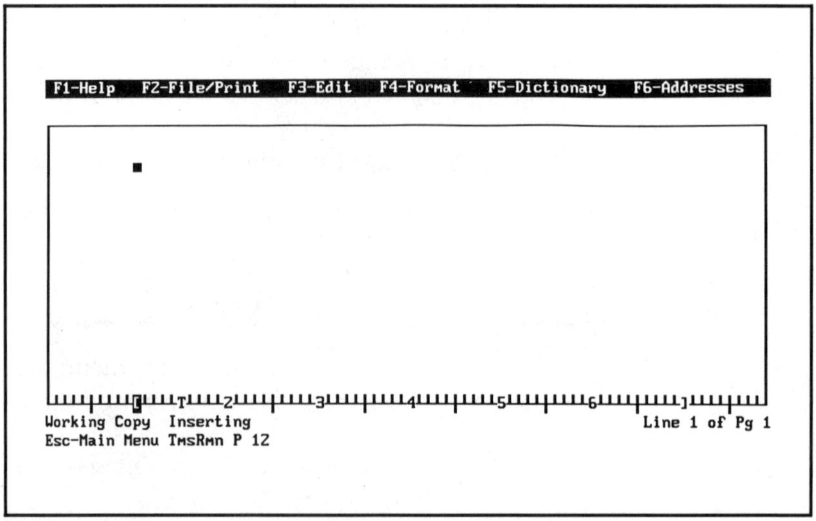

Figure 1.3: The Edit screen, where you enter and edit text

TEXT CURSOR

The text cursor is the blinking box or line that appears on-screen. Any text you enter will appear exactly where the cursor is positioned on the screen. By the same token, when you want to delete text, you must first move the cursor to the appropriate place on the screen.

RULER

The Ruler is the third line up from the bottom of the screen. It displays the following information:

- **Column numbers**. The columns on the screen are numbered from 1 (the leftmost column) to 80 (at the right-hand end of the screen). Each column is indicated by a short vertical line on the Ruler. For example, column number 20 is indicated by the number *2*, column 30 by *3*, and so on.
- **Margin settings**. The left and right margins are indicated by square brackets ([and]). Initially, these margins are set by Professional Write at columns 10 and 70.
- **Tab settings**. Each setting is indicated by a T or D on the Ruler. As you can see, one tab is preset at column 15.
- **Cursor position**. The current cursor position is always indicated by the solid box on the Ruler. As you move the cursor, the box also moves, so that you always know the cursor's exact column position.

STATUS LINE

The status line is the second line from the bottom of the screen. It provides information that will be helpful to you when working with a document:

- **Document name**. If you are working with a document retrieved from a disk file, the name of that document is listed here. (You'll learn how to name a document later on.) If you're creating a new document, then the title "Working Copy" appears. (See later in this chapter for a discussion of the working copy.)

- **Insert/Overwrite mode**. If you are in the Insert text-editing mode, the word *Inserting* appears. On the other hand, if you are in the Overwrite mode, this part of the Status line is blank. These two text-editing modes are discussed later in this chapter.
- **Line** *n* **of page** *m*. The line and page numbers tell you exactly where the cursor is at any instant. The default page length is 54 lines. When you start the word processor, the cursor is positioned at column 10 of the first line of the first page.
- **0%**. This indicator tells you how much computer memory is available for your document. Initially, when you first begin a new document, the memory is empty, or 0% full. See later in this chapter for a discussion of the maximum possible document size that you can generate.

MESSAGE LINE

The message line is the bottom line on the screen. It contains the following bits of information:

- The words *Esc-Main Menu*, which simply remind you how to exit from Professional Write.
- Information about the current font (only if you're using a font printer). For example, in Figure 1.3, the entry "TmsRmn P 12" means that the current font is Times Roman 12 point Portrait.

See Chapters 8 and 9 for details about fonts.

MENU BAR

The top of the screen is called the *menu bar*. Each of the six items on the bar (except the first one) represents a pull-down menu. To select one of these menus, press the corresponding function key and that menu will appear.

The first item on the menu bar is special case: Press F1 to get help with what you are doing at the moment.

The menu bar is easy to use. For example:

1. Press the F3 key to select the Edit menu (Figure 1.4).
2. You can move from one pull-down menu to another simply

```
▸ 1. Insert blank line  Ctrl-I
  2. Delete word        Ctrl-W
  3. Delete line        Ctrl-L
  ------------------------------
  4. Mark text          Ctrl-T
  5. Mark rectangle     Ctrl-R
  6. Paste              Ctrl-P
  ------------------------------
  7. Boldface word      Ctrl-B
  8. Underline word     Ctrl-U
  ------------------------------
  9. Draw lines
  ------------------------------
  A. Find & Replace     Ctrl-F
  ------------------------------
  B. Calculate          Ctrl-M
```

Figure 1.4: The Edit pull-down menu

by pressing one of the function keys F2 through F6. For example, press the F4 key to select the Format menu.

3. You can also move from one menu to another by pressing the ← and → cursor keys. For example, if you are in the Format menu and you press the ← key once, the Edit menu reappears.
4. To exit from a menu, press Esc.

AN OVERVIEW OF THE EDIT SCREEN MENUS

Professional Write's pull-down menus, listed on the Menu bar, provide access to the program's features. This section will briefly describe the contents of each menu. You might want to select each menu as you read about it. The descriptions will contain a number of terms that may be unfamiliar, but they will become clear as you read through the text.

The File/Print menu contains several different types of selections. From this menu you can retrieve an existing file, save a duplicate of your current work, delete files, or insert another document into your current work. From this menu you can also print your work in progress or display an on-screen preview of how the printed page will appear. You can also use this menu to delete your current work from the computer's memory. Finally, the File/Print menu can be used for working with macros.

The Edit menu is used primarily for making changes to your current work, but it has other functions as well. Selections are available for inserting blank lines, deleting various bits and pieces of text, and changing the style of individual words (boldfacing and underlining). You can also initiate block operations from this menu. Other operations with the menu include drawing straight lines, finding and replacing selected text strings, and using the built-in calculator.

The Format menu contains selections that control the physical layout of a document. These include margin, tab, and indent settings, insertion of headers and footers, single or double spacing, and line justification.

The Dictionary menu is used for spell-checking and finding synonyms. You can check the spelling of a single word or all or part of a document.

The Addresses menu is used for working with Professional Write's address book feature. You can create a new address book or work with an existing one, adding or deleting entries. You can also control the content and format of information copied from an address book into the working copy.

GETTING ON-LINE HELP

No matter what you are doing in Professional Write, you can get help by pressing the Help key, F1. This Help system is called *context sensitive* because the information that you get depends on what you're doing at the moment. This system is comprehensive, and through it you can learn a great deal about the software's capabilities.

HELP FOR PULL-DOWN MENUS

When you're working with a menu, the Help key (F1) can be used to remind you of the purpose of any particular menu item: Simply highlight the desired item with the ↑ and ↓ keys, and then press the Help key.

The following exercise will show you how Help works:

1. Press F3 to pull down the Edit menu (Figure 1.4).
2. Use the cursor keys to highlight *7. Boldface word.*
3. Press F1, and you'll see a screenful of information about this item, as shown in Figure 1.5.

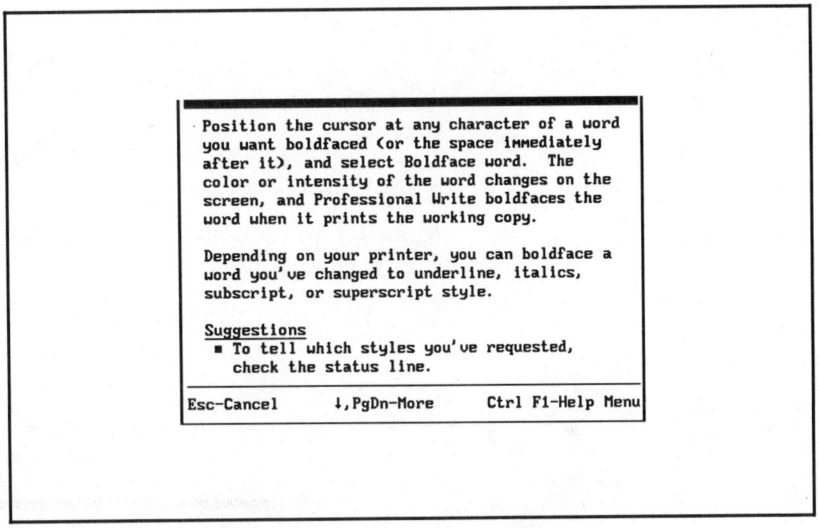

Figure 1.5: A Help display with information on boldfacing

At the bottom of this display, you'll see a list of keys that can be used for various purposes:

- Press the Esc key to exit from the Help display.
- Press the ↓ or PgDn keys to display more information. This is called *scrolling* down. You can also use the ↑ and PgUp keys to scroll back up.
- Press the Ctrl-F1 key combination to display a complete menu of topics for which on-line help is available.

When you're through reading the on-line help about boldfacing, press the Esc key to return to the Edit screen.

GETTING HELP ABOUT A PARTICULAR TOPIC

If you want to find out about a particular subject, the Help facility may be useful to you. To begin, display the Help menu. Then select the topic you want, and relevant information about this subject will be displayed.

For example, suppose you want to learn about printing envelopes. Here's how you would use the Help system:

1. Display the main Help menu by pressing Ctrl-F1 (Figure 1.6).
2. Select the topic you want: Use the ↓ and ↑ keys to highlight the appropriate entry (in this case, *Printing*) and then press ↵ to select it.
3. Another menu appears, displaying a list of topics dealing with printing (Figure 1.7).
4. Select the appropriate entry (in this case, *Printing envelopes*), and a screenful of useful information will appear (Figure 1.8).
5. When you are done scrolling through this information, press Esc to return to the Edit screen.

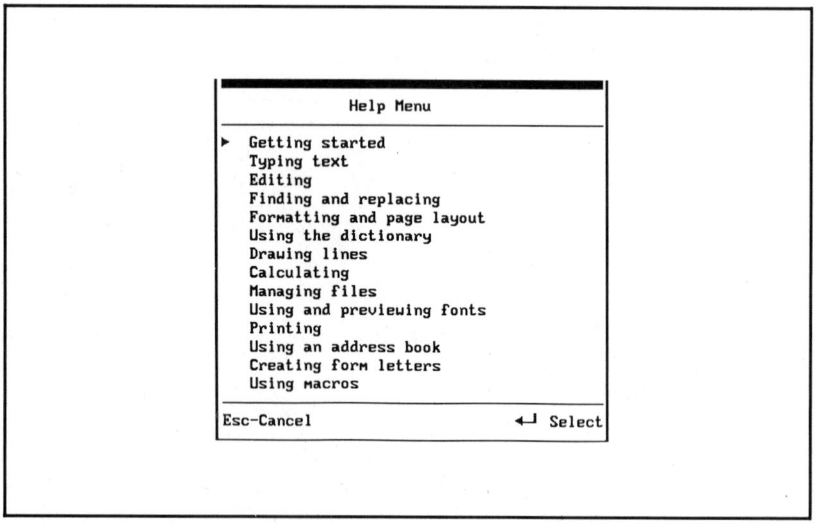

Figure 1.6: The main Help menu

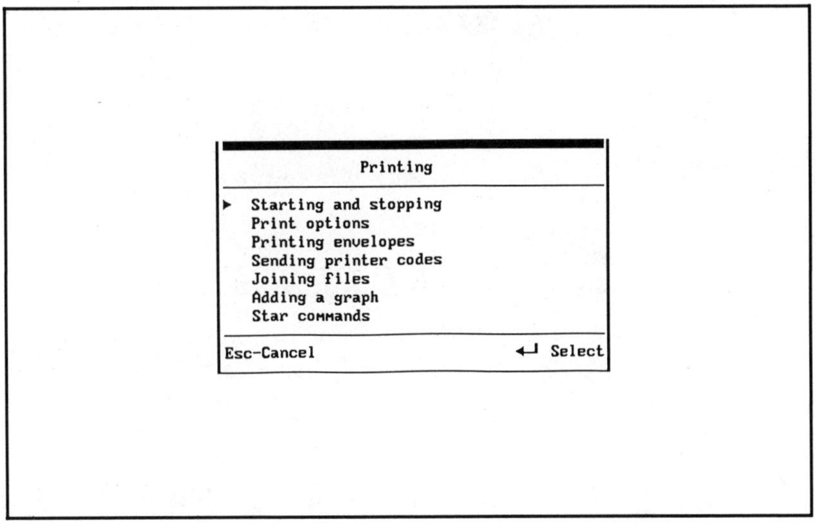

Figure 1.7: A menu of topics related to printing

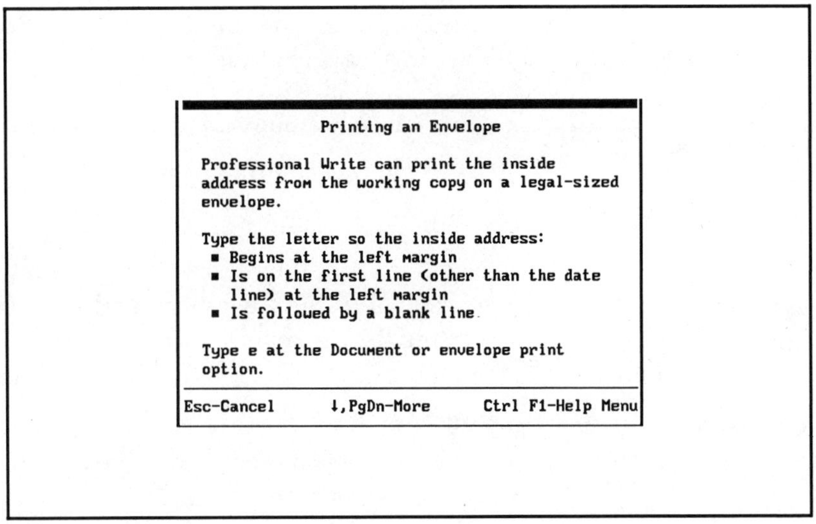

Figure 1.8: A Help display with information about printing

OTHER TYPES OF HELP

If a menu is not being displayed when you press the Help key, you'll see a screenload of information relevant to what you're doing at the moment. For instance, if you're editing text and you press F1, you'll see a list of keystrokes that can be used for cursor movement.

WORD PROCESSING BASICS

The first time that you begin to enter text into a word processor, you may find that strange and unexpected things happen. The following sections will give you some helpful hints.

INSERT AND OVERWRITE MODES

Professional Write can operate in either of two editing modes: Insert and Overwrite. The default mode—the mode that is automatically selected each time Professional Write begins running—is initially set to Insert. You can change the default mode by calling the Setup program from the Main menu (See Appendix A for details.) You can always tell which mode is in effect by the shape of the cursor:

- In *Insert* mode the cursor is a blinking rectangle.
- In *Overwrite* mode the cursor is a blinking line.

The Insert mode is normally used for text entry and editing. On the other hand, the Overwrite mode may occasionally be more convenient. You can move back and forth between the two modes by pressing the Ins key.

If you accidentally press the Ins key and don't notice that the cursor has changed to the Overwrite mode, you'll nevertheless soon notice that your editing is not doing what you had expected. Simply press the Ins key to return to the Insert mode and continue editing.

Insert Mode

When new text is entered at the current cursor position, any existing text beyond the cursor (to the right and down) is pushed over to make room for the new text. If text runs over beyond the right margin, Professional Write will automatically reformat that line and any lines after that if necessary, to the end of the paragraph.

Overwrite Mode

In this mode, new text overwrites existing text at the cursor position. In other words, existing text is not pushed over to accommodate new text. If you want to overwrite existing text, move the cursor to the beginning of the material to be replaced and then enter the Overwrite mode by pressing the Ins key. Enter the new text, which will replace the old text character for character. This method of text editing is useful provided that the new text is exactly the same length as the original.

This mode is also useful when editing columns of text or numbers. Otherwise, for general text editing, the Insert mode is usually more convenient.

THE WORKING COPY

Whenever you are working on a document—either creating a new one or editing an old one—it resides in the computer's memory (RAM). This document is called the *working copy*. If you have just retrieved a document from a disk file, then the working copy is an exact duplicate of that document. However, as you make changes to the working copy, adding or deleting text or changing numbers, *the original document on disk remains unchanged.* If you accidentally erase the entire working copy (it's not hard to do), you can still fall back on the original document on disk: Simply retrieve the orginal back into Professional Write and begin editing again.

Whenever you are working with a document in the working copy, you should take care to protect it by periodically saving a duplicate of it. For example, if you are working on a new document and you accidentally erase the working copy, you can fall back on the last version of the working copy you saved. You'll learn how to save documents in Chapter 2.

The working copy is preserved until you exit from Professional Write. For example, suppose that during the editing of a document you decide to change one of Professional Write's default settings. You can safely exit from the Edit screen back to the Main menu, select *Setup* to change the default, and then finally return to the Edit screen. Your work will be displayed because the working copy hasn't been touched.

LIMITATIONS ON DOCUMENT SIZE

Because any document on which you're working must reside in the computer's memory, there is an upper limit to the size of document that you can create. The maximum possible size depends on the amount of free memory in your computer. For example, with left and right margins set to one inch and with every line completely filled with text, you can generate a document of approximately 50 single-spaced pages. This is for a computer with 640K of memory and with no memory-resident programs. Generally, for a 640K machine the maximum size will actually be somewhat longer than 50 pages because of the amount of unused space on most pages.

If your computer has a LIM extended memory board (if you don't know what this is, don't worry about it), the maximum size document may be considerably larger than 50 pages. Again, the length will depend on the amount of available RAM memory, which in turn depends on what memory-resident programs exist when Professional Write is running. You can easily find out the maximum size document that you can create with your particular hardware setup by using the following steps, the details of which are described later in Chapter 3:

1. Fill an entire single page with characters.
2. Copy this page to Professional Write's clipboard.
3. Copy the contents of the clipboard back into the document over and over, until the % indicator on the Edit screen reaches 100%.
4. Move the cursor to the end of the document.

The status line will indicate the page number, which tells you approximately how lengthy your documents can become.

2 Working with a New Document

NOW THAT YOU'VE BEEN INTRODUCED TO THE keyboard, to the word processor's Edit screen and Help menu, and to some of the basic concepts of word processing, it's time to begin using the software to create a simple document.

This chapter describes the basic techniques for creating and editing documents. You'll also learn how to print and save a document that you have created. Finally, you'll learn the steps for retrieving an existing document back into Professional Write.

If possible, follow along on your own computer by duplicating the examples in this chapter.

GETTING STARTED

Each time you begin a session with Professional Write, you'll need to go through the procedure described at the beginning of Chapter 1 for getting the software running. If you're going to be using a document that you previously created and saved, you'll need to read it into Professional Write; see "How to Retrieve an Existing Document" later in this chapter.

Generally, the term *document* describes any type of text that you create with Professional Write—a letter, a report, or a memorandum, for example. Creating a document requires these basic steps:

- Starting up Professional Write and then selecting *Create/Edit* from the Main menu
- Entering the text at the keyboard
- Making corrections as needed, using the editing features of the word processor
- Periodically saving a duplicate of the working copy to a disk file
- When finished, saving a copy of the working copy to disk and then (if you wish) printing a copy of the document
- Exiting from Professional Write or beginning work on another document

CREATING A NEW DOCUMENT

To create a new document, you simply begin entering text into a blank working copy. If the working copy isn't blank, see "How to Start Over" later in this chapter.

Keeping in mind a few simple things as you are working at the keyboard will save you considerable trouble. You might want to make a note of these—mental or otherwise—before you begin typing:

- The cursor moves along with new text on the screen; and it's always exactly at the spot where the next character will appear on the screen.
- If you make errors as you type, you can either stop to fix each one, or you can wait until you have typed for a while and then go back and edit the errors all at once.
- If you notice a typing error as soon as it occurs, you can delete the last characters that you just entered by pressing the ⟵ key one or more times.
- As you enter text, you do not press ↵ at the end of each line. One of the advantages of using a word processor like Professional Write is that it keeps track of lines for you. When a word is too long to fit on the current line, it is automatically moved down to the next line. This is called automatic *wordwrap* or *reformatting*. These two terms are interchangeable.
- When you reach the end of a paragraph or when you want to enter a new element (a line in a street address, for example) *then* press ↵. This key will automatically start a new paragraph.

Example

Make sure that the Edit screen is displayed (Figure 1.3). Then begin by entering the following paragraph at the keyboard:

> **Hi, Tom. I just wanted to let you know that our monthly sales meeting will be held on Monday at the Fish Grotto restaurant. Hope to see you then!**

When you finish, your screen should resemble Figure 2.1. Don't worry about errors that you notice after you've finished; you'll learn how to take care of these shortly.

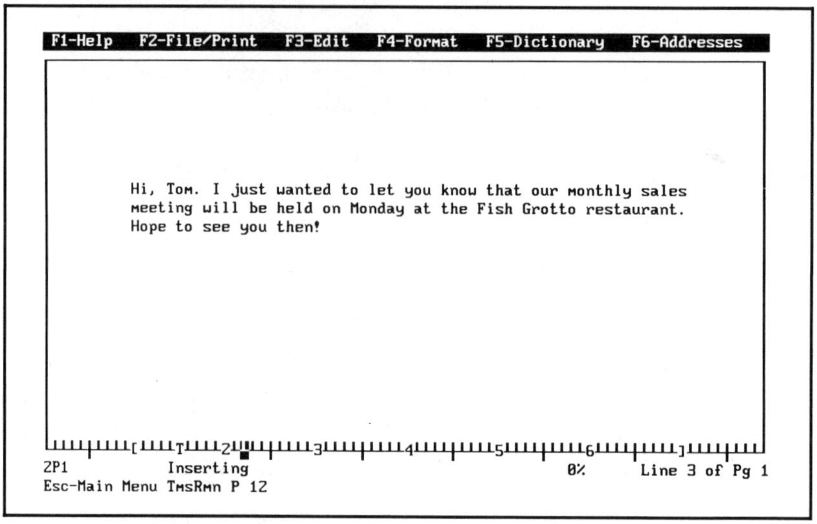

Figure 2.1: A simple document

MAKING CORRECTIONS TO YOUR TEXT

After you've entered some text, you'd probably like to make changes or improvements, such as replacing text, adding a sentence, splitting one paragraph into two, or deleting text. In order to make any of these changes, you must move the cursor around the screen. Let's look at some cursor movement techniques.

MOVING THE CURSOR

The four cursor keys, ←, →, ↑, and ↓, can be used to move the cursor one character at a time in any direction. If you hold one of these keys down, the cursor will pick up speed.

If you have two or three text lines on the screen, practice using the cursor keys:

1. Press the ← key several times. Notice how the cursor moves.
2. Continue pressing the ← key until the cursor is at the beginning of a line.
3. Now press the ← key once more. Notice how the cursor jumps to the end of the previous line.
4. Hold the ← key down: This is one way to move the cursor rapidly.
5. Practice using the other cursor keys.
6. If you hold the ↓ key down, you'll see your text scroll off the top of the screen. You can scroll it back by holding down the ↑ key.

The end of each line is determined by the right margin setting.

Other Ways to Move the Cursor

The inside cover of this book lists all of the cursor-movement keystrokes.

In addition to the four basic cursor keys, there are several other methods of moving the cursor around the screen. Table 2.1 lists some of them. You may want to become familiar with the keystrokes in this table, because many of the examples later in this chapter emphasize their use.

Note that by continuing to press the → key, you can move the cursor beyond the last character of a line, as far as the right margin. Similarly, if the cursor is positioned at the right margin, pressing the ↑ key moves the cursor straight up to the end of the previous line—even if no character is there. This feature is somewhat different from many other word processors, but although it takes a little getting used to, it's usually not a problem when editing text.

CHANGING EXISTING TEXT

In order to change a specific part of the text, you must move the cursor to that location. First, be sure the word processor is still in the Insert mode—the word *Inserting* should appear on the Status line. If it doesn't, press the Ins key once.

Example

In the paragraph shown in Figure 2.1, here's how to change the word *Monday* to *Thursday*:

1. Move the cursor to the beginning of the word *Monday*.
2. Using the Del key, remove the entire word. Did you notice that pressing the Del key deletes the character at the cursor position and that the remaining text automatically moves left to fill in the space created by the deleted characters?
3. Now enter the word *Thursday*; make sure that there's a space after the word. Notice how the text automatically moves to make room for the new characters.

Table 2.1: Cursor Movement Operations

KEYSTROKE(S)	CURSOR MOVES TO
←	left by one character
→	right by one character
↑	up by one line
↓	down by one line
Ctrl-→	beginning of next word
Ctrl-←	beginning of previous word
Tab	next tab setting
Shift-Tab	previous tab setting
Home	beginning of current line
End	end of current line
Ctrl-Enter	beginning of next line
PgDn	beginning of next screen (down)
PgUp	beginning of previous screen (up)
Ctrl-PgDn	beginning of next document page
Ctrl-PgUp	beginning of previous document page
Ctrl-Home	beginning of document
Ctrl-End	end of document

Example

Here's an example of how the Overwrite mode can be used:

1. Switch to the Overwrite mode by pressing the Ins key once. Note that the word *Inserting* disappears from the Status line.
2. Move the cursor to the beginning of the word *Thursday*.
3. Enter the word *Saturday*, watching what happens on the screen.
4. Return to the Insert mode by pressing the Ins key.
5. Move the cursor to the beginning of the word *Saturday*. Using the Del key, delete *Saturday* and reinsert *Monday*.

QUESTION: What happens if you skip step 4?

CREATING BLANK LINES AND NEW PARAGRAPHS

You can use the ↵ key to create a new paragraph or add blank lines wherever you wish within a document. The end of a paragraph is called a *paragraph break*.

- **To create a new paragraph:** Simply press the ↵ key, and the cursor will immediately jump to the beginning of the following line.
- **To add a blank line:** Move the cursor to the end of the line after which a blank line is to be added, and then press ↵.

In a similar manner, you can split a single paragraph into two paragraphs: Move the cursor to the position in the original paragraph where you want the break to occur, and then press ↵. If you want a blank line between the two new paragraphs, press ↵ again. When you press ↵, a special character called a *hard return* is inserted into the text. You can't see this character, but it's there. The hard return is always treated by Professional Write as an instruction to begin a new paragraph.

You can split one paragraph into two, as described above, only if you are in the Insert mode. In the Overwrite mode, pressing ↵ simply moves the cursor to the next line.

Example

The document shown in Figure 2.1 has one serious flaw: There should be a new paragraph after the opening salutation. Here's how to fix this:

1. Make sure that the Insert mode is on.
2. Move the cursor to the third word in the document (*I*).
3. Press ↵, creating a paragraph break.
4. Press ↵ again to create a blank line, and the document should look like the one in Figure 2.2.

COMBINING PARAGRAPHS

You can't combine two paragraphs if they have different margin settings, because Professional Write can't reformat adjacent lines with different margins. For information about margin settings, see Chapter 5.

You can combine two paragraphs into one by deleting the invisible hard return that separates them: Position the cursor *immediately* beyond the last character in the first paragraph, and then press the Del key until the second paragraph joins the first one. (Each time you press Del, you're removing either a trailing blank or an invisible hard return character at the end of the paragraph.) Notice that the text is automatically reformatted as the two paragraphs merge together.

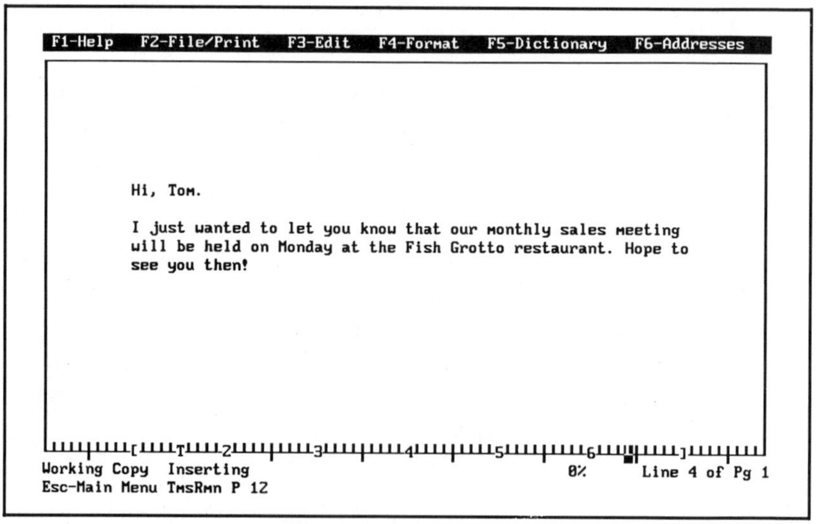

Figure 2.2: A two-paragraph document

ENTERING MORE TEXT

You can add text anywhere in your document. Simply move the cursor to the desired location and enter the new text. As you enter text, Professional Write automatically makes room for it by moving existing text.

Example

Make sure that Professional Write is in the Insert mode. Add the following sentence after the word *restaurant* in your practice document:

We'll be discussing next year's salary increases.

When you're done, the document should look like the one shown in Figure 2.3. If you've made any errors, you may want to correct them before going on.

DELETING TEXT

You can use either of two keys for deleting text one character at a time. Pressing the Del key deletes the character *at the cursor*. Pressing

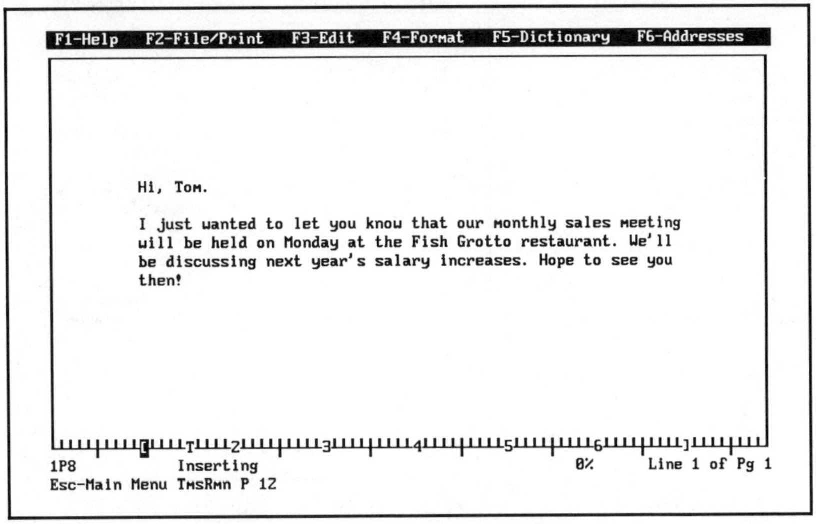

Figure 2.3: The document with a new sentence added

the ⟵ key deletes the character *to the left of the cursor.* The Del key always behaves the same, but the ⟵ key behaves differently in the Insert and Overwrite modes. You may want to experiment to see the difference.

In addition, you can delete an entire word, line, paragraph, or block of text in a single operation. To do this, you'll need to use the Edit menu, as described in the next section.

Deleting a Word

One way to delete an entire word uses the Edit menu:

1. Move the cursor to any letter in the word to be removed.
2. Select the Edit menu by pressing F3. The menu then drops down, as shown in Figure 2.4.
3. Select item 2, *Delete word*, in either of the following ways:
   - Press the key numbered 2.
   - Use the ↓ key to highlight item 2, and then press ↵ to select the item.

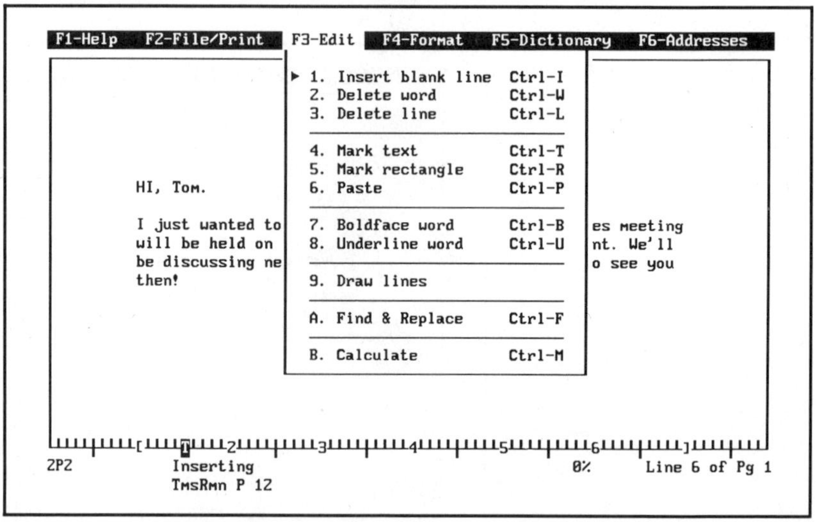

Figure 2.4: The Edit pull-down menu

When you delete a word, the space after the word is also deleted, and the remaining text is reformatted. In fact, you may see the entire paragraph wiggle around as this happens.

Using a Speed Key

Professional Write contains many speed keys, which will be introduced at the appropriate places in the book.

Because deleting a word is such a common operation, Professional Write offers a quick method: using a *speed key*. The speed key for deleting a word is the key combination Ctrl-W (W for *word*). To use it, first hold down the Ctrl key, then press W. By the way, did you notice Ctrl-W on the Edit menu?

Here's how to use this speed key for deleting a word: Move the cursor to any character of the word, and then press Ctrl-W. This method is considerably quicker than using the Edit menu, although the menu is handy if you can't remember which speed key to use.

Example

Here's how to delete the word *Fish* from the practice document in Figure 2.3, by using the speed key:

1. Move the cursor to any character in the word.
2. Press Ctrl-W. The word *Fish* disappears, and the remaining text is reformatted to fill in the space.

Deleting a Line

You can delete an entire line at once, using methods similar to those for deleting a word; you can either use the Edit menu or press the appropriate speed key.

To delete a line using the Edit menu:

1. Move the cursor to any location on the line.
2. Press F3 to pull down the Edit menu.
3. Select item 3, *Delete line*, and the line is deleted from the document.

The speed key for deleting a line is Ctrl-L (L for *line*). To use this speed key, move the cursor to the line to be removed and then press

Ctrl-L. Again, if you forget which speed key to use, you can always use the Edit menu to delete a line. (The menu will also remind you of the correct speed key.) You may want to practice by entering a new line at the bottom of your document and then using the speed key Ctrl-L to delete the line.

To delete a blank line, you can press either Ctrl-L or the Del key. The latter works because Professional Write treats a blank line as a single hard return, which can be deleted just like any other character.

OTHER EDITING FEATURES

This section describes some of the more advanced editing features that are useful from time to time.

HARD SPACES

Normally, Professional Write begins a new line when a word is too long to fit on the current line. This *line break* occurs between whole words.

Sometimes, you may not want to split two separate words between lines. Consider, for example, the name *Sir Richard Holmes*. To avoid the possibility of separating *Sir* and *Richard* on two lines, you would enter a *hard space*, instead of an ordinary space, between the two words. A hard space is recognized by Professional Write as a character other than an ordinary space, so a line break won't be made at a hard space.

To enter a hard space, press Ctrl-Spacebar. The hard space appears on the screen as a little dot. For instance, here's how *Sir Richard* appears with a hard space: Sir·Richard.

You can also use one or more hard spaces to force a printer to underline blank spaces on a page. Some printers will underline only non-blank characters. If you need to underline one or more blanks, write them as hard spaces. Many printers will recognize these as non-blank characters and will cheerfully underline them.

SPECIAL CHARACTERS

You can use a great many characters that are not found on your keyboard. These include Greek characters, letters from other languages, line-drawing characters, mathematical symbols, and some others as well. These characters are built into your computer and are recognized by Professional Write, but you have to be a little tricky to access them.

To enter a special character, you use the ASCII code for that character, which is a number between 1 and 255. Here's how to enter this code: Hold the Alt key down, then enter the ASCII code *using the numeric keypad*. You don't have to press the Num Lock key first, but you can't use the numbers at the top of your keyboard.

You can use the following ASCII codes with Professional Write: 20, 21, and 32 through 255. For example, while holding down the Alt key enter the number 156, and you'll see the symbol £ appear on your screen.

Here's how to display a complete list of all of the special characters and their corresponding ASCII codes:

1. Press Ctrl-F1 to display the main Help menu.
2. Select *Typing text*, then select *ASCII chart for special characters*. When the character list appears, you can scroll through it, making a note of the codes for the character(s) you want.
3. Press Esc until the Edit screen reappears.

Although you can incorporate dozens of different special characters into a document, you may or may not be able to print them, depending on your printer. For example, the characters that a laser printer can output depends on which font sets are currently available to the printer. For more information about printers and fonts, see Chapter 8.

If you are using a dot-matrix printer, a little experimentation may be the fastest way to find out its capabilities: Just enter the special characters you want and then see if your printer will output them.

HOW TO START OVER

If the working copy is a new document, there is no prior version of it on a disk file; if you erase the working copy, it's gone forever (or until you reenter all the text).

Occasionally you may decide that the current version of the working copy is hopeless and that the best thing to do is to begin again. You can easily do this, simply by deleting the entire working copy: First display the File/Print menu, then select item 7, *Erase working copy*.

Erasing a working copy is such a crucial choice that if the contents of the working copy is brand new, Professional Write asks you if you really want to do it (see Figure 2.5). At this point, you can change

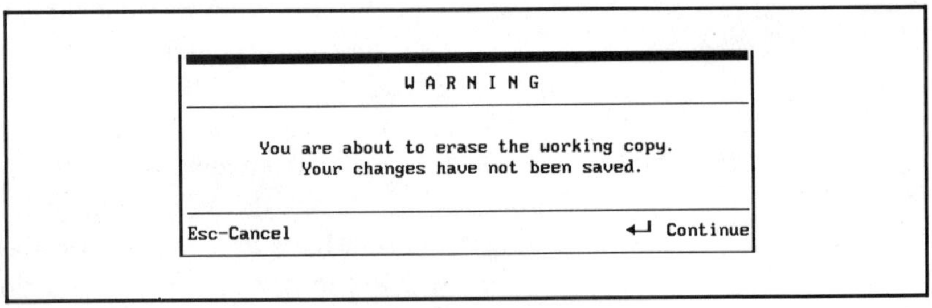

Figure 2.5: Do you really want to erase your work?

In Professional Write, you can usually stop what you are doing by pressing Esc.

your mind by pressing the Esc key. Be warned that once you've erased the working copy, there is no way to retrieve it, unless you happen to have recently saved a copy of it to a disk file.

If your working copy was originally retrieved from a disk file, that file remains unchanged when you erase the working copy. This means that you can retrieve a copy of a document into Professional Write, work with it for a while, and then decide to abandon all of your changes by deleting the working copy; the original document file remains unchanged.

SAVING A COPY OF YOUR DOCUMENT

One of the advantages of using a word processor is that you can save your work, turn off the computer, then come back at a later time and pick up where you left off. You can save your work either to a hard disk (if you have one) or to a floppy. If your work is very long or important, you can choose to save copies both to a hard disk and also to a floppy for added safety.

As you work with a document (that is, with the working copy), it's kept in the computer's main memory. However, if the computer accidentally loses power, or if you make certain types of mistakes, you can easily lose your working copy. You will then have to begin again from the last version that you saved to disk. Even worse, if you are working with a brand new document, there will be no disk file from which to recover your document, and you will need to reenter the entire document.

To prevent this type of disaster, it's a very good idea to copy your document to a disk file periodically. How often you do this is a matter of how much of your work you're willing to risk, but the few seconds spent saving are usually a good investment.

If you're planning to store your document on a new floppy disk, make sure that it's formatted.

To begin the process of saving your work, select *Save working copy* from the File/Print menu. Alternatively, press the speed key Ctrl-S (S for *save*). The Save File dialog box is displayed (Figure 2.6). Within this box, you enter the name of the disk drive, directory, and file name where you want the document to be saved. You can also enter a short description of the file, as well as the data format in which the file is to be saved.

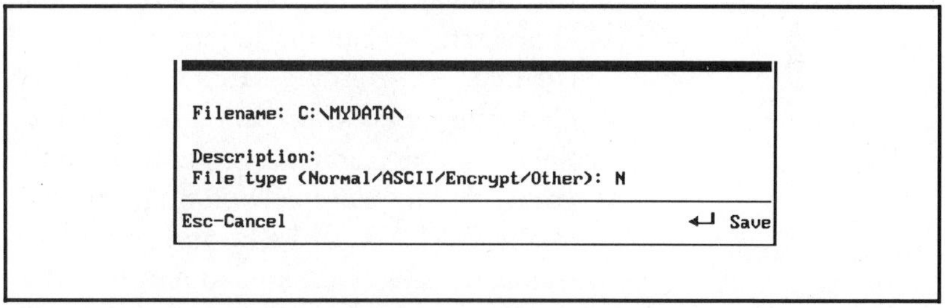

Figure 2.6: The Save File dialog box

Note that when the Save File dialog box first appears, the cursor is positioned at the line labeled *Filename*. This line shows the *current disk drive and/or directory*, that is, where Professional Write expects to read and write document files.

You can overwrite the current contents of the Filename line: Press the speed key Ctrl-E (E for *erase*) to erase the line, then enter the new values for the current disk drive and/or directory.

ENTERING THE DISK DRIVE AND DIRECTORY NAMES

If you're planning to save the working copy to a file on a hard disk, then the default data directory that you specified during the initial setup of Professional Write will normally appear on the Filename line, along with the disk drive name. The default data directory is where you normally save your work. For instance, in Figure 2.6 drive C is indicated, along with the default directory \MYDATA. If you want to select a different directory from that shown on the Filename line, erase the line, then enter the name of that directory. For example, to indicate the directory \HERWORK, enter **C:\HERWORK**.

If you're using a floppy-disk computer, use drive B.

If you plan to use a floppy-disk drive for storing the document, press Ctrl-E to erase the line, then enter the name of that disk drive (either **A:** or **B:**) on the Filename line. *Don't press ↵ yet.*

ENTERING THE FILE NAME

After you enter the name of the disk drive and/or directory, enter the name of the file to be saved. File names can contain up to eight characters—including letters, digits, and various special characters (@ or $, for example). In addition, you can optionally add a three-character *extension*, preceded by a period, to the end of the name. A file name extension is a way of helping to identify the nature of a file's contents. For example, you might name a group of files BALANCE-.JAN, BALANCE.FEB, and so on. Some software packages automatically add extensions to files that they create. Professional Write does not.

Here are a few examples of how different entries should appear on the *Filename* line, assuming that you want to save a file named FIRST:

DISK DRIVE FOR STORING DATA	***NAME OF DATA DIRECTORY***	***ENTRY APPEARING ON THE FILENAME LINE***
C:	\DATA	C:\DATA\FIRST
B:	--	B:\FIRST
A:	--	A:\FIRST

After you've entered the file name, press the Tab key, and the cursor jumps down to the line labeled *Description*. Here you can enter a short summary (up to 40 characters) of the contents of the file.

The last line can be used for specifying the format in which the document is to be stored. Initially, the entry **N** (for Normal) appears, and this entry is usually correct. (Chapter 7 will describe when and how to use other formats.)

You can move back and forth between the entries on the screen with the Tab and Shift-Tab keys, until you're satisfied that everything is correct.

You may want to try saving your practice document to a disk file. Then you can practice retrieving it as you read the section "How to Retrieve an Existing Document" later in this chapter.

To begin the saving process, press ↵. Professional Write saves the file, then redisplays the Edit screen.

A Special Warning

You can accidentally overwrite an existing file with junk, effectively wiping out that file.

If the file name that you specified is the same as that of the file from which the document was originally retrieved, Professional Write automatically replaces the existing contents of that file with the current working copy. This is a dangerous step, *so be sure that it's all right to go ahead with the save before you press* ↵.

SAVING TO HARD DISK OR FLOPPY?

If you're using a hard-disk computer, you have the option of saving your documents either to the hard disk or to a floppy. Here are some general guidelines that may help you decide when to use one or the other:

- Saving to a hard disk is *much* faster than to a floppy. The same is true for reading files.
- Hard disk crashes (in which *everything* gets lost) are not unknown. On the other hand, data can be lost from a floppy without too much difficulty—either from natural causes (dirt, fingerprints, etc.) or from human error.

Here's a good rule to follow: For your daily work, save your files to the hard disk. However, periodically—perhaps once a day or so—back up to a floppy disk any files on which you've worked and then store that disk in a safe place. In this way, even if you lose one or more files on the hard disk, you'll have a backup that's not too out of date.

For really important (or long) documents, you may want to save two backups—just in case one of them is somehow damaged. This may seem a bit *too* careful, but once you have lost a lot of work (it happens to everybody), your concept of what's too careful and what's just reasonable changes drastically.

For more complete information about saving files, refer to Chapter 7.

PRINTING YOUR DOCUMENT

You can print your working copy at any time during an editing session. There are many print options from which to choose, but in many cases you can simply use the standard default values supplied by Professional Write.

Before you attempt to do any printing, make sure that your printer is ready to receive what Professional Write will try to send to it. Check that

- The printer is attached to the correct port (connector) of the computer.
- The printer is on and the *Ready* or *On-line* or *Select* light is on.

Here are the steps for printing your current working copy:

1. Select the File/Print menu (F2).
2. Choose *Print working copy* from this menu. The Print Options menu will appear (Figure 2.7). Professional Write comes with standard options preselected in this menu. For now, print the document using these options, except:
3. If you are using a laser printer or a dot-matrix printer with a proportional font, enter the value **1,5** for the *Print style* option.
4. Press ↵ to accept the standard options and begin printing.
5. Follow any subsequent instructions that appear on the screen.

If your document fails to print, the reason could be one of the following:

- The printer is not ready to receive input from the computer. Is the correct indicator light on?
- The printer is not properly connected to your computer.

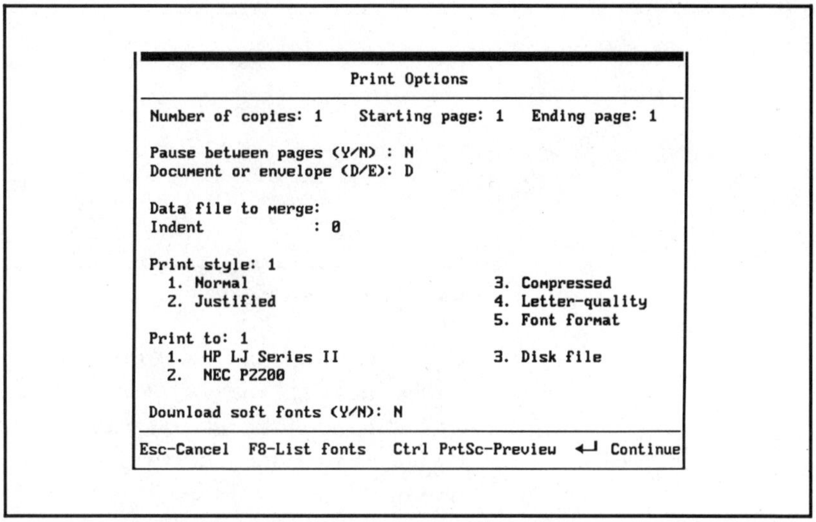

Figure 2.7: The Print Options menu

- An incorrect port or printer type was selected when Professional Write was customized for your computer.

Chapter 10 will cover printing in more detail. If you have trouble printing, you might want to consult the appropriate parts of this chapter. Also, Appendix A contains details about customizing Professional Write for your computer.

HOW TO RETRIEVE AN EXISTING DOCUMENT

For more information about retrieving files, see Chapter 7.

Here is a simple way to retrieve a file either from the hard disk or from a floppy.

To begin retrieving a file, select *Get file* from the File/Print menu. The Get File dialog box appears, as shown in Figure 2.8.

If you specified the name of a default data directory during the initial setup of Professional Write, then this directory name will usually appear in the Get File dialog box.

If necessary, you can overwrite the contents of this window: Press Ctrl-E to erase the line and then enter the correct information.

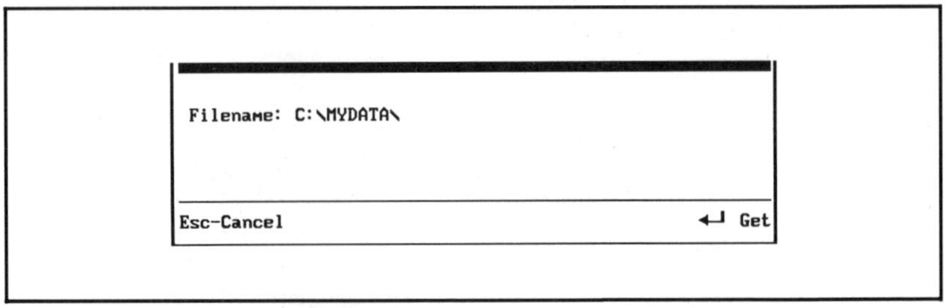

Figure 2.8: The Get File dialog box

If you're retrieving a file from a hard disk, make sure that the correct disk drive and data directory appear in the dialog box. Then enter the name of the file you want to retrieve.

If you're using a floppy-disk computer, use drive B.

If you're retrieving a file from a floppy, place the correct data disk in one of the floppy drives. Press Ctrl-E to delete the current contents, then enter the name of the drive, followed by the name of the file to be retrieved. Press ↵, and Professional Write will retrieve the file.

ENDING A WORD PROCESSING SESSION

When you have finished editing a document and you are ready to exit from Professional Write, first make sure that you have saved the latest version of the working copy to a disk file. You can save the working copy either to the same file as an earlier version, or to a new file. (See "Saving a Copy of Your Document".)

After you have copied the working copy to disk (if you want to do so), press the Esc key once or twice, and Professional Write's Main menu will appear. Select Exit, and you'll leave Professional Write and return to DOS. However, if you have made any changes to the working copy since the last time that a duplicate of it was saved to a disk file, Professional Write displays a message to that effect, giving you a chance to return to the word processor: Press the Esc key to abort leaving Professional Write. Otherwise, press ↵ and you'll exit to the DOS prompt.

3 Working with Blocks

ANY GROUP OF ADJACENT CHARACTERS, LIKE A sentence or a paragraph or several paragraphs, is called a *block*. You can work with two different types of blocks in Professional Write: *text blocks* and *rectangular blocks*.

A text block is *any* group of adjacent characters—a word, sentence, paragraph, or even several pages of text. Text blocks that cover more than one line, however, always go to the end of a line before continuing on to the next line. In other words, you cannot create a single text block from, say, two words on one line, six words on the next, and the entire next line. (Figure 3.1 shows an example of a text block.)

Unlike a text block, a rectangular block is always just that: shaped like a rectangle. This type of block can be as long as you like, even extending across page boundaries. Figure 3.2 shows an example of a rectangular block.

TEXT BLOCKS

To define a text block, you select the beginning and the end of the group of characters. Once you have selected a text block, you can perform any of the following operations on it:

- Erase it
- Move it from one part of a document to another
- Copy it to a different part of the document
- Change its style (bold, underline, italics, superscript, subscript, or normal)
- Change its font
- Change its indentation, left or right margins, or tab settings
- Set the line spacing to single or double
- Copy it to a separate disk file
- Print it
- If the block defines a group of numbers, perform calculations on them, using the built-in calculator.

The following sections will describe how to delete, move, and copy text blocks. Later chapters will describe other block operations.

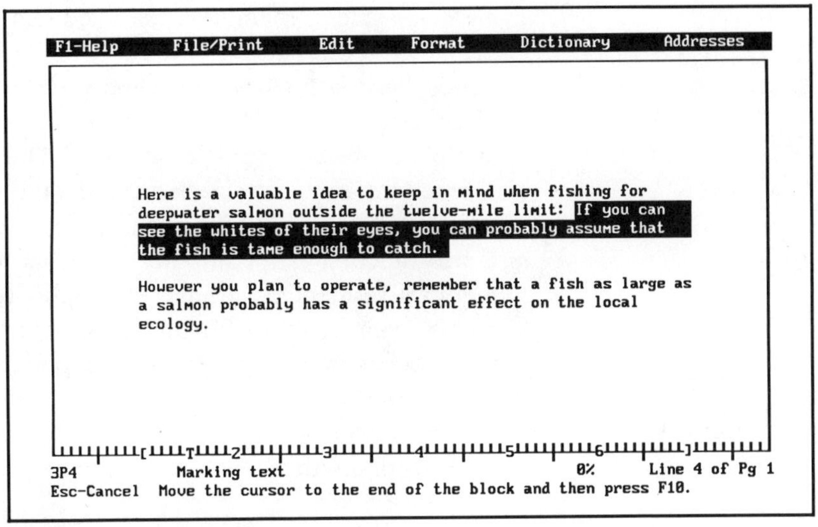

Figure 3.1: A text block

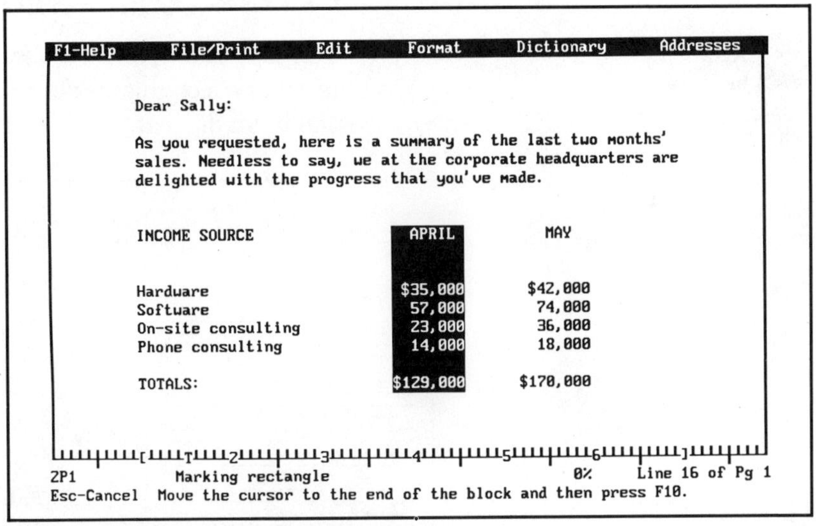

Figure 3.2: A rectangular block

THE CLIPBOARD

In order to carry out some of the above block operations, you must make use of Professional Write's built-in *clipboard*. This is a special area set aside in memory where you can temporarily store any text block.

You never actually see the clipboard, but when you are performing block operations for the first few times, it helps to visualize the clipboard as a place where you temporarily hold a block of text (see Figure 3.3). The maximum block size that can fit on the clipboard depends on the amount of free RAM (random access memory) in your computer. For instance, if your computer has 640K memory and if there are no memory-resident programs, the clipboard can hold approximately 30,000 characters, or about nine completely full pages of text. If a text block is too long to fit on the clipboard, you can work with it in smaller parts.

After a block of text has been copied to the clipboard, it remains there until another block is put there. The clipboard can hold only one block at a time.

HOW TO DEFINE A TEXT BLOCK

Remember: A text block can be any group of consecutive characters.

Before you can copy, move, or erase a text block, or do anything at all with it, you must first select, that is, define it. To do this, move the cursor to the beginning of the text, mark it as the beginning of the block,

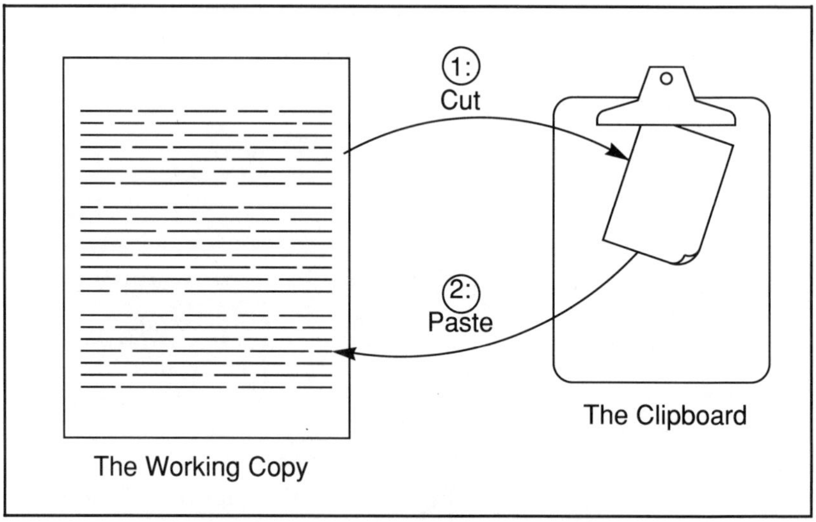

Figure 3.3: The clipboard temporarily holds a block

move the cursor to the end of the text, and then mark it as well. After these steps, you can carry out any of the operations listed above.

After you have defined the beginning of a block, you can move the cursor in any direction. For instance, if you move the cursor up, the block expands up and to the left of the cursor's original position.

Example

Using the document shown in Figure 3.4, let's define as a block the entire sentence beginning with "We'll be...".

1. Move the cursor to the beginning of the sentence (the *W* of the word *We'll*).
2. Mark this as the beginning of the block by selecting *Mark text* from the Edit menu. Notice that the Message line now contains instructions for you: If you want to cancel the operation press Esc; otherwise use the cursor keys to continue.
3. Expand the block with any of the cursor-control keys until the entire sentence is highlighted (see Figure 3.5).
4. To cancel the block operation, press the Esc key.

> Notice that the cursor stops blinking after you have defined the beginning of the block, and the block is highlighted as it expands.

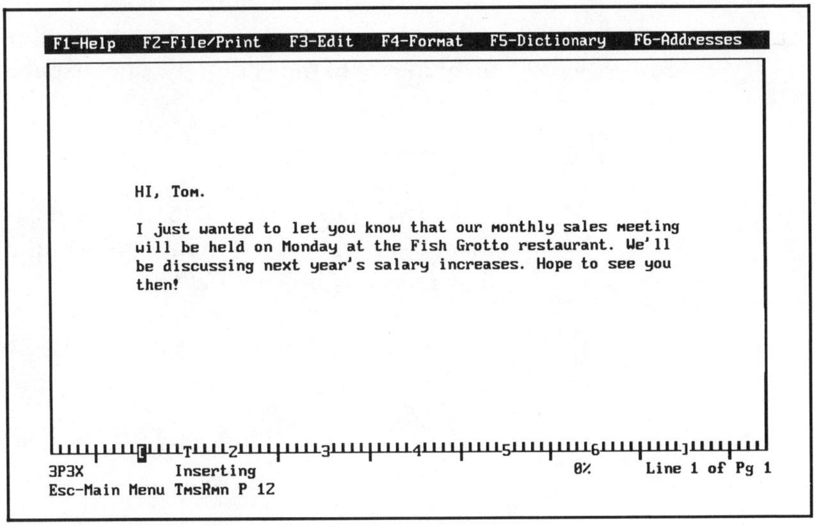

Figure 3.4: Text to be defined

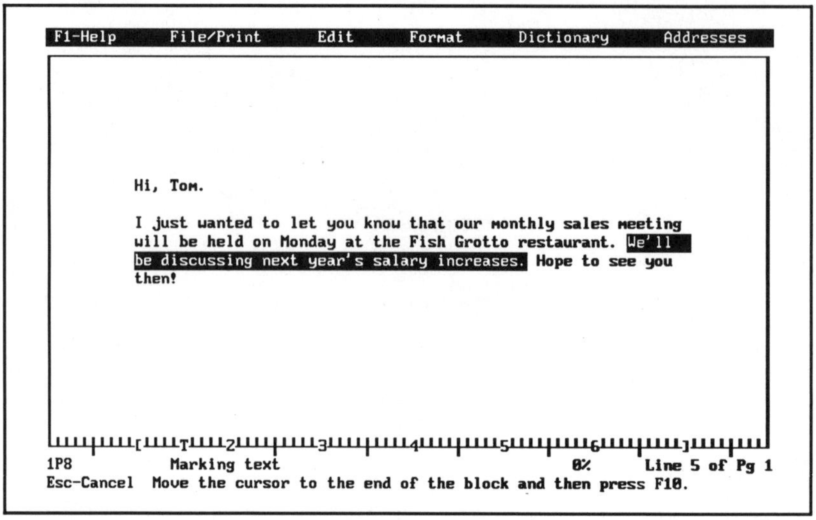

Figure 3.5: A complete sentence defined as a block

See the inside book cover for a list of cursor-control keystrokes.

Example

Any of the cursor-control keys can be used to expand a block. For example, here's how to define an entire line to be a text block: Move the cursor to the beginning of the line, select *Mark text* from the Edit menu, and then press the End key. Notice that the cursor immediately moves to the end of the line, expanding the block to that point.

MOVING A BLOCK

Suppose that you want to move some text from one part of a document to another. Here's an outline of the steps to follow (Figure 3.3 illustrates this process):

- Define the desired text as a block, following the steps described above.
- Move the block onto the clipboard.
- Place the cursor at the new position where the block is to be placed.
- Paste (that is, insert) the block from the clipboard to the new location.

Example

Using the practice document shown in Figure 3.4, here are the steps for moving the sentence that begins, "We'll be discussing..." to the end of the paragraph:

1. Define the sentence as a block, following the procedure described above.
2. Press the F10 key (see the Message line). The Text Block Operations menu then appears (Figure 3.6). You select the block operation that you want from this menu.
3. Move the block to the clipboard: Select *Cut* from the Text Block Operations menu. The sentence will be removed from the document, but don't worry; it's stored safely on the clipboard.
4. Move the cursor to the start of the sentence's new location, after the words *see you then*.
5. Select the Edit menu, and then choose *Paste*. The contents of the clipboard will appear as the last sentence in the paragraph (Figure 3.7).

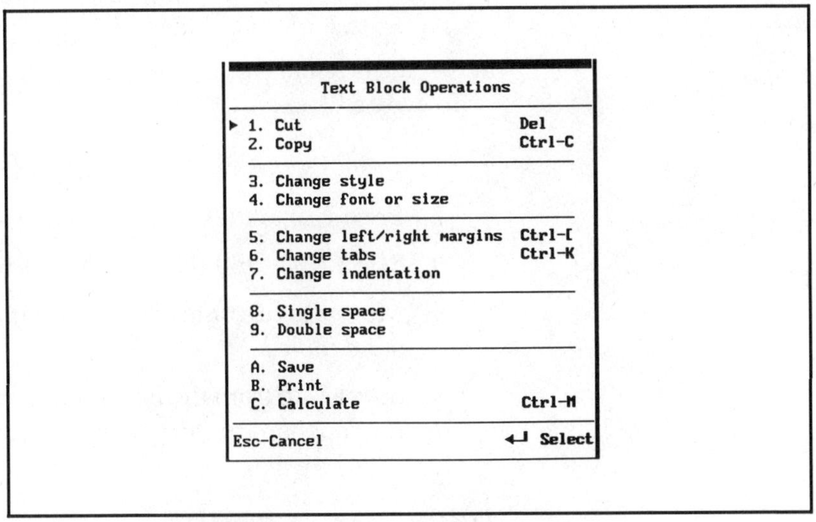

Figure 3.6: The Text Block Operations menu

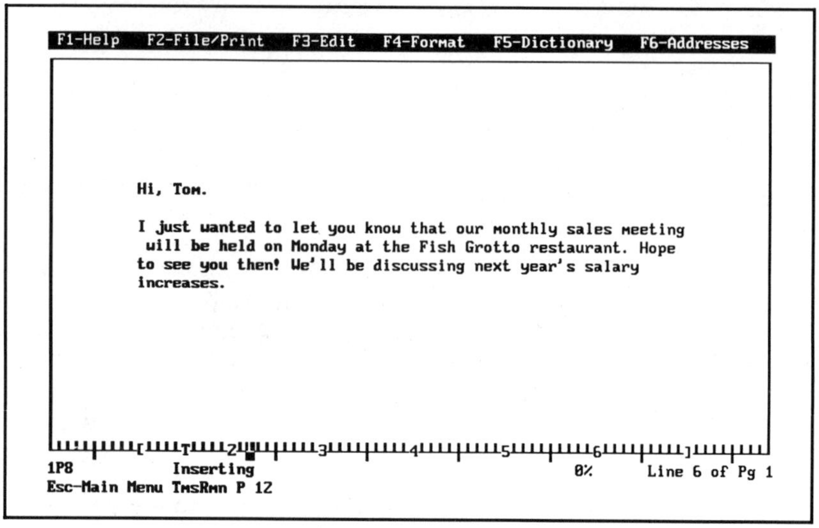

Figure 3.7: The practice document with the text rearranged

COPYING A BLOCK

The procedure for copying a block is almost identical to that for moving a block. The only difference between a block *copy* and a block *move* is that with a copy the original text remains in place; with a move, the original text is deleted.

To copy a block:

1. Begin by defining the block, as described above.
2. Press F10, and the Text Block Operations menu appears.
3. Select *Copy*, and the text block is written to the clipboard.
4. Move the cursor to the position in the text where the block is to be copied.
5. Select *Paste* from the Edit menu, and the block is copied from the clipboard to the cursor position.

DELETING A BLOCK

To delete a text block you perform the first three steps that you used in moving a block: First define the block, press F10, and then select *Cut* from the Text Block Operations menu. Note that this operation writes the block to the clipboard.

Retrieving a Deleted Block

Suppose, after you have deleted a block, that you change your mind and want to put the block back where it was. Or suppose you accidentally delete the wrong block of text—and such things do happen. Because the *Cut* operation writes the deleted block to the clipboard, you can easily recover from what might otherwise be a serious error: Simply move the cursor back to where the block was before the erasure and then select *Paste* from the Edit menu. The block will be pasted back to its original position. Remember that a block remains on the clipboard *until* another one displaces it, and thus you're protected against an accidental erasure until either you write another block to the clipboard or exit from Professional Write.

USING SPEED KEYS WITH BLOCK OPERATIONS

In order to make working with blocks easier, Professional Write offers several speed keys that can be used instead of the corresponding selection on the Edit and Block Operations menus:

SPEED KEY	*BLOCK OPERATION*
Ctrl-T	Defines the beginning of a text block
Ctrl-R	Defines the beginning of a rectangular block
Ctrl-C	Copies block to the clipboard
Del	Moves the block from the working copy to the clipboard
Ctrl-P	Pastes the block from the clipboard to the working copy, beginning at the cursor position

Example

Here are the steps for using the speed keys to move the last sentence in the document in Figure 3.7 back to its original position:

1. Move the cursor to the beginning of the sentence "We'll be...".
2. Define the beginning of the block: press the speed key Ctrl-T.
3. Move the cursor to the end of the sentence.
4. Move the block to the clipboard: press the Del key.
5. Move the cursor to the space immediately following the word *restaurant*.
6. Paste the block from the clipboard to the working copy by pressing Ctrl-P.

When a block is pasted and the end of the block contains a period, extra spaces may be inserted at one end or the other. Check your text after a paste and remove any extra spaces.

Try to get into the habit of using speed keys whenever possible; they'll greatly enhance your editing speed. Remember that a list of all speed keys appears inside the cover of this book.

Notes on Automatic Reformatting

When you insert a text block into the text or delete a block from the text, Professional Write automatically reformats the text as necessary. For example, when a text block is deleted, the remaining text is moved to fill the gap created.

When a block is written to the clipboard and later pasted into the document, the left and right margin settings for that block are also transferred. For example, if a block is pasted into a part of the document with margin settings that differ from the block's settings, the original margin settings of the block are pasted as well. This variation in margin settings can be a handy way of creating special effects within a document.

Professional Write will not automatically reformat text across a *change* in margins, however. See "How to Change Margins" in Chapter 5 for more information on this topic.

RECTANGULAR BLOCKS

Rectangular blocks can be very useful when working with columns of text or numbers. See Figure 3.2 for an illustration of a rectangular block. The following operations can be performed on a rectangular block:

- Erase it
- Move it from one part of a document to another
- Copy it to a different part of the document
- Change its style (bold, underline, italics, superscript, subscript, or normal)
- Change its font
- If the block defines a set of numbers, perform calculations on them using the built-in calculator.

Like text blocks, rectangular blocks sometimes require the use of the clipboard. This limits the maximum block size for certain operations.

There is one important difference between text and rectangular blocks: Whenever you delete an ordinary text block, Professional Write automatically reformats the text. For instance, if you delete a text block, the blank space is filled in by shifting the adjacent text. By contrast, you can choose to delete a rectangular block without having the remaining text reformatted. You'll see how this works in the following sections, where you'll learn how to erase, copy, and move this type of block.

DEFINING A RECTANGULAR BLOCK

Before you can do anything with a rectangular block, you must first define it. Here are the steps:

1. Move the cursor to one corner of the block you wish to define.
2. Select *Mark rectangle* from the Edit menu. Note that the cursor stops blinking, and instructions appear at the bottom of the screen.

You can also use the speed key Ctrl-R to define the block's beginning.

3. Move the cursor to the opposite corner of the block. Note that the block is highlighted as it expands.
4. When you have finished defining the block, press F10, and the Rectangular Block Operations menu appears (Figure 3.8).

DELETING A BLOCK

In order to delete a rectangular block, you must first define it, following the steps described above. Once you have defined the block, you can delete it in either of two ways: by *cutting* or *erasing* it from the working copy. Here's the difference between the two operations:

- When you *Cut* the block, it's deleted from the screen (and the working copy), and the text to the right of the block moves over to fill in the vacant space created by the block's removal.
- When you *Erase* the block, it's deleted from the screen, but the adjacent text is not moved over.

The Erase feature is especially handy when working with columns of text or figures: You can delete the contents of one or more columns without disturbing the layout of the document.

As an example, Figure 3.2 shows a document with a rectangular block defined. Figure 3.9 shows the same document with that block *erased*. Note that the position of the original right-hand column remains unchanged.

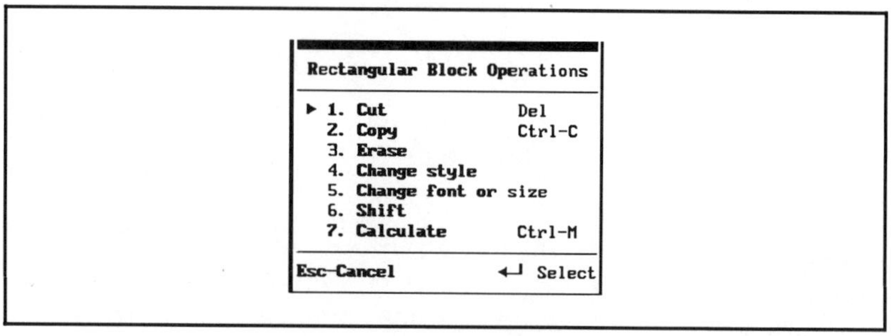

Figure 3.8: The Rectangular Block Operations menu

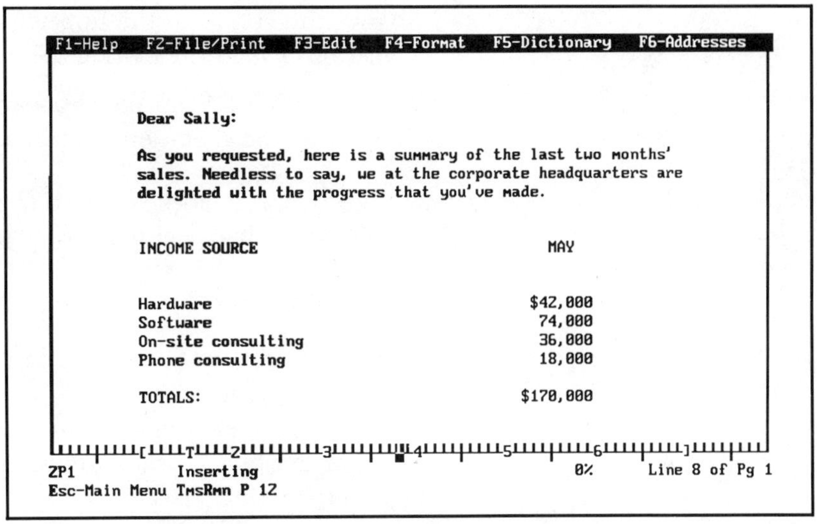

Figure 3.9: The document in Figure 3.2 with the defined block erased

Here are the steps for deleting a rectangular block:

1. Define the block as described above. After you press F10, the Rectangular Block Operations menu appears (Figure 3.8).
2. Select either *Cut* or *Erase* from this menu, depending on whether you want the remaining text to fill in. In either case, the block will be deleted from the screen.

You can press the Del key to cut the block.

Note that when you cut or erase a block, it's copied to Professional Write's clipboard. This is handy in the event that you accidentally delete a block: You can paste the block from the clipboard back into the document. See below for details about pasting from the clipboard to the working copy.

MOVING A BLOCK

Moving a block is similar to deleting it, except that an additional paste operation is added at the end of the process. Here are the steps for moving a rectangular block:

1. Define the block, following the steps described above.
2. Delete the block by selecting either *Cut* or *Erase* from the Rectangular Block Operations menu.

3. Move the cursor to the upper left-hand corner of the area where you want the block to be pasted.
4. Paste the block from the clipboard to the document: Select *Paste* from the Edit menu or press the speed key Ctrl-P.

When a rectangular block is pasted from the clipboard, the existing text is always pushed over to the right to make room for the block.

Restrictions

Professional Write won't let you paste a block if existing text would be pushed past the right margin. Also, you can't paste a block into an area that contains one or more double-spaced lines. On the other hand, you can paste a block containing double-spaced lines into single-spaced text.

If your block is too large to fit on the clipboard, you won't be able to use the Cut or Erase operations. However, you may be able to do what you need to by working with small parts of the block.

There is no way to paste a rectangular block over existing text—even a block consisting of blank spaces. If you want to insert a rectangular block into a document without changing the existing format, you'll need to do some careful column manipulations.

Example

If you paste a new column into Figure 3.9 between the two existing columns, the result looks like Figure 3.10. Notice that the right-hand column has been pushed over to make room for the new pasted column.

Suppose that you have entered the three columns of figures shown in Figure 3.11, and you then realize that the first two columns must be interchanged. There are several ways in which you could do this (including reentering the data), but here's one that requires only a few careful steps:

1. Select the middle column as a rectangular block, including all of the spaces up to the beginning of the next column (Figure 3.12).
2. *Cut* this column from the text. The right column moves over to fill in the vacated space (Figure 3.13).

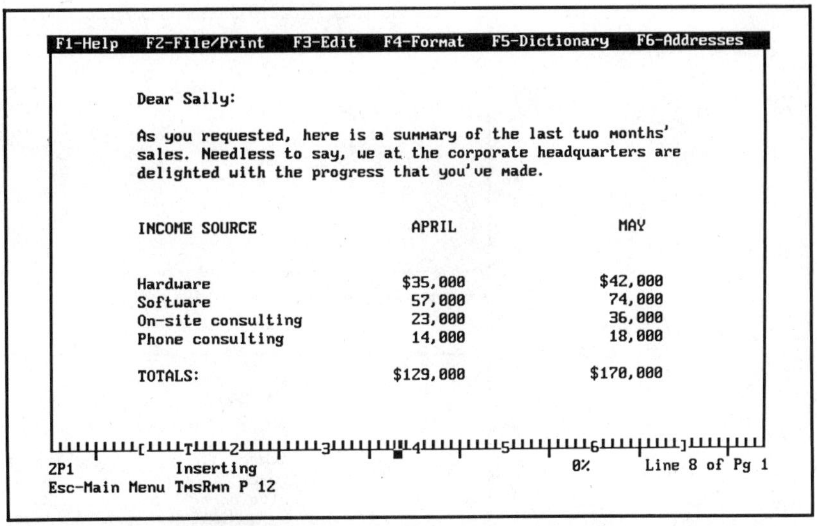

F1-Help F2-File/Print F3-Edit F4-Format F5-Dictionary F6-Addresses

Dear Sally:

As you requested, here is a summary of the last two months' sales. Needless to say, we at the corporate headquarters are delighted with the progress that you've made.

INCOME SOURCE	APRIL	MAY
Hardware	$35,000	$42,000
Software	57,000	74,000
On-site consulting	23,000	36,000
Phone consulting	14,000	18,000
TOTALS:	$129,000	$170,000

2P1 Inserting 0% Line 8 of Pg 1
Esc-Main Menu TmsRmn P 12

Figure 3.10: The document shown in Figure 3.9, with a new column pasted in

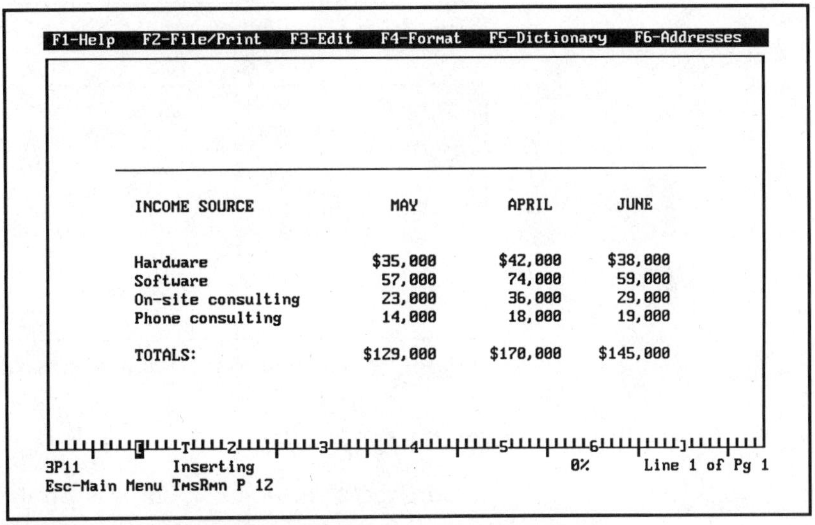

F1-Help F2-File/Print F3-Edit F4-Format F5-Dictionary F6-Addresses

INCOME SOURCE	MAY	APRIL	JUNE
Hardware	$35,000	$42,000	$38,000
Software	57,000	74,000	59,000
On-site consulting	23,000	36,000	29,000
Phone consulting	14,000	18,000	19,000
TOTALS:	$129,000	$170,000	$145,000

3P11 Inserting 0% Line 1 of Pg 1
Esc-Main Menu TmsRmn P 12

Figure 3.11: Two of these columns need to be interchanged

3. Position the cursor just to the left of the column labeled *MAY*.
4. Paste the column you cut back into the document. The two existing columns will be pushed over to make room. The result is shown in Figure 3.14.

INCOME SOURCE	MAY	APRIL	JUNE
Hardware	$35,000	$42,000	$38,000
Software	57,000	74,000	59,000
On-site consulting	23,000	36,000	29,000
Phone consulting	14,000	18,000	19,000
TOTALS:	$129,000	$170,000	$145,000

Figure 3.12: Select the middle column as a rectangular block

INCOME SOURCE	MAY	JUNE
Hardware	$35,000	$38,000
Software	57,000	59,000
On-site consulting	23,000	29,000
Phone consulting	14,000	19,000
TOTALS:	$129,000	$145,000

Figure 3.13: The middle column in Figure 3.12 has been cut

INCOME SOURCE	APRIL	MAY	JUNE
Hardware	$42,000	$35,000	$38,000
Software	74,000	57,000	59,000
On-site consulting	36,000	23,000	29,000
Phone consulting	18,000	14,000	19,000
TOTALS:	$170,000	$129,000	$145,000

Figure 3.14: The columns shown in Figure 3.11 have been rearranged

COPYING A BLOCK

Copying a rectangular block is similar to the process of moving one. The difference is that with a *copy* operation, the original block remains in place. Here are the steps for copying a block:

1. Select the block, following the steps described above.
2. Copy the block by selecting *Copy* from the Rectangular Block Operations menu. A duplicate of the block is written to the clipboard.

You can also copy the block by pressing the speed key Ctrl-C.

3. Move the cursor to the upper left-hand corner of the area in which you want the block to be copied.
4. Paste the block from the clipboard to the document: Select *Paste* from the Edit menu or press the speed key Ctrl-P.

When the block is pasted from the clipboard, the existing text is pushed over to the right to make room for the new block.

SHIFTING A BLOCK

Sometimes you may want to move a block by only a few spaces—either up, down, left, or right. When this is the case, you can use a shortcut. Here's how:

1. Define the desired rectangular block and then press F10.
2. Select *Shift* from the Rectangular Block Operations menu.
3. Use the ↓, ↑, ←, or → cursor keys to move the block in the desired direction.
4. When you have finished, press the Esc key to undefine the block.

Restrictions

You can't shift a block over existing text, past the existing margins, or over a double-spaced line. Also, you can't shift a block that contains double-spaced lines.

4 Enhancing the Page Appearance

EVEN THE MOST ORDINARY BUSINESS DOCUMENT can be made more interesting-looking, more attention-getting, by varying the appearance of its text. Professional Write offers several ways in which you can improve the appearance of your document, not only to give it a professional look, but also to direct the reader's attention to some aspect of the document you want to emphasize.

You can focus attention on a particular group of characters by giving it a style that makes it stand out from the surrounding text. Boldfacing is the strongest way to highlight text, whereas italics lend a more subtle emphasis. Underlining can also be used to call particular attention to all or part of a line. Superscripts and subscripts are additional styles that can be used for increasing the flavor of a page.

To add variety to the appearance of a page, you can also use different types and sizes of text for various parts of a document. To make a heading stand out, print it in a larger text size. To call particular attention to a special heading, use not only a larger text size, but also a different typeface.

By using various different text styles, typefaces, and sizes, you can bring life to what might otherwise be a bland, ordinary page. This chapter will focus on these useful topics.

ENHANCING YOUR DOCUMENT

Professional Write offers six text styles that enable you to control the appearance of one or more characters:

- Boldfacing
- Underlining
- Italicizing
- Superscripts
- Subscripts
- Normal

Normal, the last of these, means ordinary text, that is, without any of the other five styles. Boldfacing, underlining, and italicizing significantly change the appearance of normal text. Superscripts and subscripts, as you will see in a later section, are mostly used in footnotes and scientific notation. You can apply one or more of these styles to any character, word, sentence, or to any block of text. Any combination of styles can be applied to a block, with one exception: a character can't be both superscripted and subscripted at the same time (how would you write it?).

To experiment with some of these styles, you'll work with the document shown in Figure 4.1.

BOLDFACING AND UNDERLINING

Once you have created some text, you can selectively boldface or underline parts of it. You can quickly boldface or underline (or both) any desired word by using speed keys. In addition, you can boldface or underline any group of adjacent characters. To do this, you first select the desired text to be either a text block or a rectangular block and then boldface or underline the entire block.

Note that you can't select a style for text *as it's being entered.* You must first enter the text and then choose parts of it to be boldfaced, etc.

If you place the cursor on a character that's been boldfaced or underlined, the words *Bold* or *Und* appear on the Status line at the bottom of the screen. This is true for any of the styles: The Status line always displays the style or styles assigned to the character at the cursor.

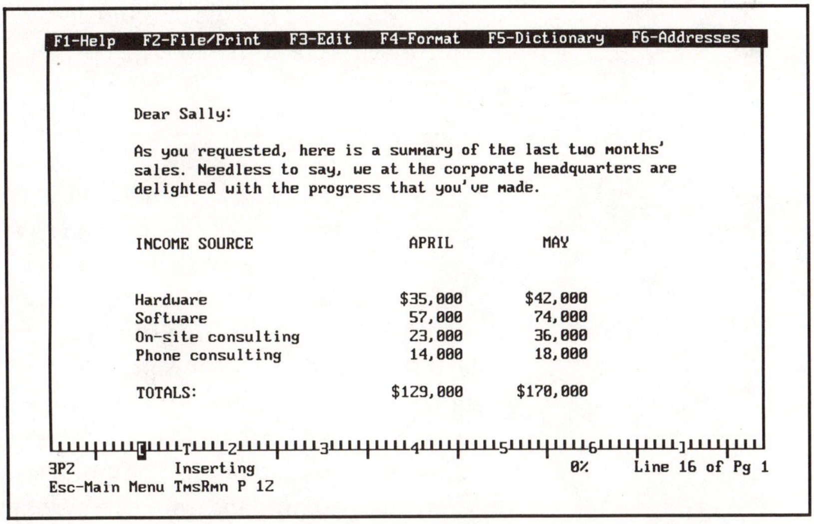

Figure 4.1: The sample document in normal, unenhanced text style

Boldfacing and Underlining Words

Professional Write makes it especially easy to boldface or underline individual words:

1. Move the cursor to any part of the desired word.
2. Select *Boldface word* or *Underline word* from the Edit menu.

Watch the status line for the style of the current character.

Most computer monitors will display both styles so that you can see which words have been boldfaced or underlined. If boldfacing doesn't show on your monitor, you may need to adjust the brightness and contrast controls.

Boldfacing and Underlining Blocks

You can either boldface or underline (or both) a selected text or rectangular block:

1. Select the block whose style you want to change.
2. To boldface the block, press the speed key Ctrl-B.
3. To underline the block, press Ctrl-U.

As soon as you press one of these speed keys, that style is assigned to the block, and the block is deselected. To assign both styles to the same block, repeat the above steps.

OTHER STYLES FOR TEXT

Besides boldfacing and underlining, you can assign any of the following styles to a block: italics, superscript, or subscript.

Some printers can't output in all of these styles. For example, some older dot-matrix printers can't generate output that's italicized. For a laser printer, the styles that can be output depend on which fonts are currently available to the printer. For instance, in some circumstances a laser printer may not be able to boldface and italicize the same text (see Chapters 8 and 9 for more details about printers and fonts). If your printer can't output a style that you have assigned, it ignores any commands from Professional Write to print in that style.

To assign a particular style to a group of characters, first select those characters as a block and then assign that style to the block. Here are the steps:

1. Select the text or rectangular block and then press F10 to display the Operations menu.
2. Select *Change style* from this menu, and the Style menu then appears (Figure 4.2), offering six options.
3. Select the style or styles that you want to be applied to the selected block:
   - For each style that you want, press the appropriate number. For example, to boldface and underline the block, press the numbers **1** and **2**. As you select each style, it's marked with an arrow.
   - To deselect a style, press its number again.
   - To remove any or all of the other five styles, select *Normal*.
4. Press ↵, and the selected block will be assigned the styles that you chose.

You can also select a style by using the ↑ and ↓ keys to highlight that style and then pressing the spacebar.

Note that you can use this method to assign the boldfacing or underlining styles, both of which appear on the Style menu.

PREVIEWING YOUR STYLES

For more information about the Preview feature, see Chapter 12.

By using the Preview feature, you can see how the styles that you have selected affect the appearance of a page. Preview gives you a

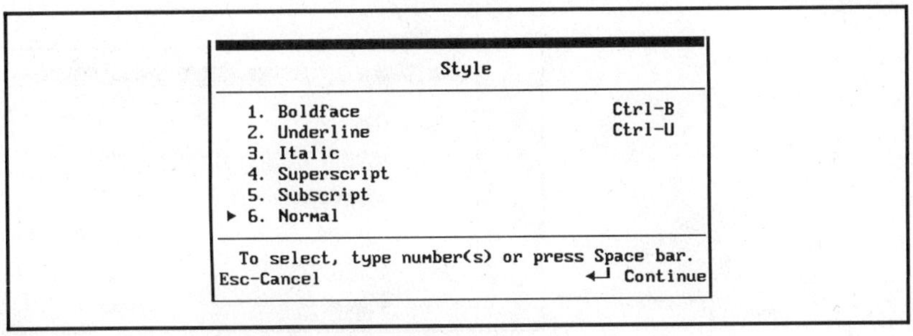

Figure 4.2: Select a text style from this menu

close representation of how the printed page will look, including boldface, underlining, and other styles. To use this feature:

1. Make sure the page you want to preview is displayed on screen.
2. Select *Preview working copy* from the File/Print menu (F2) or press the speed key Ctrl-PrtSc. After a few seconds the page display will appear.
3. If you want to expand the detail of the display, press the key combination Alt-V.

For example, Figure 4.3 shows the document in Figure 4.1 as Preview displays it, with selected text boldfaced and underlined. Figure 4.3 also illustrates a limitation of the Preview feature: Although the different text styles are accurately shown, the screen display will usually be somewhat fuzzy. This limitation *does not* necessarily reflect the actual quality of the printed document.

Example

Using the rectangular block is a handy way to emphasize a single column in a table. For instance, here's how to boldface the middle column shown in Figure 4.1:

1. Move the cursor to the upper left corner of the column marked *APRIL*.
2. Mark that position as the beginning of a rectangular block: press the speed key Ctrl-R.

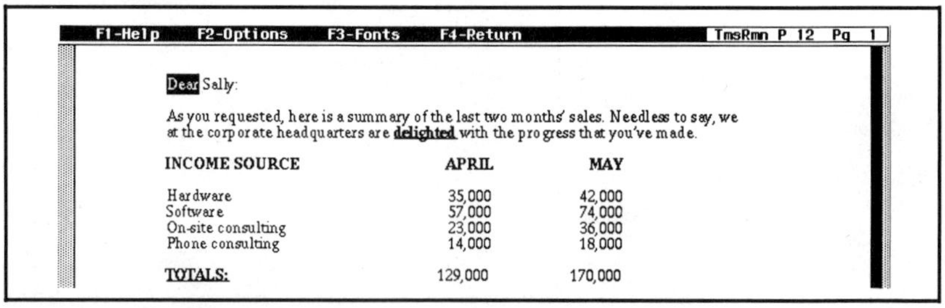

Figure 4.3: The sample document as Preview displays it

3. Move the cursor to the lower right corner of that column, that is, after the text *$129,000*.
4. Press F10 to display the Operations menu.
5. Select *Change style* from this menu.
6. When the Style menu appears, select *Boldface* and then press ←┘.

Figure 4.4 shows the results of this operation, again using the Preview mode.

USING SUPERSCRIPTS AND SUBSCRIPTS

Superscripts are most commonly used for indicating footnotes and endnotes. Subscripts are most often used in scientific notation, although there are other uses as well. The techniques for using superscripts and subscripts are identical.

You can create a superscript consisting of a single character or a group of characters. In either case, you must first create a text block and then select the superscript style for the block.

To see how this works, append the number 1 directly after the word *Sally* in Figure 4.1 and then assign it to be a superscript. Here are the steps:

1. Position the cursor directly after the colon that follows the word *Sally:* then enter the number **1**.
2. Press the ← key to reposition the cursor on the number 1.

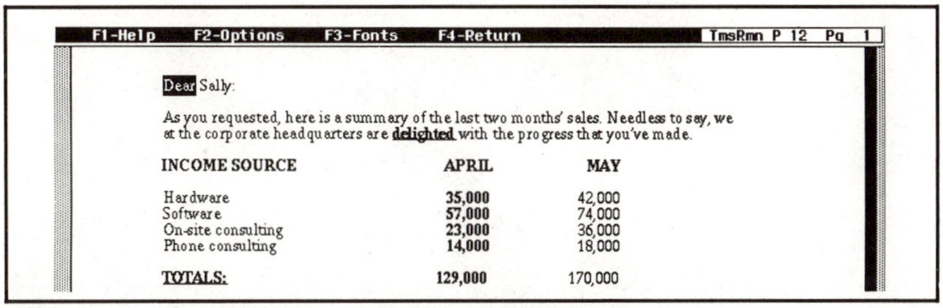

Dear Sally:

As you requested, here is a summary of the last two months' sales. Needless to say, we at the corporate headquarters are **delighted** with the progress that you've made.

INCOME SOURCE	APRIL	MAY
Hardware	**35,000**	42,000
Software	**57,000**	74,000
On-site consulting	**23,000**	36,000
Phone consulting	**14,000**	18,000
TOTALS:	**129,000**	170,000

Figure 4.4: The Preview mode shows a boldfaced column

3. Define the number 1 to be a block: press the speed key Ctrl-T to define the beginning of the block; then immediately press F10 to mark the block and display the Text Block Operations menu.
4. Select *Change style* from the menu.
5. When the Style menu appears, select *Superscript* by pressing the number **4**.
6. Return to the Edit menu by pressing ↵.

When you return to the Edit menu, notice that the cursor is still on the number 1, and that the word *Super* appears on the Status line at the bottom of the screen. If you move the cursor off of the number 1, you'll see that the number is highlighted, which indicates that it has been assigned some type of style. However, you can't tell what that style is unless you move the cursor back to the number and then look at the status line.

You can see the actual appearance of the superscript by using the Preview feature as described earlier. Figure 4.5 shows how Preview displays a superscript.

USING DIFFERENT FONTS

For more information about fonts, see Chapters 8 and 9.

You can change the size and appearance of a selected block of text by assigning to it a different *font*, provided that your printer will cooperate. Some printers can print in only one font, and you're stuck with it. If your printer does print in various fonts, the Message line of the Edit screen will display the name of the current font, such as *TmsRmn P 12*, immediately to the right of the words *Esc-Main Menu*.

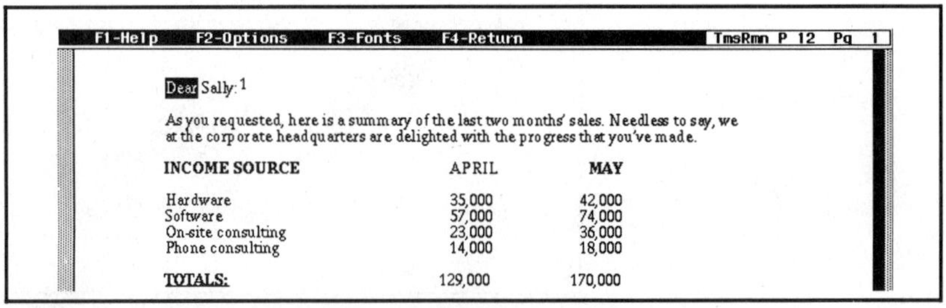

Figure 4.5: The Preview mode shows a superscript in place

If your printer can't print in different fonts, the spaces to the right of these words will be blank.

Your printer must also be able to print the particular font or fonts that you assign to text in your document. Again, refer to Chapter 9 for details concerning this important topic.

A font is a specific typeface, size, style, and orientation. As an example, consider the font called *Times Roman 12 point Normal Portrait*. This name contains all the vital information about the font:

Typeface: The name of the typeface is Times Roman (this happens to be one of most frequently used typefaces).

Type size: The size is 12 point. The *point* is the basic unit of type measurement. There are 72 points per inch, and thus a 12-point font occupies approximately one-sixth of a vertical inch on the printed page.

Style: This indicates whether the font is normal, boldface, or italics.

Orientation: A page can be printed in either *portrait* (vertical) or *landscape* (horizontal) orientation. Most pages (like the one you are now reading, for example) are printed in portrait orientation.

SELECTING DIFFERENT FONTS

To change the font of a particular group of characters, you must first select them as a block and then assign a new font to the block. Here are the steps:

1. Select the text as either a text or rectangular block and then press F10. When the Block Operations menu appears,
2. Select *Change font or size*. When the next menu appears,
3. Select the font you want: highlight it using the ↑ and ↓ cursor keys. If necessary, use the PgDn key to display other fonts

that aren't shown on the screen. Finish by pressing ↵, and the Edit screen will reappear.

Different fonts don't show on the Edit screen. However, any text that has been assigned a font that is different from the regular font appears boldfaced on the screen, to indicate to you that something is abnormal about the text—it might be in a different font or a different style.

You can see which font is assigned to a particular character by moving the cursor to that character. The name of the font assigned will appear on the Message line, just to the right of the words Esc-Main Menu.

VIEWING THE NEW FONTS

Although different fonts don't display on the Edit menu, you can get an idea of how they will appear when printed by using the Preview feature. This will show relative character and line spacings, as well as an approximation to the actual shapes of the various fonts. The section "Previewing Your Styles," above, describes how to use the Preview feature.

Example

Here's an example of how the Preview mode can be helpful when creating a document with different font sizes. Using the document in Figure 4.1, suppose that you want to emphasize the word *TOTALS:* by enlarging it to the font Roman 18 point Normal. To see the results of this operation, you can use the Preview mode, as shown in Figure 4.6.

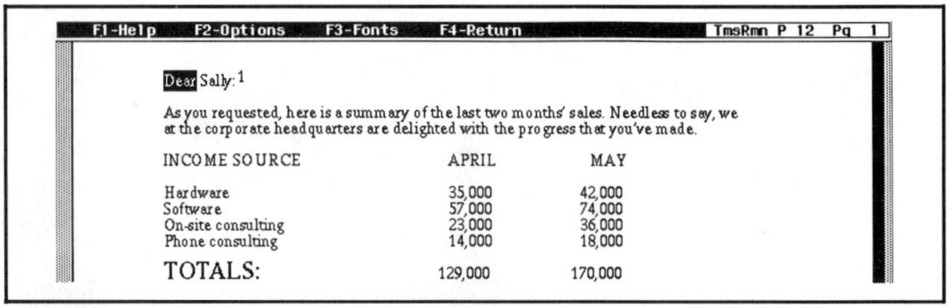
F1-Help F2-Options F3-Fonts F4-Return TmsRmn P 12 Pg 1

Dear Sally: 1

As you requested, here is a summary of the last two months' sales. Needless to say, we at the corporate headquarters are delighted with the progress that you've made.

INCOME SOURCE	APRIL	MAY
Hardware	35,000	42,000
Software	57,000	74,000
On-site consulting	23,000	36,000
Phone consulting	14,000	18,000
TOTALS:	129,000	170,000

Figure 4.6: Preview mode shows change in font

5 Setting the Page Layout

THE PREVIOUS CHAPTER DECRIBED HOW YOU could improve the appearance of a document by using different text styles and fonts. This chapter will discuss some of the other ways in which you can control the look of a document. These include the setting of margins, tabs, headers and footers, page numbering, and line spacing.

SETTING THE LEFT AND RIGHT MARGINS

Margin settings have a strong influence on the appearance of the printed page. Margins that are too small make the page look crowded. Margins that are too big give the page an unbalanced feeling, as well as wasting paper. You can change the left and right margins to suit your particular needs, as follows:

- Set the basic margins (called the *default margins*) of the entire working copy before you begin entering a new document.
- Change the margins as you are entering new text within a document. You can do this as often as you wish.
- Add a new section within an existing document, using margins that are different from those of the surrounding text.
- Change the margins of existing text blocks.
- Insert text from the clipboard or from another document with margins that differ from those of the existing text.

HOW MARGINS ARE MEASURED

The left and right margins are indicated by left and right brackets ([and]) on the Ruler line. Normally, the vertical lines on the Ruler measure in *tenths of an inch from the left edge of the printed page*. In some circumstances, you may want to use the Ruler to measure in *number of characters*, instead of tenths of an inch. To do this, you need to deselect a parameter called the *Font Format Print Style*. This is done from the Print Options dialog box, which is explained in Chapter 10.

Suppose you want to use $8^{1}/_{2} \times 11$-inch paper with left and right margins of 1 and $1^{1}/_{2}$ inches, respectively. In this case, the left margin should be set to 10 (ten tenths equals one inch), and the right margin to 70 (70 tenths, or 7 inches, leaving $1^{1}/_{2}$ inches of margin).

If you are printing with a 10-pitch monospaced font (that is, each character takes up one-tenth of an inch), then each mark on the Ruler will correspond to the position on the printed page of one character. Therefore, the edit screen shows the position of each character exactly as it will appear on the printed page. For other fonts, such as a 12-pitch monospaced font or a proportional font, this will not be the case. Consequently, the line breaks shown on the screen will not be the same as those on the printed page. However, you can use Professional Write's Preview feature to see how the printed page will actually appear.

When setting the margins, you can use values between 1 and 250. This large upper limit is useful when using a compressed font with a wide-carriage dot-matrix printer.

SETTING THE MARGINS FOR A NEW DOCUMENT

Before you begin working on a new document, you can change Professional Write's default margin settings of 10 and 70. You might want to make this change because you are using a non-standard size paper, or for aesthetic reasons. You can set the new margins by either of two methods, depending on your own preferences:

- Set the margins directly on the Ruler.
- Use a special menu in which you enter the numeric values for the margins.

Setting the Margins on the Ruler

This method is a visual approach to margin setting. Here are the steps to follow, assuming that the Edit screen is displayed and that the working copy is empty:

1. Make sure the cursor is at the beginning of the working copy (press Ctrl-Home).

2. Select the Format menu (F4) (Figure 5.1).
3. From this menu, select *Set left/right margins*. The Set Left and Right Margins menu then appears (Figure 5.2).
4. Select *Insert new margins*.

At this point, the Margin Selection display appears (similar to that shown in Figure 5.3) and you are ready to select new margins. Notice that this display looks almost the same as the normal Edit display, but with two differences:

- The cursor is not blinking (just a reminder that you are not doing normal editing at this point).

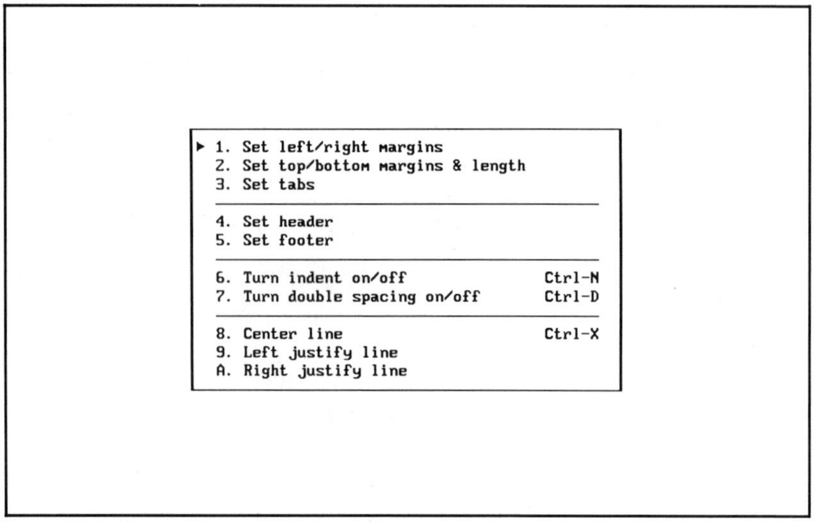

Figure 5.1: The Format menu

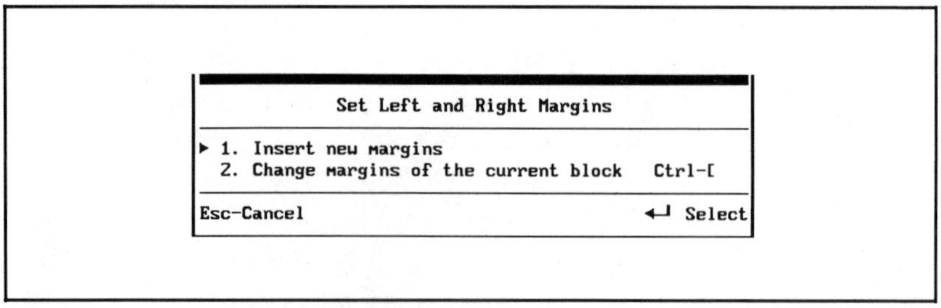

Figure 5.2: The Set Left and Right Margins menu

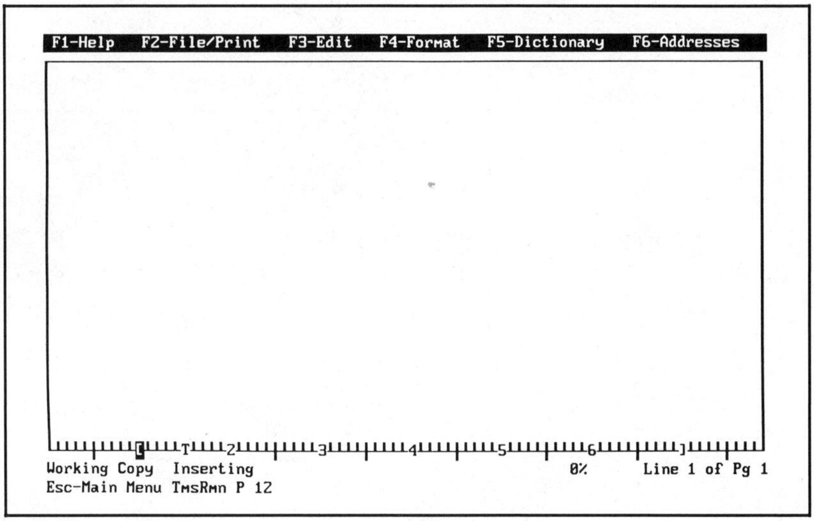

Figure 5.3: The display for selecting new margins

- The following message appears at the screen bottom: *Type [or] on the Ruler, or press F8.*

5. Move the cursor on the Ruler to the position for the new left margin (see Table 5.1).
6. Set the margin, by pressing the [key.
7. Move the cursor on the Ruler to the position for the new right margin.
8. Set the margin, by pressing the] key.
9. Press ⟵ to establish the new margins and return to the regular Edit screen.

In steps 5 and 7 above, you can use several keys to move the cursor on the Ruler. Table 5.1 lists them.

Setting the Margins by Menu

Instead of setting the new margins by moving the cursor on the Ruler, you can use the Margin Settings menu (Figure 5.4), where

Table 5.1: Cursor-Control Keys for Setting Margins

TO MOVE THE CURSOR:	**PRESS:**
One space to the right	→
One space to the left	←
Five spaces to the right	Ctrl-→
Five spaces to the left	Ctrl-←
To the current right margin	End
To the current left margin	Home
To the next tab setting	Tab

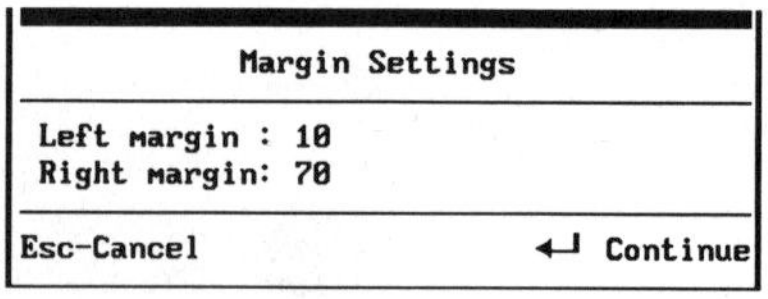

Figure 5.4: The Margin Settings menu

you can enter the numerical values of the new margins. To begin, follow steps 1 through 4 in the above section. Then

You can move between the menu settings with the Tab key.

1. Display the Margin Settings menu by pressing F8.
2. Enter the new value for the left margin and then press Tab.
3. Enter the new value for the right margin.
4. When you are satisfied with the new settings, press ↵ to make the new margins take effect.

CHANGING THE MARGIN AS YOU ENTER TEXT

You can change the margin settings for new text that you enter into an existing document. This can be anywhere in the document—

either at the end, the beginning, or anywhere in between.

For example, you may want to change margins while you are entering text to create a temporary left and right indent. The document shown in Figure 5.5 was created by introducing two margin changes: one after the first paragraph was entered and another after the second paragraph was entered.

As you enter the new text, it will remain within the new margin settings. These settings will remain in effect for all lines that you enter, as well as any lines that you insert within the new lines.

You can see this by watching the Ruler while moving the cursor back and forth between the original text and the text entered with the new margins. You will see the margin settings change as the cursor moves from one area to the other.

Here are the steps for creating new margins:

1. Make sure that the cursor is on a blank line. (If it isn't, Professional Write won't let you proceed).
2. Select *Set left/right margins* from the Format menu (F4). When the Set Left and Right Margins menu appears:
3. Select *Insert new margins*.
4. Set the new margins, as described earlier.

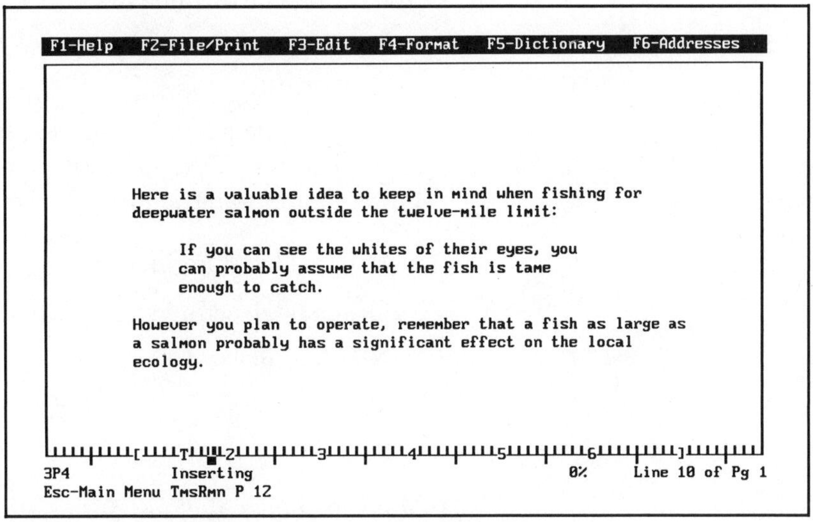

Figure 5.5: A document with two margin changes

Points to Ponder

When setting new margins, here are some things to keep in mind:

- Generally, unless you have a specific reason to do otherwise, assume that the Ruler measures in tenths of an inch. For this to be true, when you print your documents you'll then need to select the Font Format print style from the Print Options dialog box (for details about how to do this, see "The Print Options Dialog Box" in Chapter 10).
- Remember that unless you're using a 10-pitch font, the positions of the letters on the screen won't correspond to those on the printed page. For instance, if you're printing with a 12-pitch font (12 characters per inch) on $8\frac{1}{2} \times 11$-inch paper and 1-inch margins, the screen will show at most 65 characters on a line; whereas on the printed page as many as 78 characters per line may be printed.
- If you're using a printer that holds extra-wide paper, you'll need to reset the right margin. For instance, with a paper width of 11 inches and with 1-inch margins, the right margin would be at 10 inches from the left paper edge. Therefore, use a right margin value of 100 (tenths of an inch).
- You can set one margin only, or both margins at the same time.
- Once you have set margins, they stay in effect until you change them.
- When you change the left margin, the tab settings remain the same, relative to the new left margin. For instance, here's how a change to the left margin would affect the tab settings:

For more information on tabs, see "How to Use Tabs" in this chapter.

Original left margin:	10
Original tab settings:	15, 20, 25
New left margin:	15
Readjusted tab settings:	20, 25, 30

- You can change the margins as often as you wish while you

enter new text, but each time you do, be sure that the cursor is on a blank line.

CHANGING MARGINS OF EXISTING TEXT

You can adjust the margins of any group of adjacent lines within an existing document. These lines may initially have the same margins, or several different sets of margins may exist within these lines. To change the margins, first select those lines as a text block and then change the margins of that block.

For instance, suppose you want to change the margins of area B in Figure 5.6a. Here are the basic steps:

- Define the lines within area B as a text block.
- Select the appropriate menu items for changing the margins.
- Enter the new margin settings.

All of the lines within area B will be assigned the new margin settings. Lines outside the selected block (areas A and C) will retain their original margin settings.

Don't change the margins of just part of a paragraph.

When you select a block for margin alterations, make sure that you select only entire paragraphs. The reason is that if you change the margins of just part of a paragraph, the wordwrap will probably look wrong because Professional Write can't reformat across a change in margins.

If you later enter one or more new lines of text within area B, their margins will be those assigned to that area.

Example

Let's suppose that you have entered the document shown in Figure 5.7. Upon close examination, you decide that it would look much better if the middle paragraph were set off by having larger margins, such as those shown in Figure 5.8. Here are the steps for changing the margins:

1. Move the cursor to the beginning of the line "If you can see...".

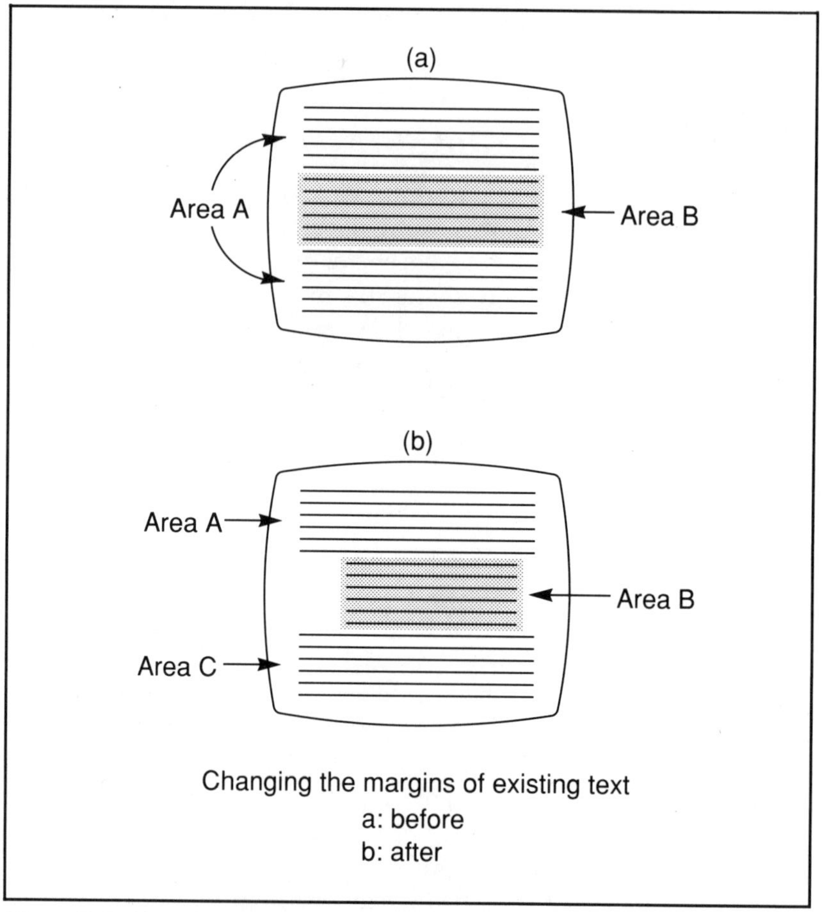

Figure 5.6: Changing the margins of existing text

2. Select the entire paragraph to be a text block. For a review of how to define a block, refer to Chapter 3.
3. Press F10. When the Text Block Operations menu appears:
4. Select *Change left/right margins*; the Margin settings display will appear, and the block you selected will appear highlighted.
5. Change the margins from 15 to 60, either directly on the Ruler or by pressing F8. In either case, remember to finish by pressing ↵.

Instead of steps 3 and 4, you can press the speed key Ctrl-[.

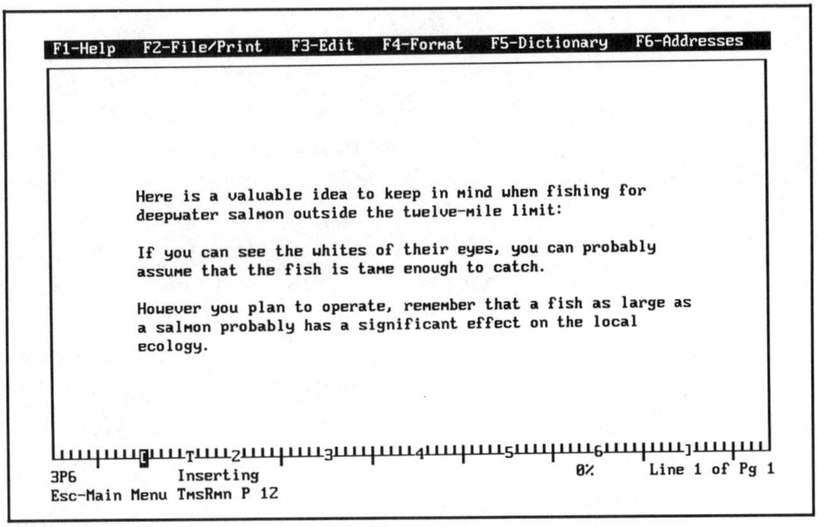

Figure 5.7: A document that could benefit from reformatting

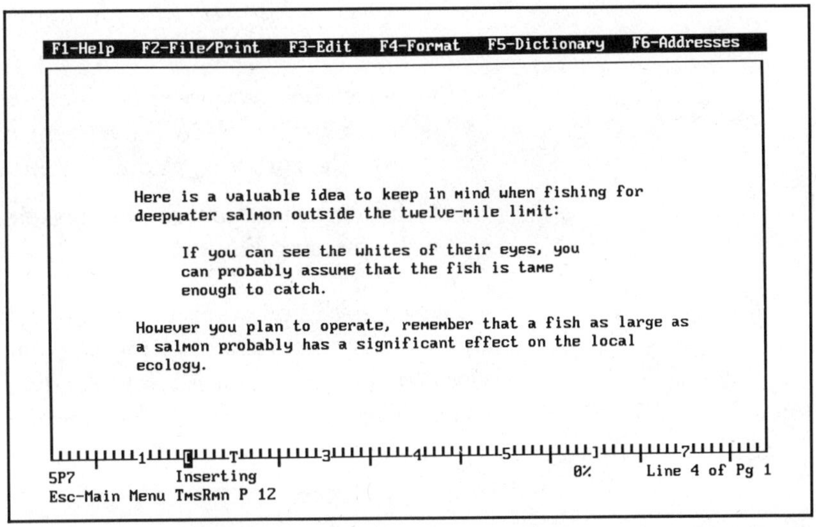

Figure 5.8: The document in Figure 5.7, with the middle paragraph readjusted

In this example, you could use the speed key Ctrl-[instead of steps 3 and 4. The meaning of this key is: *change the margins of the current block.*

MARGIN AREAS

The term *margin area* refers to any group of adjacent lines that have the same left and right settings. For instance, Figure 5.6b has three separate margin areas. Even though areas A and C have the same margins, they are two separate margin areas because they are separated by another margin area, that is, one with different margins.

Margin areas are often a convenient tool when you want to change margins of existing text. For example, suppose that you want to change the margins of the middle paragraph shown in Figure 5.7. You can do so by using the technique described in the above section, "Changing Margins of Existing Text," but because this paragraph defines a distinct margin area, you can instead use one of Professional Write's shortcuts. Here's how it works:

1. Place the cursor anywhere within the middle paragraph of Figure 5.7.
2. Select *Set left/right margins* from the Format menu (F4). When the Set Left and Right Margins menu appears:
3. Select *Change margins of the current block.* Professional Write immediately selects the current margin area (that is, wherever the cursor is) as the current text block.
4. Enter the new margin settings, either directly on the Ruler or by pressing F8.

The key to this process is in the third step, where Professional Write automatically selects as a block the *entire* margin area in which the cursor is located. This technique is a very handy way of changing the margins of any adjacent group of lines that have the same margins.

Using Speed Keys

You can streamline the above process for changing the margins of a margin area by using the speed key Ctrl-[:

1. Place the cursor anywhere within the margin area whose margins you want to change.

2. Press Ctrl-[. Professional Write immediately selects the current margin area as a text block and then brings up the Margin Selection display.

Professional Write offers two convenient speed keys for moving about within a given margin area:

- Ctrl-Q: Moves the cursor to the beginning of the current margin area (that is, the area in which the cursor is located).
- Ctrl-Z: Moves the cursor to the end of the current margin area.

EDITING TIPS WHEN USING DIFFERENT MARGIN SETTINGS

As you are working with a document, some of the editing operations may require a little care if you are manipulating groups of text with different margins. As long as you keep in mind certain small details, however, these operations shouldn't present any problems.

Combining Paragraphs

You can usually combine two paragraphs into a single one by deleting the invisible hard return that separates them. However, if the two paragraphs have different margins settings, you won't be able to combine them because Professional Write can't reformat across two lines with different margin settings.

To get around this problem, you will first need to make the margins of both paragraphs the same: Select both paragraphs as a single block and then assign margins to the block. After this operation, you can delete the hard return between the paragraphs, and Professional Write will then be able to reformat them.

Inserting Text Blocks and Files

Chapter 3 described how to copy and move text blocks within a document. Here are a couple of things to keep in mind when you work with this type of block:

- When a block is written to the clipboard, as the result of either a cut or a copy operation, the margin settings of each line within the block are copied as well.

- When a block is pasted from the clipboard into a document, the margin settings for each line within that block are also pasted.

These two facts mean that you should be able to cut (or copy) and paste a block and retain its original margin settings. However, *this won't happen if the cursor is placed in the middle of a line when the block is pasted.* To make sure that the block's margin settings are pasted, first insert a blank line where the block is to be pasted. Place the cursor at the beginning of that line and then paste the block.

You can insert the contents of another document file into any part of the working copy. When you do so, the margin settings of that document are preserved. In this case, you don't have to worry about the cursor position or blank lines when you read in the file: Professional Write always preserves the margin settings of the file that is read in. For more information on combining files, see Chapter 7.

INDENTING TEXT

An *indent* is a temporary left margin, generally used for special emphasis. You can create an indent and then enter new text; you can also create an indent for a block of existing text.

Here are some key points to remember about indents:

- Setting an indent is quick, requiring only a couple of keystrokes.
- When you set an indent and then begin entering text, Professional Write remembers the original left margin; to return to it, you need enter only a special keystroke.
- You can move the cursor to the left of the temporary margin created by an indent. This is a handy way of entering a heading after you have created a paragraph of indented text.
- Generally, an indent is the fastest way to temporarily change the left margin.

CREATING AN INDENT FOR NEW TEXT

To enter new text with an indent:

Always start the indent on a blank line.

1. Move the cursor to the place in the existing text where you want to enter the new indented text.
2. Create a blank line at this spot, and place the cursor at the point on that line where you want the indent to be set.
3. From the Format menu (F4), select *Turn indent on/off*, or press the speed key Ctrl-N (N for iNdent).
4. Begin entering the text. Each line will begin at the position established as the indent.
5. When you want to return to the normal left margin, select *Turn indent on/off* again from the Format menu or press Ctrl-N.
6. Press ↵ to start a new paragraph.

The symbol > appears on the Ruler when an indent is set.

Points to Ponder

- When you establish an indent, as in step 3 above, the temporary left margin is indicated on the Ruler by the > character. Thus a glance at the Ruler can always tell you whether or not an indent has been set.
- You can actually turn on the indent mode in the middle of a line of text. If you do, however, the indent will take effect beginning with the *following* line.
- If you turn off the indent mode in the middle of a line, indenting will continue until you start a new paragraph.
- The speed key Ctrl-N is a toggle for turning an indent on and off.

CHANGING THE INDENT OF EXISTING TEXT

You can change the indent of existing text within a document in two ways. First, you can create an indent for a group of lines, each of which starts at the left margin. In addition, you can change the indentation of a group of lines that have been previously indented.

To create an indent for a group of lines:

1. Select the lines as a text block (for a discussion of text blocks, see Chapter 3) and then press F10. When the Text Block Operations menu appears:
2. Select *Change indentation*.
3. Move the cursor on the Ruler to the new indent position and press ↵. The left margin of all lines in the block will be adjusted to the indent setting, and these lines will be reformatted.

As an example, the above steps could be applied to the middle paragraph shown in Figure 5.9. The result is displayed in Figure 5.10.

HOW TO USE AUTOMATIC INDENTING

You can use Professional Write to help create automatic indentation. With this feature, each paragraph automatically wraps so that the next line indents at the same position as the previous line. This is

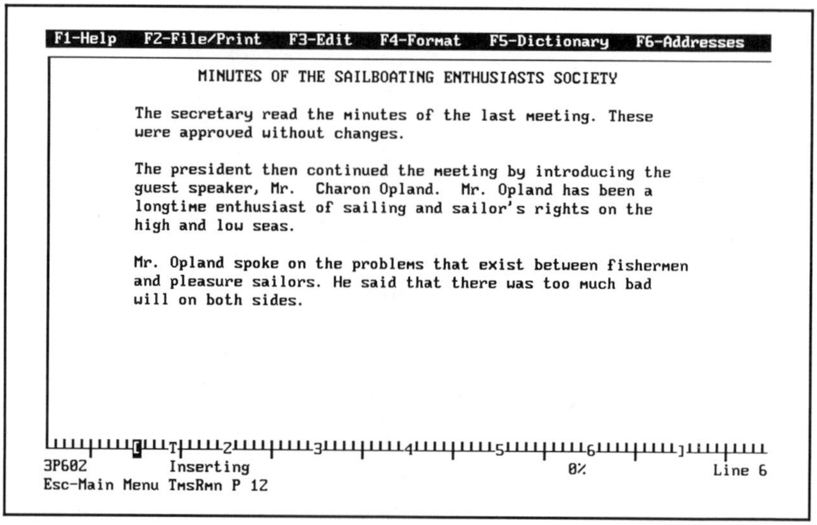

Figure 5.9: Sample text to be reformatted

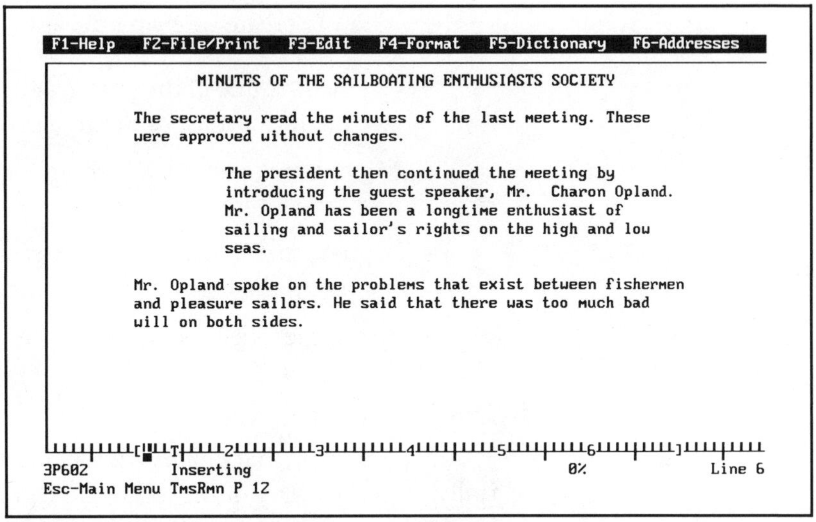

Figure 5.10: Figure 5.9 with the middle paragraph indented

a convenient way of creating itemized lists, outlines, and other text that falls naturally into this type of format. You can use this feature to create several levels of indentation. For example, the page shown in Figure 5.11 was created using Professional Write's automatic indenting feature.

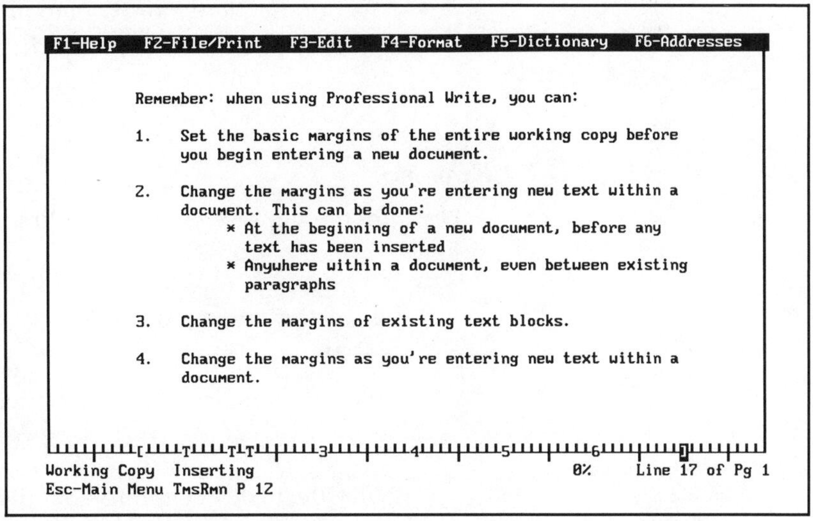

Figure 5.11: This page was created using the automatic indent feature

Here's how to create a new paragraph with automatic indentation:

- On the first line of the paragraph, enter a special *item delimiter* (see below for a list of delimiters).
- Move the cursor to where you want the left margin of the paragraph body to begin.
- Begin entering text. The paragraph will automatically wrap around to the left margin you established in the last step.
- To end the indentation, begin a new paragraph by pressing ↵.

Item Delimiters

Any paragraph that begins with an item delimiter will be automatically indented. Any of the following can be used as a delimiter:

- Any of the these characters:

  – o * + ■ .

  When used in this way, these characters are sometimes called *bullets*. In this list, "o" is the lowercase letter, and ■ is the special character Alt-254 (hold Alt down, then enter 254 on the numeric keypad).
- Any number, letter, or Roman numeral that is *immediately* followed by one of these special characters:

  : – .) > / \

Example

Here are the steps for creating the first indented paragraph shown in Figure 5.11.

The text will automatically indent as it wraps around.

1. Move the cursor to a blank line, where the text is to be placed.
2. Enter the item delimiter, **1.** (Remember to include the period.)
3. Move the cursor to the right a few spaces.
4. Enter the text, beginning "**Set the basic margins....**

5. When you have finished with the text, end the paragraph by pressing ↵.

Points to Ponder

Note that Figure 5.11 uses two different types of item delimiters—numbers and asterisks—and two levels of indentation at item 2: The first level starts with "Change the margins...", and the second level begins with the asterisks.

For automatic indenting to work properly, you must adhere to the following rules:

- Each item delimiter must begin a new paragraph.
- An item delimiter must be followed by at least one space.
- Automatic indentation won't work properly if you have also created an indent for the same paragraph.
- If the text is to be output using a proportional font, you must insert a tab setting at each position where you want the paragraph bodies to begin. In addition, these tab settings must be entered *before* you begin entering the text to be automatically indented. Otherwise, the paragraphs won't line up correctly when printed. For example, the tab settings in Figure 5.11 were created before the text was entered.

You can create the necessary space or spaces after entering an item delimiter either by moving the cursor manually or by pressing the Tab key to move the cursor to the next tab setting. For instance, in the above example you can use the Tab key in step 3 because tabs have been previously set at appropriate positions in the document.

HOW TO USE TABS

You use tabs within Professional Write much as you would have used them on a typewriter (what's that?): Each time you press the Tab key, the cursor jumps to the next tab setting. You can return to the previous tab setting by pressing Shift-Tab.

The current tab settings appear on the Ruler: Each setting appears either as a T, for a typewriter setting, or a D, for a decimal setting.

Initially, Professional Write sets one default tab setting at position 15 on the ruler. However, before you begin a new document, you can change this by adding as many new tab settings as you wish. In addition, you can change the existing tab settings anywhere within a document, adding new ones and deleting unwanted ones. Once you have created a group of tab settings, they remain in effect until you create new ones.

You can't change the position of existing text by changing tab settings.

When you assign new tab settings at some point in a document, they affect only text that's subsequently typed in. That is, these new settings have no effect on any text already in the document. However, you can change the tab settings of existing text, but it's a two-step process that involves moving the text to the new tab settings.

When you enter a line of new text within an existing document, the tabs of that line are set to those of the adjacent lines.

TYPES OF TAB SETTINGS

You can use two different types of tab settings within Professional Write: *typewriter* and *decimal*. A typewriter tab setting appears on the Ruler as a T, and a decimal tab setting as a D. Both types of settings can be used at the same time.

Typewriter Tabs

This type of tab setting is used for aligning columns of text. To move the cursor to the next setting, press the Tab key. To move it to the previous setting, press the Shift-Tab key combination. You can then continue entering text.

Decimal Tabs

This type of tab setting is used for aligning columns of numbers on their decimal points. Here's how it works: press the Tab key or Shift-Tab to position the cursor at the next or previous setting. As you enter a number, the cursor remains fixed and anything that you enter gets pushed to the left of the cursor—*until you enter a decimal point*. The decimal point is entered at the tab setting, and subsequent characters are entered normally—that is, to the right of the decimal point.

Figure 5.12 shows a page with decimal tabs at columns 32 and 49. Notice that in each of the two columns, the decimal points line up with the decimal tab setting (D) displayed on the Ruler.

CHANGING THE TAB SETTINGS FOR NEW TEXT

You use the same procedure for creating new tab settings, whether you are starting a new document or entering new text into an existing document.

When you first start up Professional Write, one tab setting is preset at position 15 on the Ruler, and thus you can indent paragraphs without having to worry about tab settings. However, you may want to delete this tab setting and create new ones before beginning work on a new document.

You can change the tab settings at any time while you are entering text. Any new text that is entered *immediately beyond the new settings* will conform to these settings.

To create a new set of tabs:

Make sure the cursor is on a blank line.

1. Position the cursor at the point in the text where you want the new tabs to take effect. This must be a blank line.

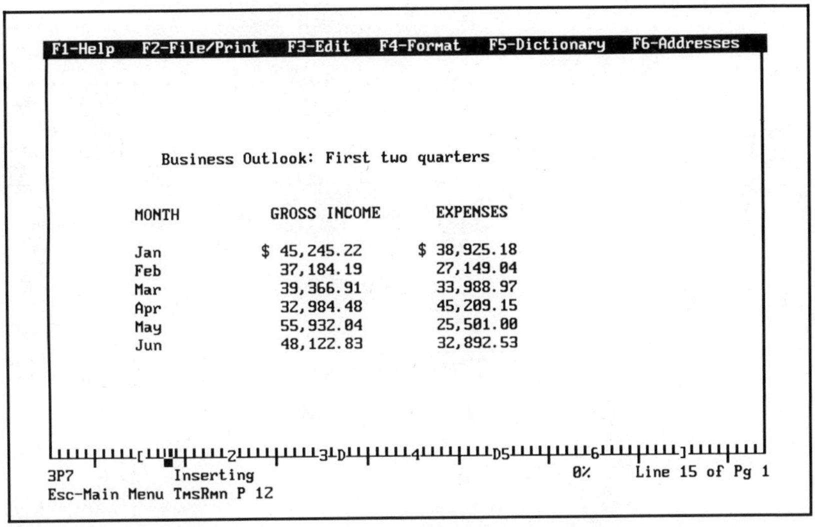

Figure 5.12: You can use decimal tab settings to align columns on decimal points

The current column number is displayed on the Status line, and instructions are on the Message line.

2. Select *Set tabs* from the Format menu (F4). When the Set Tabs menu appears (Figure 5.13):
3. Select *Insert new tabs*. At this point, you can use the Ruler to delete old tab settings and insert new ones:
4. To delete an existing tab, move the cursor to that tab and then press the spacebar; the tab mark (either a T or D) will disappear.
5. To insert a new tab, move the cursor to the desired spot on the Ruler and then press either T (for a typewriter tab) or D (for a decimal tab).
6. When you are finished entering tabs, press ↵ to return to the Edit screen.

You can use any of the keystrokes shown in Table 5.2 to move the cursor.

```
                    Set Tabs
▸ 1. Insert new tabs
  2. Change tabs of the current block      Ctrl-K
Esc-Cancel                              ↵ Select
```

Figure 5.13: The Set Tabs menu

Table 5.2: Cursor-Control Keys for Setting Tabs

To Move the Cursor:	**Press:**
One space to the right	→
One space to the left	←
Five spaces to the right	Ctrl-→
Five spaces to the left	Ctrl-←
To the current right margin	End
To the current left margin	Home
To the next tab setting	Tab

You can enter new text somewhere in the middle of a document, assigning new tab settings to this text. To understand how this works, consider the two-column page of text in Figure 5.14a, and suppose that you want to enter additional text at the position shown in this figure, but with different tab settings. Here are the steps:

- Move the cursor to the desired position on the page and insert a blank line at that point.
- Enter the new tabs using the steps described above.
- *Starting on that same line*, enter the new text.

The result is illustrated in Figure 5.14b. The new text, represented by area C, conforms to the new tab settings. Here are the key points to consider:

- Areas A and B contain the original tab settings. Any time that you enter new text into either of these areas, that text will conform to the original settings.
- Area C contains the new tab settings. Any time that you enter new text into this area, that text will conform to the new settings.

Points to Ponder

- Tab settings can be created only within the current margins.
- At any time while you are entering new settings, you can abort the whole operation and restore the original tab settings by pressing the Esc key.
- The new tab settings will remain in effect until you enter a new group of settings farther on.
- When you enter a new line of text, that line takes on the tab settings of the adjacent lines.
- When you create a new blank line by pressing ↵, the tab settings of this new line will be the same as those of the line immediately above.

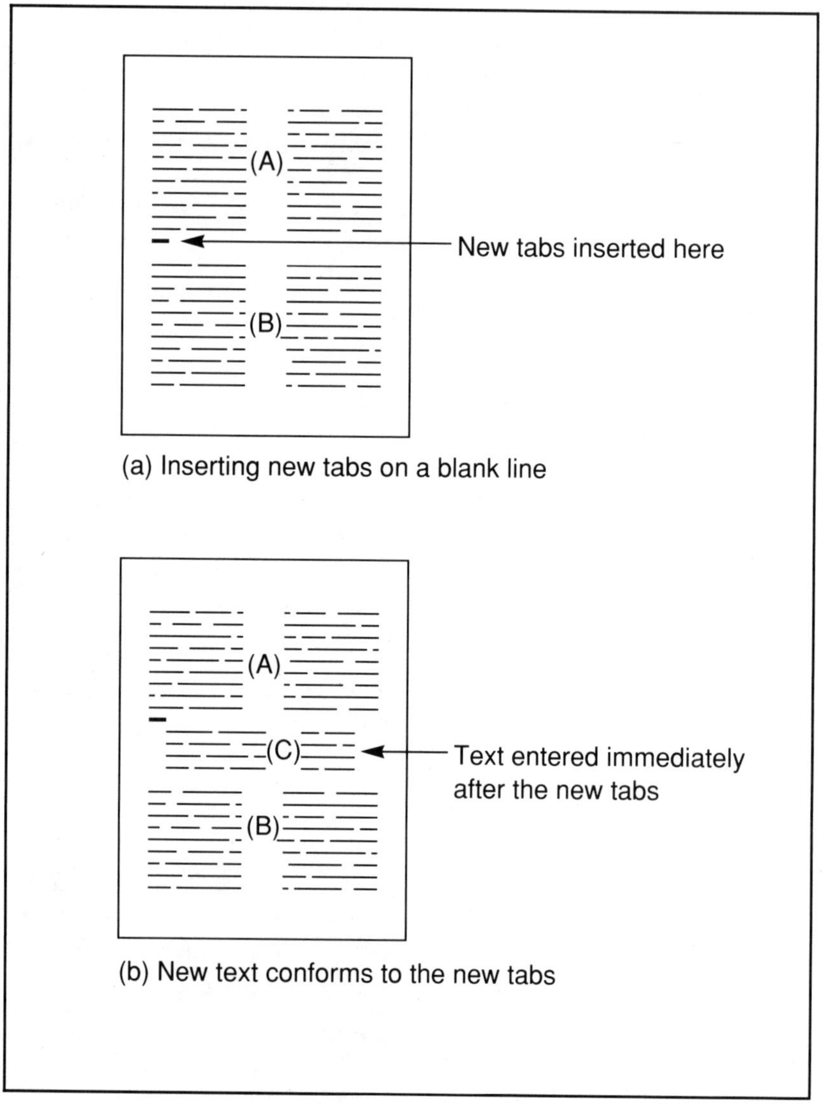

Figure 5.14: New text can be entered with different settings

CHANGING THE TAB SETTINGS OF EXISTING TEXT

You can change the tab settings of existing text, but the process may sometimes be tedious. First, you must manually move each column to the position that you want. Then you assign new tab settings to the text in these columns, matching the new positions of the columns. You must go through this two-step process for two reasons. The first is that you can't change the position of a group of text lines simply by changing the tab settings of those lines. Try it, and you'll see that this is true.

The second reason, which is less obvious, has to do with the fact that for many printers, what you see on the screen is not the same as what is printed out. For instance, if you are printing with a proportionally-spaced font, different characters occupy different amounts of horizontal space on the printed page. On the other hand, every character on the *screen* has the same width, and therefore the screen can't show you the true printed positions of the various characters.

To deal with this limitation, Professional Write adopts the following rules when working with tab settings:

- The Ruler normally shows the actual measurements of tab settings in inches as they will appear on the printed page (the same is also true of the margins).
- If a word is positioned at a particular tab setting on a line, then when the line is printed that word will be placed at the position on the line dictated by that tab setting, *regardless of the widths of the various characters on that line.*

The process of changing tab settings can be a little confusing, and an example will help illustrate how it works. Figure 5.15 shows a page containing three columns. Suppose that you want to reposition the two rightmost columns, as shown in Figure 5.16. Here are the steps you need to go through:

For a discussion of rectangular blocks, see Chapter 3.

1. Reposition each column (including the column heading): Define it as a rectangular block and then move or shift it. Finish up by pressing ↵.
2. Select a text block, consisting of all lines containing the columns (including the headings).
3. Select *Change tabs* from the Text Block Operations menu.

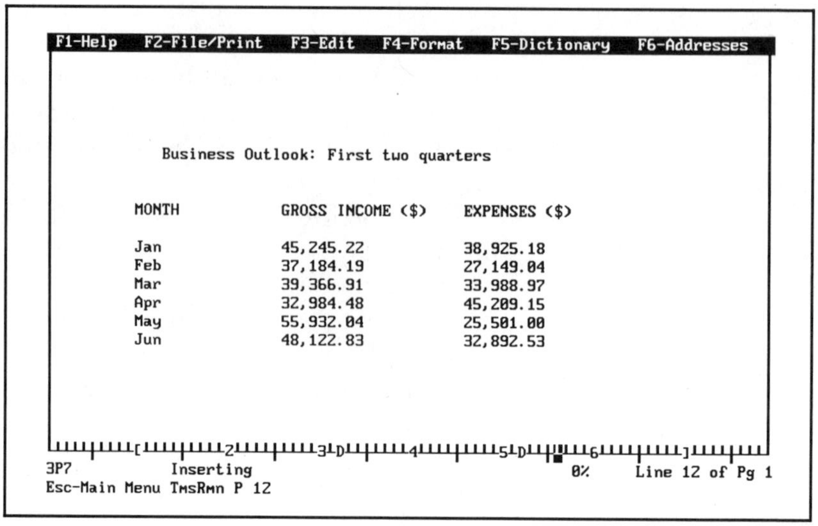

Figure 5.15: A page with three columns

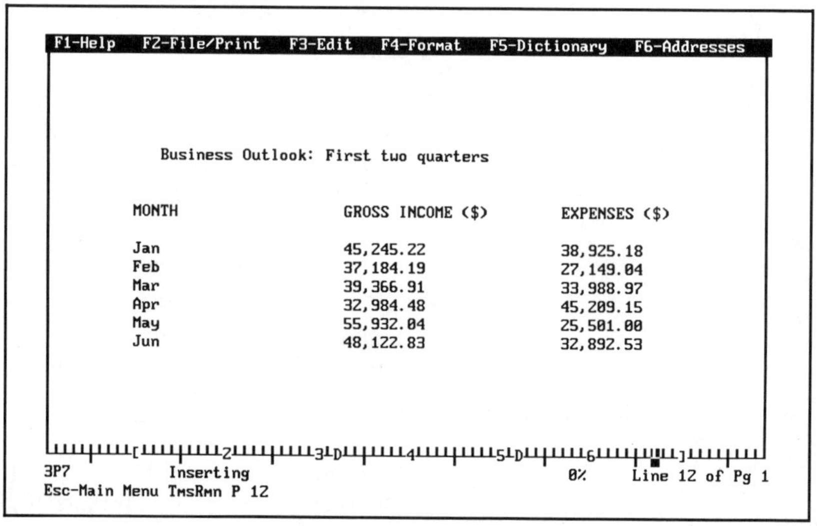

Figure 5.16: Figure 5.15 with two of the columns shifted

4. Delete the original tab settings, then enter the new ones:
    - Add decimal tabs to line up with the decimal points of the columns.
    - Add two new typewriter positions to line up with the beginning of each column heading.

5. Press ↵ and the Edit display reappears.

Points to Ponder

What this series of five steps does is to ensure that when the page is printed, the columns will line up properly on the decimal points, using the tab settings as guides. They will line up no matter what type of font is used for printing.

The two typewriter tabs guarantee that the column headings are positioned properly relative to the rest of the columns.

After completing the above process, you can then enter additional lines within the existing columns. Professional Write will line them up properly with their upper and lower neighbors.

You can change the tab settings of ordinary text columns by using the same process. In this case, you'd use typewriter tabs instead of decimal tabs, and each tab setting would correspond to the beginning of a column.

INSERTING BLOCKS AND FILES

When you paste a text block into the working copy, you need to be aware of tabs. Here are some things to keep in mind:

- When a block is written to the clipboard, either as the result of a cut or copy operation, the tab settings of each line within the block are copied as well.
- When a block is pasted from the clipboard into a document, the tab settings for each line within that block are pasted as well.

To preserve tabs, always paste to a blank line.

Thus you can reasonably expect that when you cut and paste a text block from one location to another within a document, the tab settings within that block will be preserved. This will be true, *provided that the cursor is on a blank line when you do the pasting*. If you paste into the middle of a line containing text, some or all of the tab settings of the pasted block may be lost.

You can insert the contents of another document file into the middle of the working copy. When you do so, the tab settings of that document are preserved. In this case, you don't have to worry about the cursor position when you read in the file: Professional Write always preserves the tab settings of the file that's read in. For more information on combining files, see Chapter 7.

SETTING THE PAGE LENGTH AND THE TOP/BOTTOM MARGINS

You can control the appearance of your document by adjusting the top and bottom margins. On the other hand, the page length is normally set to match the physical dimensions of the paper in your printer. Whenever you change the length of the printer paper, you will need to reset the page length within Professional Write.

PAGE LENGTH

The page length is equal to the maximum number of *lines* that can fit on a printed page. This number is determined by the size of the page and also by the printer.

For dot-matrix printers, here's how to calculate what this number is:

> Page length = (number of lines printed per inch) × (paper length in inches)

Most dot-matrix printers are set to print at 6 lines per inch, and therefore the most common size of printer paper, $8^1/_2 \times 11$ inches, is equivalent to 66 lines per page. Table 5.3 lists the more popular sizes of paper, along with the equivalent page lengths. These lengths apply only for printers that output 6 lines per inch. For printers that output at line spacings other than 6 per inch, the numbers in Table 5.3 won't apply.

Most laser printers can print on only 10 of the 11 inches of a standard full-size sheet ($8^1/_2 \times 11$). Using the above formula, and assuming 6 lines per inch, the correct page length to use is 60 lines. For most laser printers with standard paper, this is the correct value to use for the page length. Remember: The default page length for Professional Write is 66, so you need to change this before printing a document on a laser printer.

Table 5.3: Common Paper Sizes

PAPER SIZE (INCHES)	TOTAL LINES PER INCH
$8^1/_2 \times 11$	66 {assuming 6 lines per inch}
$8^1/_2 \times 14$	84
$8^1/_2 \times 17$	102

If you're using a laser printer, you can avoid having to change the page length for each document by setting a new default value for the page length. For details, see "How to Create New Automatic Formatting Defaults" in this chapter.

TOP/BOTTOM MARGINS

The top margin is equal to the number of *lines* between the top edge of a sheet and the first printed line of text (not including the header, which is printed in the top margin). Similarly, the bottom margin is equal to the number of lines between the bottom of a sheet and the last printed line (not including the footer, which is printed in the bottom margin).

Figure 5.17 illustrates the basic components of a printed page.

When you select values for page length and the top and bottom margins, Professional Write automatically calculates the number of lines available for text on each page. For example, here are the default values that Professional Write uses when it's installed:

Page length:	66
Top margin:	6
Bottom margin:	6

The number of lines available for normal text on each page is then 54 (66 – 12).

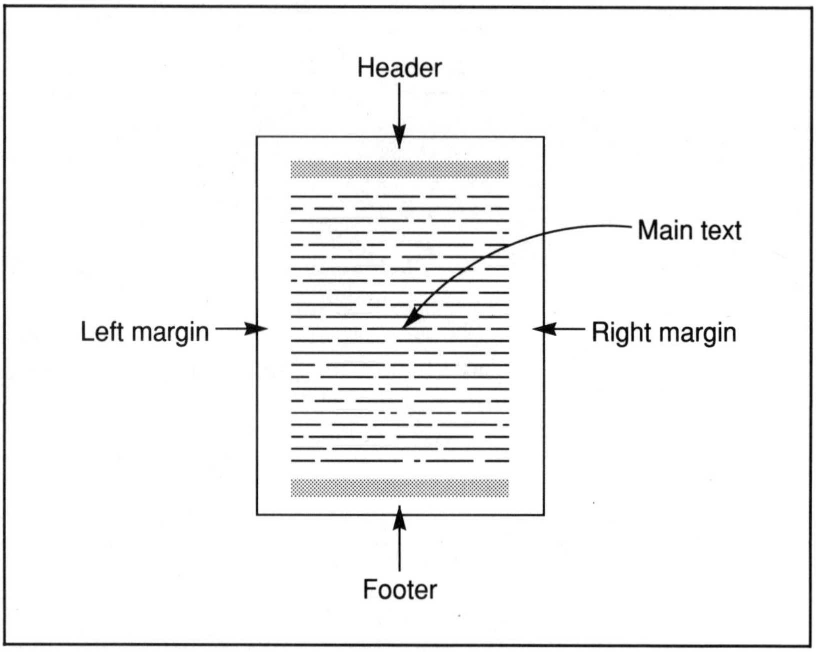

Figure 5.17: The components of a printed page

SETTING NEW VALUES

To change the value of the page length and top and bottom margins, Select *Set top/bottom margins & length* from the Format menu (F4). On the margins menu that appears (Figure 5.18), enter the value(s)

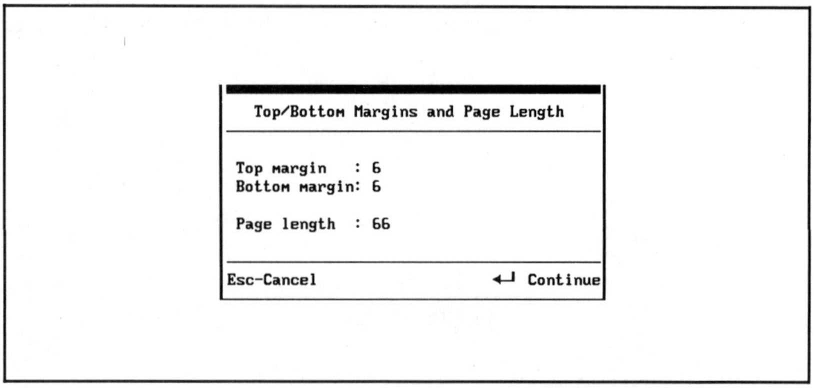

Figure 5.18: Menu for setting page length and top and bottom margins

that you want:

1. Move the cursor to the desired item using the Tab, ↑, or ↓ keys.
2. Enter the new value, overwriting the original one (Professional Write automatically shifts into the Overwrite mode when this menu is displayed).
3. When you have finished, press ↵ to have the new values take effect.

To return to the original values, press Esc while the menu is displayed.

Points to Ponder

- Settings for the page length and top and bottom margins affect the entire document. That is, you can't have some pages with one value for the top margin, and other pages with another.
- You can change any of these values anywhere within a document.
- The maximum value you can assign for a top or bottom margin is 18. The maximum page length is 999.

USING HEADERS AND FOOTERS

A *header* is a section of text that appears at the top of each page of a document. A *footer* appears at each page bottom. Headers and footers are handy ways of including document identification as part of each page. For example, if you're generating an annual report, you might want something like *XYZ Corp. 1989 Report* to appear at the bottom of each page. Headers and footers are also convenient places to insert page numbers.

You can include a one- or two-line header or footer (or both) in a document, and you can create or edit a header or footer from any place within a document. However, when you enter a header or footer, it applies to the entire document—not just to the page on which you happened to create it.

When you create a header or footer, Professional Write will display it along with each page on the Edit screen, and thus you have some idea how the header or footer will look when printed. For an even better idea of how the final printed page will appear, you can use the Preview feature. You will see the headers and footers almost exactly as they will appear on the printed page.

If there is enough room in the top or bottom margin, Professional Write will insert a blank line between the text body and the header or footer. If there's even more room in the margin, a blank line will be inserted between the edge of the paper and the header or footer.

Professional Write lets you control the appearance of the header or footer. You can adjust their horizontal position on the page, as well as select their style (boldface, etc.). You can also specify the font to be used for a header or footer, provided that your printer supports different fonts.

If you want page numbers to appear in your document, they must be placed in the header or footer. You can control the horizontal placement of the numbers, and you can also select on which page the numbering begins.

HOW TO ENTER HEADERS AND FOOTERS

You don't need to be at the top or bottom of a document to create or edit a header or footer.

To create a header or footer, select *Set header* or *Set footer* from the Format menu (F4). The Header or Footer menu is displayed (see Figure 5.19). Except for the title, the menus are identical. To make an entry on a particular line, first move the cursor to that line using the Tab, Shift-Tab, ↑, or ↓ keys. Then make the new entry on that line. When you have finished, press ↵ to have the header or footer take effect.

Let's go over the various entries that appear on the Header or Footer menu:

You can switch between the Overwrite and Insert modes with the Ins key.

Lines 1 and 2: Enter the text for the header or footer on these two lines. You can enter either one or two lines of text. For single-line headers or footers, placing the text in *Line 2* instead of *Line 1* will position the header or footer one line lower on the page.

Position: You can control the horizontal positioning of the header or footer with this entry as follows:

- **C** Centered between the header or footer margins

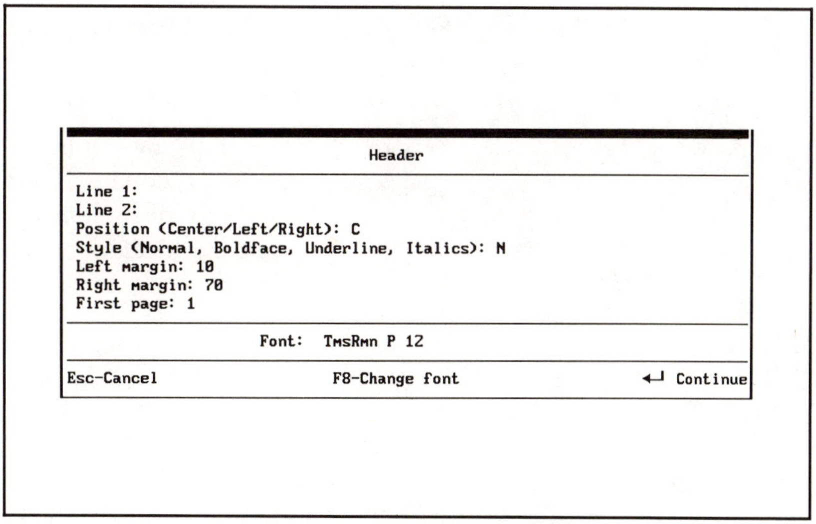

Figure 5.19: The menu for inserting header information

- **L** Left justify (that is, against the left margin)
- **R** Right justify (that is, against the right margin)

Style: The selection for this entry controls the style of the text in the header or footer, as follows:

- **B** Boldface
- **U** Underline
- **I** Italics
- **N** Normal text, that is, none of the above

You can use any combination of the last three, provided that your printer supports that style (some printers, for example, don't print italics).

Left and Right Margins: You can control the margins of the header and footer independent of the margins of the document. Thus you have the option of placing a header or footer outside of the normal document margins for special emphasis. When the Header or Footer menu is first displayed, these entries for the margins are set at the original default values (usually 10 and 70). You can change either or both margins by entering new values (any number between 1 and 250).

First page: This entry determines the first page on which the header or footer is printed. For example, if the first page of a document is a cover, you will probably want the headers or footers to appear starting on page 2.

If the **Font** entry reads *Normal Font*, then your printer can't output in different fonts, and this entry can't be changed.

Font: This entry displays the font in which the header or footer will be printed. That is, a different font can be used from that of the main text. For example, in Figure 5.19 the header font is listed as TmsRmn P 12, which translates to Times Roman Normal 12-point Portrait. To change the Font entry:

- Press F8, and the Font menu will appear.
- Move the cursor to the font that you want by using the ↑, ↓, PgUp, and PgDn keys.
- Press ↵ to select that font.

Page numbers can't appear in both a header and a footer in the same document.

If you select a font that's too large, the text on the header or footer lines may overlap either with each other or with the body text. For more information about fonts, see Chapters 8 and 9.

PAGE NUMBERING AND PAGE BREAKS

You can control a document's appearance by forcing page breaks at selected locations. In addition, you can create page numbers on each printed page, either in the footer or the header.

PAGE BREAKS

Normally, Professional Write starts a new page (called a *page break*) when the current page "fills up," that is, when the number of lines on the current page plus the lines in the top and bottom margins equals the number of lines specified in the *page length* option on the Format menu. A page break appears as a horizontal double line across the entire screen.

You can force printing to begin at the top of a new page by creating a page break in the document. This can be useful, for example, when you want a particular section of a document, such as a table, to appear entirely on the same page.

To create a page break, insert the command *NEW PAGE* (or the abbreviated command *N*) wherever you want a new printed page to begin. Normally, this command is placed at the beginning of a paragraph.

CREATING PAGE NUMBERS

Page numbers can appear within a document as part of either a header or a footer. The page number can appear by itself, or as part of other text.

To specify page numbering, simply insert the special command *n* (where n is the first page number) anywhere within the text of the header or footer. For instance, to start page numbering with the digit 2, enter ***2*** as part of the header or footer text. You can be as creative as you like when using page numbering. For example, you could enter **Page number *1*** as the text for a footer. The header for the pages of the document would then read *Page number 1*, *Page number 2*, and so on.

Suppose that you are creating a document and you want all pages except the first one (a title page) to be numbered starting with the number 1. Figure 5.20 illustrates a set of entries on the Header menu that could be used for this document. A sample output page is shown in Figure 5.21.

Note that the header consists of two lines, with the page number on the second line. Also note that the page numbering will begin with page number 1, but starting on page 2, because the title page doesn't get numbered.

The header is printed in italics and in a smaller size than the default font. This was done by selecting the header font to be Times Roman 8 Point (Portrait), and also by selecting *Italics* in the *Style* entry. Notice also that the second line includes the line numbering command *1* in addition to other ordinary header text.

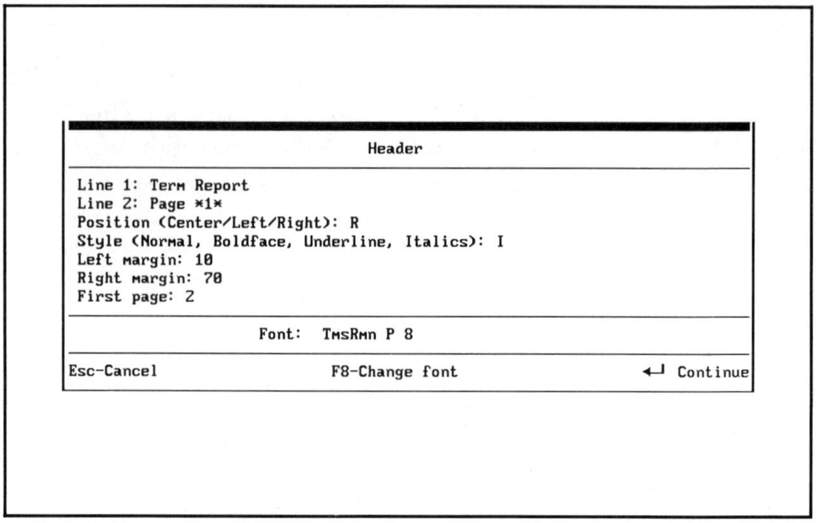

Figure 5.20: This header will be printed with Times Roman 8 Point Italic.

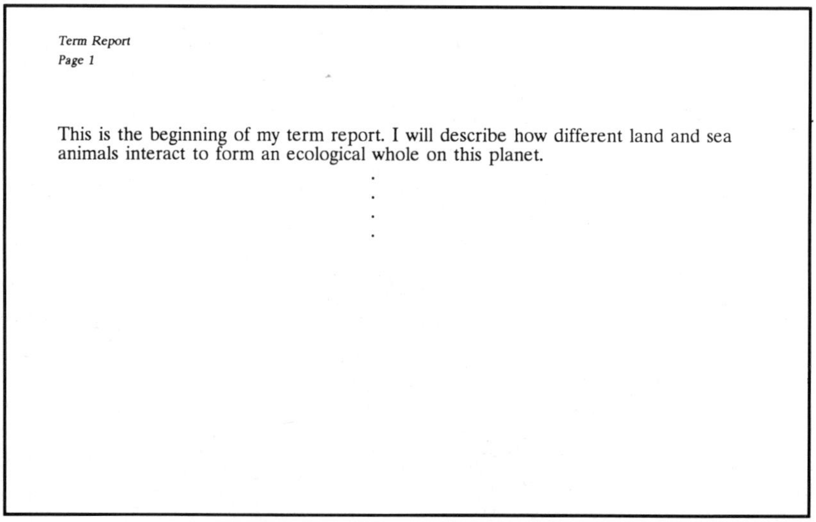
Term Report
Page 1

This is the beginning of my term report. I will describe how different land and sea animals interact to form an ecological whole on this planet.

Figure 5.21: This header was generated from the specifications in Figure 5.20.

Points to Ponder

If you create a header or footer for a document, it will appear on the screen along with each page. However, if you also create page numbers within a header or footer, these numbers may or may not correspond with the page numbers appearing on the Status line. This discrepancy is not a problem, but you should be aware of why it happens.

First, in the Header or Footer menu (see Figure 5.18), you can specify on which page the page numbers are to begin by selecting *First page*. Furthermore, you can also select the starting page number.

Professional Write always displays the page numbers for a document in the lower-right corner of the screen. These numbers are Professional Write's count of the number of physical pages scrolling by on the screen; *they are not necessarily related to any page numbers that you may be creating from within a header or footer.*

For example, suppose you make the following entries in the Header menu for a document:

Line 1: Page *2*

First page: 1

When you begin working on the document, you'll see *Page 2* appear in the header at the top of the first page, but you'll also see *Pg 1* appear at the bottom of the screen.

LINE FORMATTING

You can build your document either with single or double spacing (single is the default). You can also change the spacing of any selected groups of existing lines from single to double spacing and vice versa. This can be a useful feature when preparing a rough draft, for example: create the draft with single spacing, then, just before printing, change the spacing of the entire document from single to double and print it so that you can easily make corrections by hand. Later, when you are ready for the final printing, reset the document to single spacing.

You can also control the horizontal positioning of individual lines—for instance, you can center a title line on a page.

When working with a document on the screen, always use single spacing to maximize the amount of text that's visible.

SELECTING DOUBLE AND SINGLE SPACING

When you begin working on a document, Professional Write defaults to single spacing. At any time while you are entering new text you can switch back and forth between single and double spacing. When you switch from one to the other, the spacing of text that's already been entered remains the same. The new spacing will begin with the current line.

When double spacing is on, the word *Double* appears at the bottom of the screen.

To turn on double spacing, select *Turn double spacing on/off* from the Format menu (F4). To turn on single spacing, select the same item again. In other words, the item *Turn double spacing on/off* is a *toggle*: Selecting it switches you between single and double spacing.

You can also use the speed key Ctrl-D (D for Double) to switch between double and single spacing.

Changing the Spacing of Existing Text

To change the spacing (either to single or double) of an existing group of lines:

1. Select those lines as a text block and then press F10.
2. Select *Single space* or *Double space* from the Text Block Operations menu.

Because a line's spacing (single or double) is a characteristic of that line, when you cut and paste a group of lines, the spacing of those lines is cut and pasted as well. With double-spaced text, the last text line that's cut and pasted will always be followed by a blank line.

SETTING THE HORIZONTAL POSITION OF A LINE

Professional Write includes a set of keystrokes that allows you to quickly position a line, either to the far left, to the far right, or centered within the existing margins. To reposition a particular line, first move the cursor to any position on that line. Then, from the Format menu (F4) select one of the following options:

- To center that line, select *Center line* or press the speed key Ctrl-X.
- To move the line so that it's next to the left margin, select *Left justify line*.

- To move the line so that it's next to the right margin, select *Right justify line*.

Most text lines are left justified to begin with, and thus you would probably use the *Left justify* option only to reposition a line that had previously been adjusted to the center or to the right.

Note that because line centering is so frequently used, there is a special speed key for it, Ctrl-X.

If you select the Font Format print style from the Print Options dialog box, lines may not center or right justify properly. If this happens, you can use two special commands, *CENTER* and *RIGHT*, to force lines to behave properly. To center a line, insert the command *CENTER* either at the beginning of the line or at the beginning of a blank line just above. To right justify a line, use the *RIGHT* command. Each of these commands affects only the line immediately following.

Full Line Justification

The term *full justification* refers to a line that's both left and right justified. To fully justify a line, Professional Write inserts blanks between words until the last word on the line is against the right margin. You can fully justify an entire document, or only selected lines within the document.

To fully justify an entire document, select the *justified* print style from the Print Options dialog box, as part of the process of printing the document. For more information about this feature, see "The Print Options Dialog Box" in Chapter 10.

To fully justify a line or group of lines, the commands *JUSTIFY YES* and *JUSTIFY NO* are used (you can also use the abbreviated commands *JY Y* and *JY N*). Here's how to fully justify a group of lines:

Make sure that the Insert mode is on.

1. Move the cursor to the beginning of the first line to be justified.
2. Enter the command *JUSTIFY YES*.
3. Move the cursor to the end of the last line to be justified.
4. Enter the command *JUSTIFY NO*.

You can use the *JUSTIFY* commands as often as needed in a document. On the other hand, if you're going to justify the entire document, do so from the Print Options menu, rather than inserting a *JUSTIFY ON* command in the text.

Generally, full justification is best reserved for special situations. The reason is that a page containing fully justified text often appears to have too much white space, which is caused by the extra blanks inserted between words. Experiments have shown that this white space slows the eyes down as they read the page. (You might try this on a page of text: print it twice—once with and once without full justification.)

MATCHING DISPLAYED AND PRINTED LINE BREAKS

Normally, the line breaks displayed on the screen don't match those of the page when printed because the Ruler measures in units of *tenths of an inch*, whereas the printed characters may be either a variable-pitch font or a fixed-pitch font other than 10-pitch. However, in some cases you may want the line breaks on the screen to match those when printed. This might occur, for example, if you are entering long tables of columns, and you don't want to worry about unexpected line breaks in the table.

You can do this by temporarily turning off a parameter called the *Font Format print style*. Normally, this parameter is in effect for the entire document. However, you can turn off the Font Format print style for selected groups of lines anywhere in a document. For these lines, and these lines only, the line breaks on the screen will exactly match those when printed.

To turn off the Font Format print style somewhere in a document, enter the command *FORMAT NO* (or *F N*) on a blank line at that point in the document. Then, at the point in the text where you want to reinstate the Font Format print style, enter the command *FORMAT YES* (or *F Y*) on another blank line.

Note that when the Font Format print style is not in effect, the Ruler measures in units of *characters* instead of tenths of an inch. This means that for those sections of a document in which Font Format is not in effect, you may want to readjust the left or right margins. For example, if you were using a Courier 12 pitch font (12 characters per inch), and you wanted a right margin of 7 inches, you would select a right margin setting of 84 ($12 \times 7 = 84$).

HOW TO CREATE NEW AUTOMATIC FORMATTING DEFAULTS

When you begin a new document, Professional Write assigns default values for the various page formatting characteristics. These include the following:

- Left margin: 10
- Right margin: 70
- Top margin: 6
- Bottom margin: 6
- Page length: 66
- Tabs: One at 15

In addition, the default values for headers and footers are those shown in Figure 5.18.

You can change any of these defaults. Then, whenever you start a new document, these new values will automatically be in effect. Here are the steps for creating one or more new default values:

1. Erase the working copy by selecting *Erase working copy* from the File/Print menu (F2).
2. Change the values of all items that you want to become new default values. For example, if you want the default left margin to be 15, select *Set left/right margins* from the Format menu (F4), and then set the left margin to 15, as described earlier in this chapter.
3. After you have set all the new values, save the empty working copy to a file named PW.DEF. This file must be written to the directory where all of the Professional Write programs are stored (see Appendix A for a discussion of the Professional Write directory).

For floppy-disk computers, write the file to the disk labeled *Program disk*.

Any time in the future that you run Professional Write, the contents of the file PW.DEF will be used to set the default values that you selected. Note that after you create PW.DEF, you must exit from Professional Write and then rerun it so that it can read the new default values from PW.DEF.

To restore the original default values, simply delete the file PW.DEF and then rerun Professional Write.

If you want to restore the original default values but save the ones that you created for possible later use, rename the file PW.DEF to something else, instead of deleting it. Then, whenever you want to restore these values, rename the file again—to PW.DEF.

6

Using Professional Write's Editing Aids

AMONG THE ADVANTAGES OF MODERN COMPUTER software are the many fringe benefits that we more or less take for granted. Just a few years ago word processing programs couldn't do much more than just that: process words; moreover, you paid a great deal for one of these relatively primitive (by current standards) programs. However, when you purchase a software package like Professional Write, you get not only excellent word processing at a bargain price (compared to what you would have paid as recently as five years ago), but you also acquire a whole array of built-in tools that enormously enhance your editing capabilites.

You'll find out about some of these writing aids in this chapter. They include the following:

- A built-in spelling checker that can be used for examining an entire document for misspelled or other questionable words, or for checking the spelling of a single word. Here, a "questionable" word is one that either can't be found in a dictionary, appears as a double word in the text, or contains questionable capitalization.
- A thesaurus that can be used for finding synonyms for any word in a document.
- A search capability that allows you to find any desired word or character *string* (that is, a sequence of characters treated as a unit).
- The ability to replace automatically all occurrences of a particular character string with another string.

FINDING MISSPELLED WORDS

You can use the spelling checker along with Professional Write's online dictionary to scan part or all of an entire document for misspelled words. You can also check the spelling of any particular word. If you frequently use special words that aren't included in this dictionary, you can create a personal dictionary. Professional Write will then use this dictionary along with its own when checking for spelling errors.

When the spelling checker encounters a questionable word, you can choose to accept it as is. Alternatively, you can edit it to correct any misspelling; you can also add it to your personal dictionary.

SPELL CHECKING A WORD OR DOCUMENT

You can have the software check for spelling errors in a single word, part of a document, or the entire document. Actually, the spelling checker does more than just look for spelling errors. It will *flag* (pause with an error message) any of the following:

See "How to Create a Personal Dictionary," below.

- Any word that does not appear in either Professional Write's built-in dictionary or in your own personal dictionary.
- Some capitalization errors.
- Any word that's repeated twice in a row.

When any of the above items turns up, Professional Write pauses with an error message for you, indicating that the word is questionable. You must then decide what to do about the word. To see what options are available to you, read "Handling Questionable Words," below.

Checking a Single Word

To check the spelling of a particular word:

1. Position the cursor anywhere on the word.
2. Select *Proof word* from the Dictionary menu (F5).

Alternatively, you can press the speed key combination Ctrl-A.

If the word is found in either the on-line dictionary or the personal dictionary, the cursor is moved beyond the word. However, if the word is not found, then it is flagged with an error message, and you must decide what to do with it.

Scanning a Document for Errors

To check through a document for errors:

1. Position the cursor at the place in the document where you want the checking to start.

2. Select *Proof to end of document* from the Dictionary menu (F5).

The spelling checker begins scanning the words in the document. If a word is not found in either dictionary, or if it is otherwise questionable, the scanning pauses with an error message, and you must decide what to do with this word.

HANDLING QUESTIONABLE WORDS

The spelling checker will question a word when the word can't be found in either dictionary, when a double word is found, or when the word's capitalization doesn't agree with the corresponding dictionary entry. Whenever a questionable word is found, you must decide on a course of action. The possibilities are discussed below.

Possible Misspelling

If the word can't be found in a dictionary, it's highlighted on the screen and a menu of your alternatives is displayed (see Figure 6.1). Use the ↓ and ↑ keys to select an option and then press ↵.

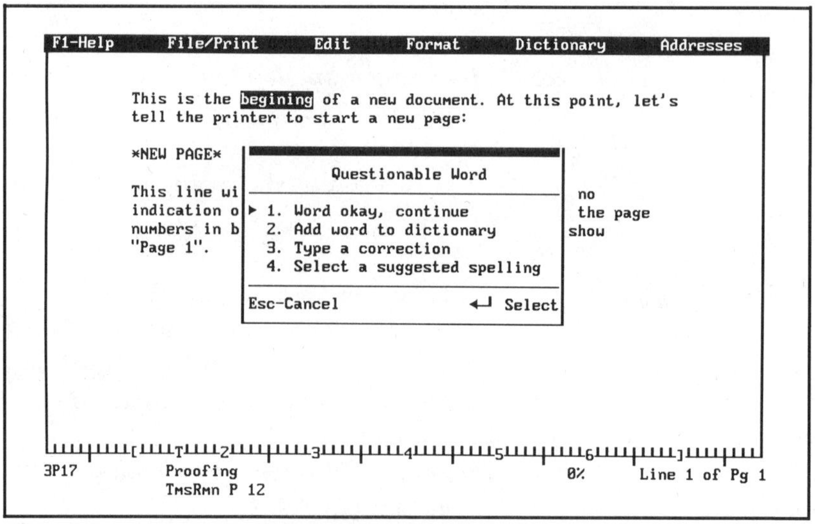

Figure 6.1: Professional Write finds a questionable word

Here are the menu options:

Word okay, continue: Accept the word as it is and continue with the scanning.

Add word to dictionary: Accept the word and continue with the scanning, *and* add the word to your personal dictionary.

Type a correction: Edit the word to correct its spelling. After you have entered the correct spelling, press ↵ and the word scan will continue.

Select a suggested spelling: Professional Write displays any possible alternative spellings that it finds in the dictionaries (see Figure 6.2). You can then:

- Reject all of these words and return to the previous menu by pressing the Esc key.
- Select one of these words and substitute it for the original word in the text. To select a word, use the ↓ and ↑ keys and then press ↵.

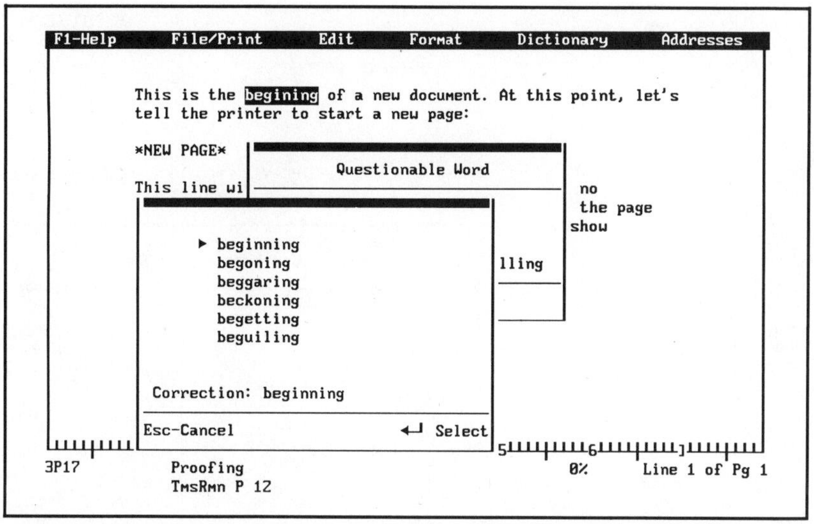

Figure 6.2: Select one of these words as a replacement for the misspelled word

Note (from the shape of the cursor) that you are in the Overwrite edit mode.

- Select a word and then edit it before substituting it for the original word. To edit a word, first move the cursor to it by using the ↑ and ↓ keys. Edit the word by using the → and ← keys to position the cursor and then make your corrections. After you have finished making changes, press ↵ and the edited word will be substituted for the original one.

The spelling checker does its best to handle plurals and verb tenses. These words, if properly spelled, generally won't be flagged by the checker. On the other hand, if a verb or plural is found to be questionable, then the checker flags the word and also tries to match the form of the word when suggesting alternative spellings. Table 6.1 gives some illustrations.

Double Words

If a double word is encountered during a word scan, the first word of the pair is flagged, and a menu of your choices appears, as shown in Figure 6.3. To make a menu selection, highlight it by using the ↓ and ↑ keys and then press ↵.

Here are your choices from this menu:

Word okay, continue: Accept the double word as is and continue with the word scan.

Delete word: Delete one of the double words and continue with the word scan.

Table 6.1: Alternative Words Suggested by Professional Write's Spelling Checker

MISSPELLED WORD	SUGGESTED ALTERNATIVES
confoorm	confirm, conform, condor
confoorms	confirms, conforms, condors
corect	correct, cornet, corrected, correctly
corected	corrected, corniced, correct, coquetted
seeeing	seeing, seine

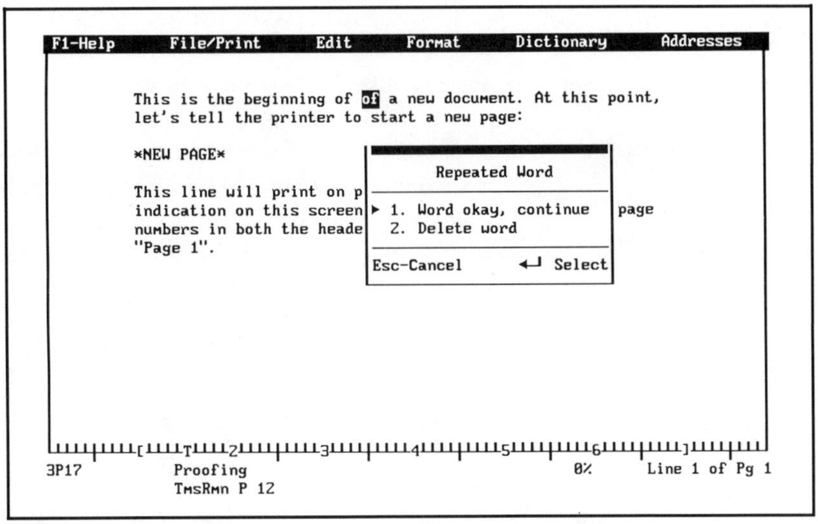

Figure 6.3: The spelling checker has found a repeated word

Note that the spelling checker will not stop for double words that are separated by any type of puncuation, as in the following phrase: "... he didn't go there. There will be...". On the other hand, the two consecutive words "...there There" will stop the scanning because the uppercase T and lowercase t are considered equivalent in this case (see the next section).

Questionable Capitalization

The entry for most words in the spelling checker's built-in dictionary is lowercased. A few special words are capitalized, such as proper names. For example, the dictionary contains an entry for *Europe*, but not for *europe*.

When the spelling checker examines a word for spelling, it looks for a corresponding word in its built-in dictionary and also in your personal dictionary. Except as noted below, a word is considered to be correctly spelled if it matches the spelling of an entry in a dictionary, and if one of the following is also true:

- The word is all lowercase.
- The word is all uppercase.
- The first letter of the word is capitalized.

If a word is capitalized in any other way, it will generally be flagged. For example, any of the following would be considered correct spelling by the spelling checker: *joker*, *JOKER*, or *Joker*. On the other hand, *joKer* would be flagged.

If a dictionary entry has any capitalization, then a corresponding document word must match this capitalization or the word will be flagged. For instance, the word *europe* will be flagged, but *Europe* will not. As another example, suppose you have the entry *dBASE* in your personal dictionary. Then a document word *dBASE* would not be flagged, but *dbase* would.

HOW TO CREATE A PERSONAL DICTIONARY

The spelling checker's built-in dictionary contains over 75,000 words—essentially all of the commonly used words in their various forms (look, looks, looked, looking, etc.). However, if you frequently use technical language in your documents, you will find that many of your words are being flagged because they are not in the built-in dictionary. You can correct this by creating your own personal dictionary, containing words that you are likely to use and whose spelling you would like checked.

When you create a personal dictionary, it's stored in the file PERSONAL.SPC on the Professional Write directory. Whenever the spelling checker scans words in a document, it also checks for the existence of the file PERSONAL.SPC. If it does exist, the spelling checker uses it, as well as the built-in dictionary.

For floppy-disk machines, the dictionary must reside on the disk labeled Dictionary, and the maximum size is about 500 words.

You can create a personal dictionary containing approximately 5,000 words on a hard-disk computer. You can edit the dictionary at any time, adding new words or deleting those that are no longer frequently used. When your dictionary fills up, Professional Write will issue a message to that effect. You can then edit the dictionary and delete infrequently used words to make room for new ones. If necessary, you can even create several personal dictionaries for different purposes.

There are a number of ways to create a personal dictionary, all of which are described in the following sections.

BUILDING A DICTIONARY BY DIRECT INSERTION

You can begin creating a personal dictionary by entering a set of words into a blank working copy, then saving it to the file PERSONAL.SPC in the Professional Write directory. For example, Figures 6.4 and 6.5 show two different styles that you can use for entering words. In Figure 6.4, each line consists of a single word. In Figure 6.5, several words have been entered on each line. Notice that the same words have been used in both figures.

Rules for Entering Words

Make sure that each word is preceded by a blank.

When you enter words into the working copy, you can enter them in any order, and as many words as you like can be entered on each line. You can even insert punctuation between words, but make sure that each word is immediately preceded by a blank. For instance, the string *aflatoxin, toxinaxis* will be treated as a single word because there is no blank space between the comma and the *t*.

If you insert any capital letters into a word, the entry in the personal dictionary will retain that capitalization. For example, if you enter *Smithitis*, then when the word *smithitis* appears in a document it will be flagged by the spelling checker.

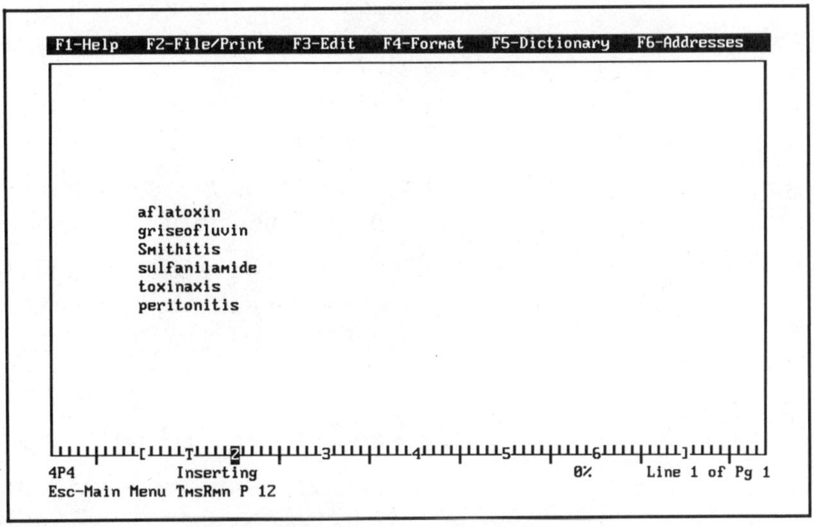

Figure 6.4: A file for generating a personal dictionary

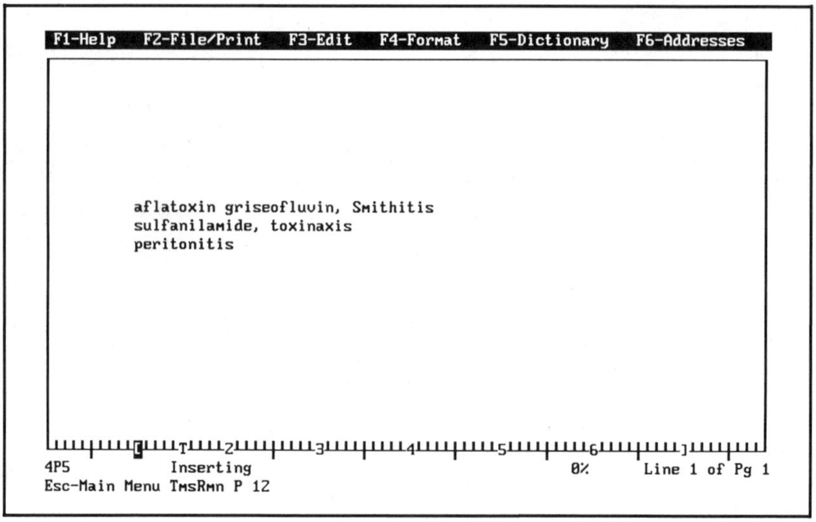

Figure 6.5: Another type of file for generating a personal dictionary

HOW THE PERSONAL DICTIONARY IS GENERATED

Figure 6.6 shows the personal dictionary that is generated by the working copy in either Figure 6.4 or 6.5. If you study these figures, you will see that before the working copy is saved, a good deal of processing is done. Here's what Professional Write does as it generates a personal dictionary from your working copy:

- All punctuation marks, such as commas and decimal points, are stripped out.
- If any word in the working copy matches an entry in the built-in dictionary, it's deleted from the working copy.
- The remaining words are alphabetized. Words beginning with capital letters are sorted first, and then the remaining words are sorted.

CREATING A DICTIONARY FROM DOCUMENTS

If you have a long, computerized document that contains a large number of the words that you want to become part of a personal

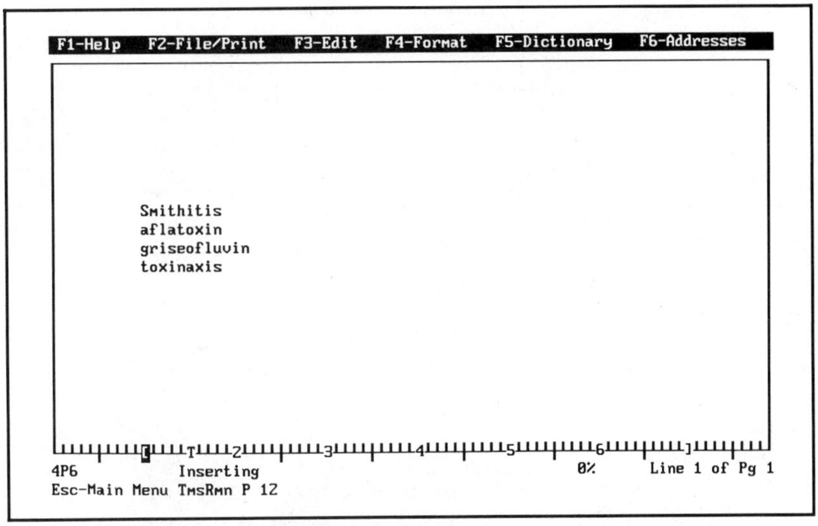

Figure 6.6: The personal dictionary created from either of the documents shown in Figures 6.4 and 6.5

dictionary, that document itself may offer the easiest way to begin creating the dictionary. Here's how:

- Retrieve this document into the working copy.
- Save the copy to the file PERSONAL.SPC in the Professional Write directory. The document will be processed before being saved, and all words already in the on-line dictionary will be deleted, as well as all punctuation marks. The remaining words will be alphabetized.
- You can view the contents of the dictionary by retrieving it back into the working copy.

For example, the tiny document shown in Figure 6.7 will generate the personal dictionary shown in Figure 6.5.

For a discussion of retrieving various types of documents, see Chapter 7.

The document that you input as a source for the dictionary doesn't necessarily have to be in a Professional Write file. Professional Write can read documents in a variety of standard word processing formats. For details, see Chapter 7.

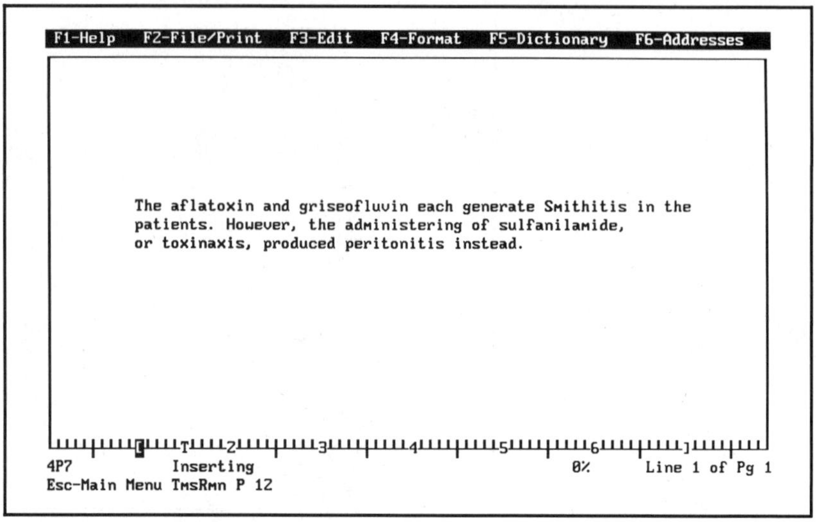

Figure 6.7: A technical document can be the source of a personal dictionary

Deleting Unwanted Uppercase Words

There is one slight problem when using a document to create a personal dictionary: If a word that was added to the dictionary is capitalized in the original document (because, for example, it began a sentence), that word will also be capitalized in the dictionary. To deal with this possibility, you may want to retrieve the personal dictionary back into Professional Write, and then scan the first part of the dictionary (where all the uppercase words are stored) for any words incorrectly capitalized. If you find such a word, just replace the capital letter (or letters) with lowercase. When the dictionary is saved, it will be re-alphabetized.

If you want to use a particular document to create the dictionary, but it's not in a format that's acceptable to Professional Write, one possible way to gain access to that file is as follows: If possible, convert the document to an ASCII file, using the software package that originally created the document. Next, read that ASCII file into Professional Write and then save the working copy to the file PERSONAL.SPC. Again, see Chapter 7 for more details on inputting ASCII files.

EDITING THE DICTIONARY

You can edit your personal dictionary just as you would any other file, adding new words and deleting others. To do so, you must first retrieve the file PERSONAL.SPC into Professional Write.

To delete a particular word, you can place the cursor on it and press the speed key Ctrl-W.

> You can move the cursor quickly to the word that you want by using Professional Write's Find function. See "How to Find and Replace Words," below.

To add new words, just enter them at any convenient place in the file. When the file is saved, it's alphabetized, as described in the section "How the Personal Dictionary Is Generated," above.

Enlarging the Dictionary with On-Line Documents

> You can enlarge the dictionary in this way only with document files in either Professional Write or ASCII format.

Here's a very convenient way to add to your dictionary: If you have one or more document files that contain words that you would like to add to the dictionary, you can merge those words directly into the dictionary. For instance, these documents might be technical articles that you have transferred from some other computer.

To add words contained in a document to the personal dictionary:

1. First retrieve the file PERSONAL.SPC into Professional Write.
2. Merge the new document file into the working copy: Select *Insert file* from the File/Print menu (F2) and then enter the complete file name, including the disk drive and/or directory.

> You can merge the document anywhere in the working copy.

3. Save the working copy back to PERSONAL.SPC.
4. Reload PERSONAL.SPC back into Professional Write.
5. Scan through the uppercase words for any that don't belong there (see "Deleting Unwanted Uppercase Words," above).

Note that you can insert the new document file anywhere into the working copy because when it's saved back to PERSONAL.SPC, all the extraneous words are deleted and it's re-alphabetized.

To merge several different documents into the dictionary, repeat the second step above for each file.

If you have a document file that contains words you would like to add to the dictionary, but the file is not in either ASCII or Professional Write format, you may still be able to use it: Try to find a way in which the file can be converted to an ASCII format, possibly by using the software that originally generated the file.

HOW TO USE SEVERAL PERSONAL DICTIONARIES

If you do a lot of technical work, you may find that you have too many words to fit into the personal dictionary, which can hold a maximum of about 5,000 for hard-disk computers. One possible way to get around this limitation is to create different dictionaries for different circumstances (each dictionary has the same maximum size of 5,000 words). For instance, if you work both with law and computers, you might create one dictionary for legal terminology and another for technical words related to computers. You could then use whichever dictionary was relevant to the document you were working on at the moment.

However, you need to be just a little tricky because the spelling checker can work only with the personal dictionary in the file PERSONAL.SPC. To illustrate, suppose that you are going to create two dictionaries, one for law and the other for computing. Here are the steps to follow, assuming that there is no other personal dictionary already named PERSONAL.SPC:

1. First, create the personal dictionary for legal terms: Follow the steps described earlier for creating a personal dictionary, and then save the file to PERSONAL.SPC in the Professional Write directory.
2. Retrieve the file PERSONAL.SPC back into the working copy, and make sure that it was properly created (there should be only one word per line, with all words alphabetized).
3. Save the working copy to a *new file* with a different name, such as PERSONAL.LAW, on the Professional Write directory.
4. Delete the file PERSONAL.SPC.
5. Create the personal dictionary for computer terminology, following the steps described earlier, and again save this file to PERSONAL.SPC.

6. Retrieve PERSONAL.SPC back into the working copy.
7. Save the working copy to another new file with a new name, such as PERSONAL.CMP, on the Professional Write directory.

At first glance, it would seem that steps 2 and 6 are unnecessary: Why retrieve a file that you have just stored? The reason is that when PERSONAL.SPC is saved, Professional Write does a lot of processing before writing the file to the disk. When you read the file back into the working copy, it's quite different from the working copy that you just saved. Note that this happens *only* when the file PERSONAL.SPC is saved.

You now have two different files, PERSONAL.LAW and PERSONAL.CMP, each of which contains a different personal dictionary.

To use either of these dictionaries, retrieve it into the working copy, and then save it to the file PERSONAL.SPC.

FINDING SYNONYMS

Sometimes when you're writing a document you know what you want to say, but you can't find quite the right word for the exact shade of meaning that you have in mind. Like many word processors, Professional Write has a handy writing aid that can usually help you: the thesaurus.

The thesaurus, which uses the same built-in dictionary as the spelling checker, allows you to find synonyms for any word in a document. Although this thesaurus isn't as large as some that are commercially available, it's more than adequate for nearly any word that you can think of.

To use the thesaurus, just select the word about which you're not sure, invoke the thesaurus from the Dictionary menu (F5), and a list of possible alternatives will pop up. If you find one that you like, you can have it automatically replace the original word in the text.

To find synonyms of a word:

The PgDn-More message at the bottom of the window indicates that there are other synonymous words to see. The phrase "Meaning 1 of 3" indicates that there are three pages of synonyms accessible by using the PgDn key.

1. Move the cursor to any part of the word.
2. Select *Find synonyms* from the Dictionary menu (F5). After a short pause, a list of synonyms appears. For example, Figure 6.8 shows a list of synonyms for the word *idea*.

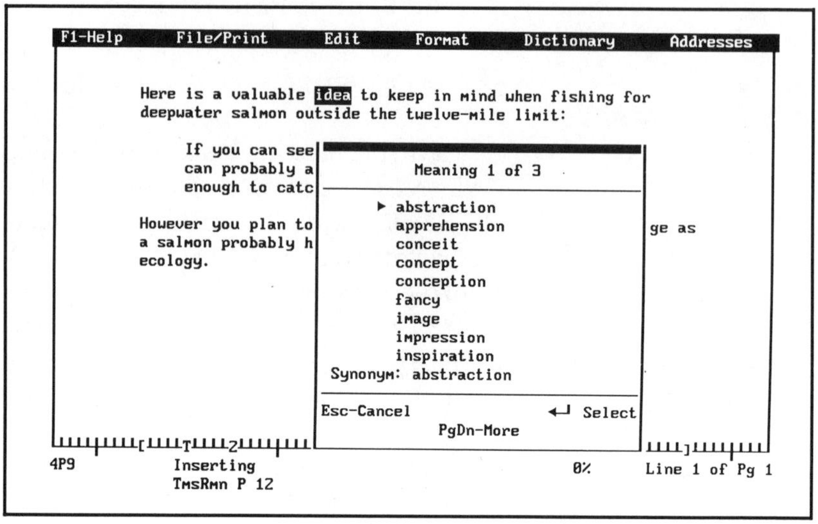

Figure 6.8: A list of synonyms for the word *idea*

3. If you find a word you prefer to the original one, highlight by using the ↑ and ↓ keys. That word will also appear on the *Synonym* line.
4. If necessary, you can edit this new word on the *Synonym* line: Move the text cursor as necessary with the ← and → keys and then enter any replacement text.
5. After the *Synonym* line displays the new word exactly as you want it, press ↵, and the new word will replace the original one in the text.

If you start typing before moving the cursor, the original word on the *Synonym* line will disappear.

Points to Ponder

If you find a synonym that's closer to your intended meaning than the original word but still not exactly right, you can search further by finding the synonyms for the synonym. Here is one way to do this:

1. Press Esc to exit from the synonym list.
2. Enter the new word into the text *right next to the original one.*
3. Find the synonyms for new word, as described above.

You can continue this process until you find the best word for your particular meaning. After you do, go back and delete the original word from the text, as well as any other unwanted synonyms that you may have temporarily placed onto the screen.

The thesaurus has certain limitations. You will find that there are no synonyms for some very common words, such as *is* and *my*, simply because such common words have no true synonyms. It isn't strictly true, therefore, that you can find a synonym for *every* word in a document.

In addition, the thesaurus does not handle irregular verb tenses or plurals very well. For example, there are many synonyms for *deposit* or *play*, but none for *deposits* or *playing*. Generally, here's what to do when you want to find synonyms of either type of word:

1. Replace the word in the original text with its root. For example, replace *playing* with *play*.
2. Find the synonyms of the root.
3. After you have found a suitable synonym, press ↵ to replace the original word.
4. Edit the replacement word to the correct form.

As you work with the thesaurus, you will find that it is by no means infallible. For example, you may find that *word 2* is a synonym of *word 1*, but not vice versa. That is, when you look up the synonyms of *word 2*, *word 1* isn't on the list. This limitation is typical of many word processing thesauri, and it doesn't mean that it's no good. It just indicates that it's not yet perfect.

You may also find that some words that you think should be in the thesaurus aren't there. Again, electronic thesauri are relatively new, and techniques for their development are still being improved. You may still want to have a copy of *Roget's Thesaurus* nearby to help you formulate those ideas whose exact expression continues to elude you.

HOW TO FIND AND REPLACE WORDS

You can use the *Find and Replace* feature to locate a particular *search string*. A search string can be a word, a group of words, or part of a word. This feature is one of the most convenient to have at your fingertips, and you will be amazed at the number of ways in which it can be used. For instance, you can use the *Find* part of Find and Replace to help you quickly locate a particular section of a long document: Just specify a word or phrase that you know is there, and the software will quickly locate the section you need.

When searching for strings, you can either specify the exact capitalization, or you can tell Professional Write to ignore case while searching.

You can also use Find and Replace to replace all instances of a particular string with another one. This replacement can be done automatically, or you can have the program pause for your verification before each replacement is made.

The Find and Replace feature also has other uses. For instance, you can delete specified words or phrases in a document. You can also count the number of words in all or part of a document.

HOW TO FIND A WORD OR A GROUP OF WORDS

Suppose that you want to find the next occurrence of *search string* in the working copy. Here's how to do it:

1. Select *Find & Replace* from the Edit menu (F3), or press Ctrl-F (F for Find). When the Find and Replace menu (Figure 6.9) appears:
2. Enter the string *search string* on the line labeled *Find.*
3. Press the Tab key to move the cursor down.
4. If you want the search to ignore capitalization, enter **Y** for *Ignore case*. Otherwise, leave N as the entry for this line.
5. Leave the other two entries unchanged.
6. Check your two entries over; if necessary, use the Tab and Shift-Tab keys to move to an entry and edit it.
7. When you have finished, press ↵.

If capitalization is important during the search, be sure to capitalize *search string* correctly here.

The cursor will then move to the next occurrence of *search string* that's found in the text. You can continue editing from the new cursor location or find the next occurrence of *search string*.

If no match is found, a message to that effect appears on screen.

```
                    Find and Replace
Find:
Ignore case (Y/N): Y
Replace with:
Manual or automatic (M/A): M

Esc-Cancel                                    ↵ Continue
```

Figure 6.9: The menu for finding and replacing strings

If no match is found, a message to that effect appears on screen.

The cursor will then move to the next occurrence of *search string* that's found in the text. You can continue editing from the new cursor location or find the next occurrence of *search string*.

Points to Ponder

When looking for a match to the search string that you enter, the software follows these rules:

- The search always starts at the current cursor position and scans forward through the working copy.
- For comparison purposes, multiple spaces are treated like a single space—both in your search string and also in the text being searched.
- A space before the first word of a group is ignored.
- If you enter **N** for the *Ignore case* option, a match will be found only if a string in the text exactly matches the capitalization of every letter in your search string.
- If you enter **A** for the option *Manual or Automatic*, Professional Write will scan directly to the end of the document without pausing and then give you a count of the number of occurrences in the text of the search string you entered.
- Whenever you are ready to search for the next occurrence of the same word(s), again press the speed key Ctrl-F, and when the Find and Replace menu appears, immediately press ↵.

The Find and Replace menu always displays the last string that you entered.

Table 6.2 shows several examples that illustrate these rules.

Table 6.2: Examples of How Find and Replace Works (Ignoring Case)

YOU ENTER	TEXT CONTAINS	MATCH FOUND?
my cat	My Cat	Y
my cat	my cat	Y
my cat	my cat	Y
my cat	mycat	N

HOW TO FIND PART OF A WORD

You can use the double-period *wildcard* (..) to search for a string that is just part of a word. This wildcard stands for *any group of characters*. For example, suppose that you want to find somebody's name within a document and you can't remember the exact spelling, although you are sure that it's something like *Peters* or *Petersen*.

Here's how you can solve this problem by using a wildcard: When the Find and Replace menu appears (Figure 6.9), make the following entries and then carry out the search:

Find: Pete..

Ignore case: N

The double period after *Pete* is the wildcard. When the search is carried out, it will pause as soon as any word that begins with *Pete* is encountered. For instance, a pause would occur for any of the following words in the text: *Pete*, *Peterson*, *Peters*, *Petersen*.

A wild card can appear either at the beginning, the end, or at both ends of your search string. However, wild cards can't appear in the middle of a search string. Table 6.3 gives several examples of using wild cards.

How to Count Words

You can use the Find and Replace feature for what would seem like unrelated tasks: Getting either the total word count of a document, or the count of a particular word. In addition, you can obtain the same counts for only part of a document.

Table 6.3: Find and Replace Examples Using Wild Cards

YOU ENTER	TEXT CONTAINS	MATCH FOUND?
rate	rate	Y
rate	operate	N
..rate	rate	Y
..rate	operate	Y
..rat	rat	Y
..rat	rate	N
..rat..	rat	Y
..rat..	rate	Y
..rat..	operate	Y
Harry Smith	Harry Smith	Y
..ry Smith	Harry Smith	Y
Harry Sm..	Harry Smith	Y
..ry Sm..	Harry Smith	Y
Ha.. Smith	Harry Smith	N

To get a partial count, position the cursor at the starting location; the count will be from there to the end of the document.

To get the total word count of a document:

1. Move the cursor to the beginning of the document.
2. Press the speed key Ctrl-F and then make the following entries in the Find and Replace menu:

Find:	..{*the wildcard*}
Ignore case:	either Y or N
Replace with:	{*leave blank*}
Manual or automatic:	A

3. Press ↵. The entire document will be scanned, and the total word count displayed on screen.

To get the count of a particular word in a document, follow the above steps, except that for *Find* enter the word whose count you want, and for *Ignore case* enter either **Y** or **N**, depending on your needs regarding capitalization.

You can also get word counts for only part of a document. First, copy the relevant part of the document to a temporary file and then work with that file. For details, see "How to Work with Only Part of a Document," below.

REPLACING CHARACTER STRINGS

While Professional Write is searching in the text for duplicates to your search string, it can also replace each match that it finds with another string that you specify. You can have every string replaced automatically, or you can selectively replace some but not others.

Suppose that you want to replace *string 1* with *string 2*. As before, you begin by selecting *Find & Replace* from the Edit menu (F3). Then, when the Find and Replace menu appears, make the following entries:

Use Tab and Shift-Tab to move between entries.

Find: Enter *string 1*.

Ignore case: Enter **Y** if you want to ignore capitalization during the search. Otherwise, enter **N**.

Replace with: Enter *string 2*. Any capitalization that you enter will be followed *exactly*, regardless of the setting for *Ignore case*.

Manual or Automatic: If you enter **M**, then as each match is found in the text, the menu in Figure 6.10 appears. You can then decide whether or not to replace *string 1* with *string 2*. The scan then continues after you make your choice.

If you enter **A**, all occurrences of *string 1* found in the text will automatically be replaced with *string 2*.

When the search ends, an on-screen message will display the number of words in the text that were replaced. (Figure 6.11.)

After you have filled in all of the entries, press ↵ and the Find and Replace operation will begin, starting at the current cursor position.

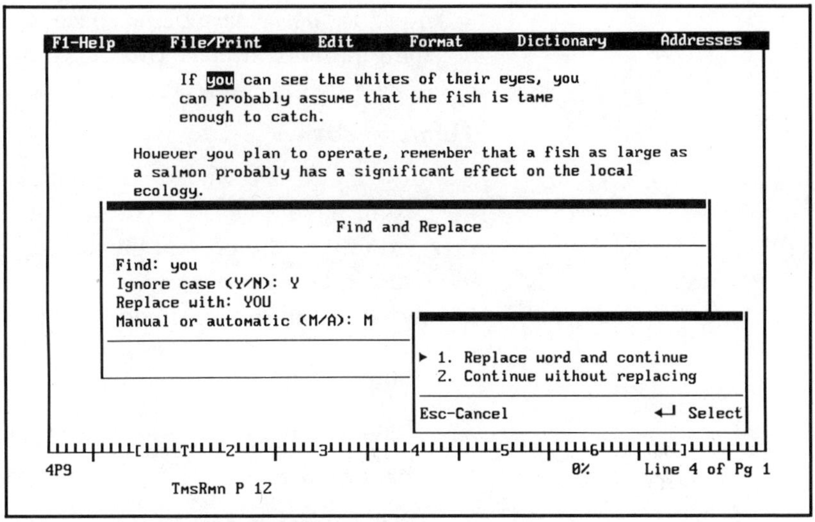

Figure 6.10: Find and Replace options

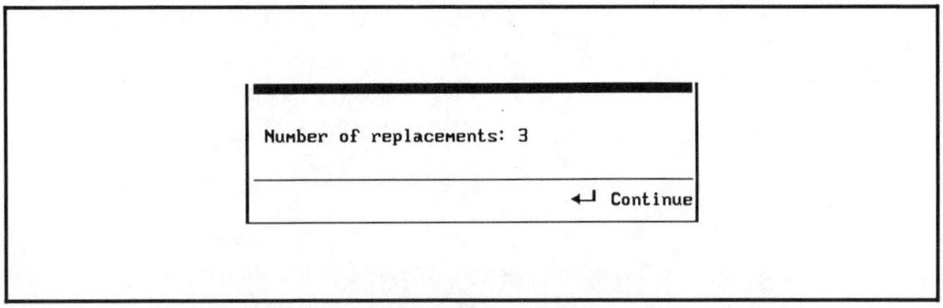

Figure 6.11: A count of the number of words that were replaced

How to Delete Words

A minor variation on the Find and Replace theme allows you to delete all occurrences of a particular word. For example, to delete every instance of *string*, use these entries in the Find and Replace menu:

Find:	*string*
Ignore case:	either **Y** or **N**, depending on what you want.
Replace with:	" "
Manual or automatic:	either **A** or **M**, depending on whether you want to monitor each deletion.

Use two double quotes right next to each other.

You can't just leave a blank space for the *Replace with* option; if you do, the Find and Replace process won't work.

Points to Ponder

Don't try to use wildcards when doing replacement operations. For instance, suppose that you want to change the tense of all verbs that end in *ry* to the present participle, that is, *ing*. Words like *try* and *fry* would end up as *trying* and *frying*. You might like to try using the following entries in the Find and Replace menu:

Find:	..ry
Ignore case:	Y
Replace with:	..rying
Manual or automatic:	A

Here's a sample of the outcome of this operation:

ORIGINAL WORD WAS	*FINAL WORD IS*
try	..rying
fry	..rying
cry	..rying

The problem is that Professional Write just doesn't execute replacements properly when a wildcard is used.

Actually, doing this type of wildcard Find and Replace would be highly dangerous, even if you could use wildcards as shown above. You're probably better off not having the opportunity to mangle your documents. For example, in the above example, what would happen to words like *ornery* and *foundry*?

Save Headaches by Using Backups

The Find and Replace option is a double-edged sword: It's extremely powerful and useful, but it's also one of the most dangerous operations you can perform on a document. Even without the capability of using wildcards in Find and Replace operations, it's not very difficult to make a mistake when you fill in the Find and Replace menu, resulting in considerable damage to your document. Sometimes it may take you quite a while before you even notice the mess that you have made.

For example, suppose you wanted to delete every occurrence of the word *the*, but you accidentally entered *the..* for the *Find* option (don't laugh—these things happen all the time!). The result would be that every word beginning with the string *the* would be deleted, including words like *these*, *them*, *therefore*, and so on.

There is one very good way to minimize the irritation and inconvenience that goes along with a ruined document: *Always make a backup (that is, a copy) of a document before you attempt to do any Find and Replace operation.*

Making a backup is easy, only taking a few seconds, and it's a good investment of your time. Here's how to do it:

For more information about saving files, see Chapter 7.

1. Press the speed key Ctrl-S to save the document.
2. Enter a different name for the backup file (the file that is to contain a copy of the document).
3. Enter a short description for the file, indicating which file this one is backing up. For example, if you are working on a document that was retrieved from the file SMITHDOC, you could name the backup file SMITHDOC.BAK.

You can't be too careful about backing up important work!

If your document is quite long, or if you have spent a lot of time building it, you might want to consider even greater caution: Make *two* backups of the document. I routinely do this for all my important computer work, and even so I have occasionally lost more work than I care to think about.

HOW TO WORK WITH ONLY PART OF A DOCUMENT

In all of the Find and Replace operations described above, you could work either with an entire document or from the current cursor position to the end of the document. However, you may on occasion want to work with some other piece of a document. For example, you might want to do extensive Find and Replace operations, but only on a middle section of your working copy.

The way to accomplish this is as follows: First isolate the block of text you want to manipulate by copying it to a temporary file. Then delete that same block from the original document. Next, retrieve the temporary file back into the working copy and perform the necessary Find and Replace operations. When you have finished, save the working copy back to the temporary file, retrieve the original document, and merge the two parts back together. Figure 6.12 shows a schematic of this process.

Here are the steps in more detail:

1. Make a backup of the original file, just in case a disaster occurs in the following steps.
2. Select as a text block the section of the document you want to edit. When you have selected the block, press F10.
3. Save this block to a temporary file: Select *Save* from the Text Block Operations menu and then give a name to the temporary file. Press ↵, and the file will be saved.
4. Delete the same block from the working copy (you'll have to reselect the block).

Make a note of where the block begins and ends.

5. Make some type of special text marker (like ZZZZZ) where the block was, so you can return to it later.
6. Save the working copy to its proper file. Remember that this is the original file *minus the deleted block*.
7. Retrieve the temporary file into the working copy.

This Find and Replace operation is a critical step, so be sure that everything is OK before going on.

8. Perform whatever Find and Replace operations you wish.
9. Make sure that the operations have worked correctly and then save the working copy back to its temporary file.
10. Retrieve the original file into the working copy and then use a Search operation to move the cursor to the special mark that you created in step 5. Delete the mark.
11. Insert the contents of the temporary file back into the working file at the cursor location by selecting *Insert file* from the File/Print menu (F2).

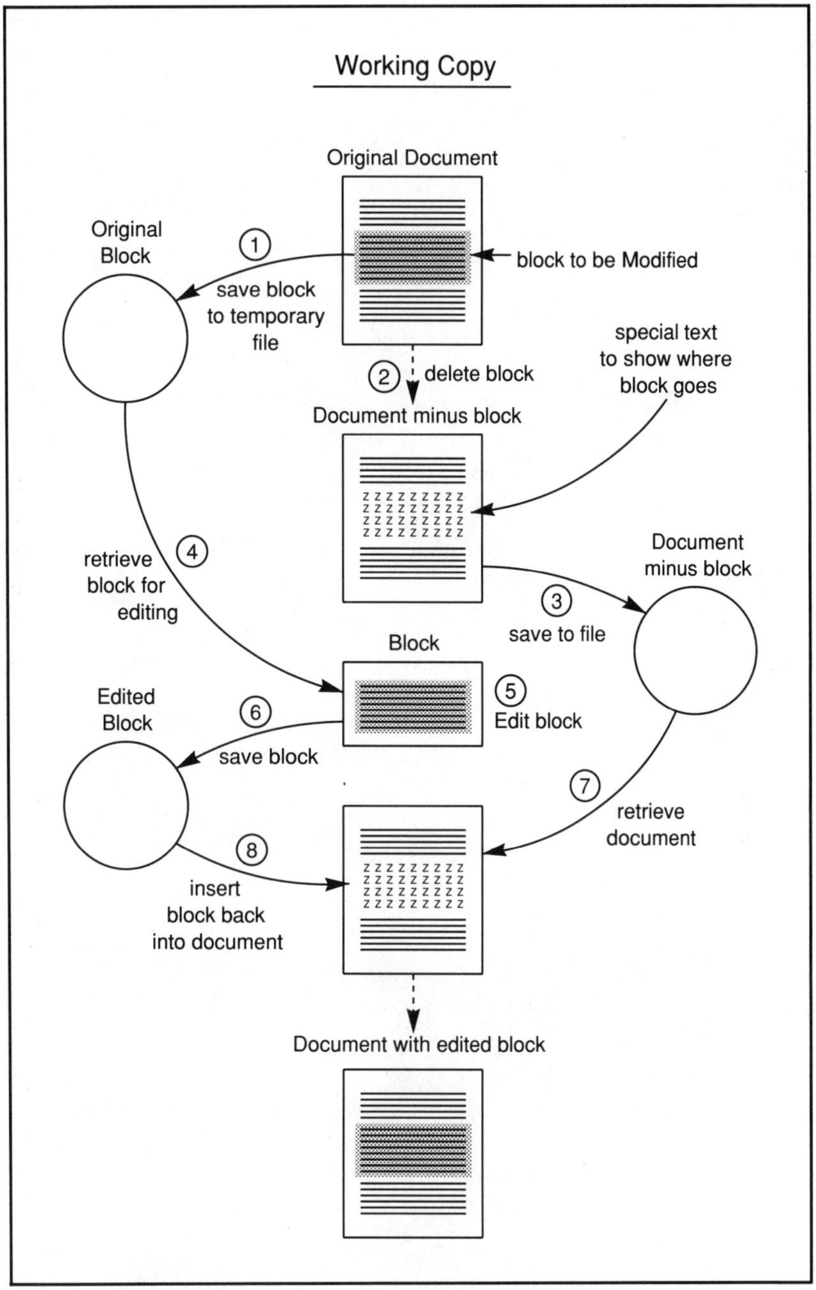

Figure 6.12: Isolate part of a file for extensive Find and Replace operations

Make sure that you save the backup copy for a reasonable period of time. Usually, when you have *completely* finished with the original file and it has been thoroughly read through, wait six months or longer (just to be safe) and then delete the backup.

7

Managing Your Files

KNOWING HOW TO MANAGE FILES EFFECTIVELY can often be as important as being able to process words. File-management skills include the ability to save and retrieve document files with Professional Write. In addition, it's important to be able to remove unwanted files so that your disks don't become overloaded. Also, you should know how to make secure backups of important files so that you are protected from disasters such as hard-disk failures, inconvenient power outages, or the worst of all possibilities—human error.

This chapter will discuss all of these topics. You will also find out how to work with files from other software packages—not only different word processors like WordPerfect, but also other types of files, such as worksheets from Lotus 1-2-3.

RETRIEVING FILES

Before you can begin working on an existing document, you must first retrieve it into the working copy. Of course you can easily retrieve any files previously created by Professional Write. But you can also retrieve files in ASCII format, as well as files in any of a number of standard word processing formats. In addition, you can retrieve the contents of a 1-2-3 worksheet file into the working copy.

PROFESSIONAL WRITE FILES

Alternatively, press the speed key Ctrl-G (G for Get) to show the file name display.

To retrieve a file that was previously stored by Professional Write, begin by selecting *Get file* from the File/Print menu (F2). The Get Filename dialog box will then appear (Figure 7.1). Initially, the name of the current disk drive and directory are listed here. For instance, in Figure 7.1 the directory is \PWFIGS on drive C.

When the Get Filename dialog box appears:

1. If necessary, delete the current disk drive and/or directory names (press Ctrl-E), and then enter the correct names. Include the full pathname for the directory.

2a. If you know exactly which file name you plan to use, enter it right after the directory name. Then press ↵. Otherwise:

For details on how to use the file directory, see "The File Directory."

2b. If you want to view the contents of the current directory (the one on the *Filename* line), *do not enter the file name*. Instead, press ↵, and the file directory will appear. Select the file that you want from the file directory.

3. If the file you want to retrieve is encrypted, a Password dialog box appears (Figure 7.2). Enter the password and press ↵.

After you have completed the above steps, the file is loaded into the working copy, and you can proceed to edit it.

Figure 7.1: The Get Filename dialog box

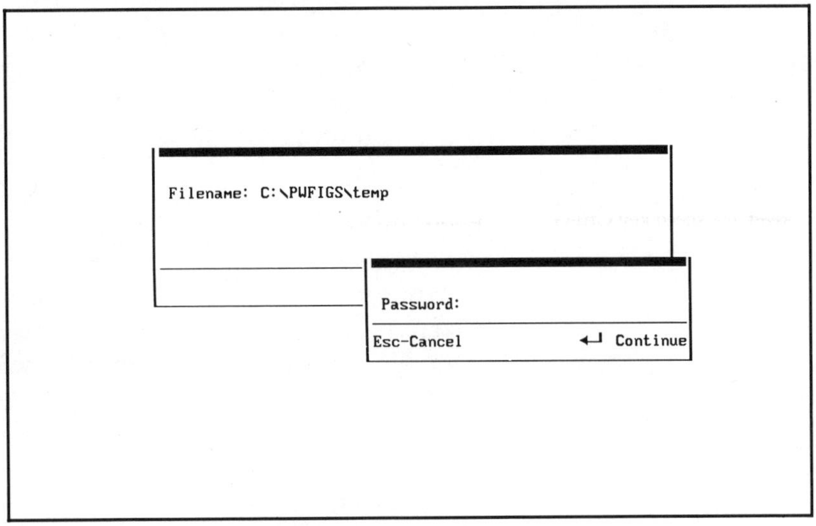

Figure 7.2: The Password dialog box

FILES IN OTHER WORD PROCESSING FORMATS

You can retrieve a file that is in any of the following word processing formats:

Microsoft Word, versions 3 and 4

MultiMate

OfficeWriter, version 6

Wang PC

WordPerfect, versions 3, 4.1, 4.2, and 5.0

WordStar, versions 3 and 4

The steps for retrieving any of these file types are nearly identical to those described in the preceding section, "Professional Write Files," except that in some cases you will be asked to identify which type of file you are retrieving. The file is then converted to Professional Write format and placed in the working copy. You can then edit the file just as you would a normal Professional Write document.

Saving to a new File

Save the working copy to a new file.

After you have retrieved a file into the working copy, save it to a new file with a different name. Then when you make changes, only the working copy is affected; the original file remains unchanged. The reason for this action is that in case anything goes wrong at some later point, you can always fall back on the original file and start over.

What Gets Converted

When any of the above types of files is converted to Professional Write format, as much formatting and style information as possible is converted, as well as the basic text itself. In general, the following will usually be successfully converted: margins, tabs, footers and headers, boldfacing, italics, underlining, superscripts, and subscripts.

Usually, however, a good deal of special coding that's specific to the originating word processor can't be translated because there is no equivalent in Professional Write documents. This coding is deleted. In some cases, Professional Write will substitute a backslash (\) for characters that it doesn't recognize.

Never trust a translated document until it has been thoroughly checked.

After you have retrieved a foreign-born document, be sure to check it completely and thoroughly; document translation can never be 100% accurate, and there are always bound to be some surprises.

ASCII FILES

ASCII files are the common denominator of most computer software. (ASCII is an acronym for American Standard Code for Information Interchange.) Nearly every word processor can translate a document from its own format into an ASCII file; most of them can also generate ASCII files directly. No matter what type of word processed document you are dealing with, therefore, ASCII can nearly always be used as a last resort for retrieving that document into Professional Write.

Moreover, other types of software, such as file management and spreadsheet programs, can often output files in ASCII format. This is frequently the best way (and sometimes the only way) that you can retrieve these types of files into Professional Write.

The steps for retrieving an ASCII file are nearly identical to those described in the section "Professional Write Files," except that after you enter the file name, you will be asked to specify what type of file you are retrieving.

When the page length is set to zero, Professional Write doesn't insert any page breaks.

When an ASCII file is retrieved into the working copy, hard returns are retrieved, as well as the rest of the text. The top margin, bottom margin, and page length are all set to 0. The left margin of the working copy is set to 1, and the right margin is usually set to the margin of the longest line in the file. Under some circumstances (such as a right margin greater than 250), the right margin will be set differently. However, after the file has been retrieved, you can always reset any of the margins or the page length. (For details on setting these parameters, see Chapter 5.)

WORKSHEET FILES

You can retrieve files that contain worksheets either in Professional Plan PFS:First Choice, or Lotus 1-2-3 formats.To import a Lotus 1-2-3 worksheet:

Follow the instructions on the screen for switching disks.

1. Select *Get file* from the File/Print menu, or press the speed key Ctrl-G. When the Filename dialog box appears,

2. Enter the disk drive and/or directory where the file you want is stored, and then enter the full file name, including the extension (either .WK1 or .WKS).
3. Select *Import entire worksheet* from the dialog box that appears.

After a few seconds, the worksheet will appear on your screen. You can then treat it as you would an ordinary document: Edit it in any way that you wish, save it to a Professional Write file, and print it out.

Points to Ponder

If you have not copied the contents of the disk labeled "Conversion Disk" to your hard disk, you'll need to insert this floppy disk into drive A *before* performing steps 1 through 3 above. Otherwise, your program might freeze up, and you'll need to reboot your computer.

You can also retrieve worksheets generated by Professional Plan or PFS:First Choice into the working copy. Professional Plan worksheets can be retrieved directly, by using the steps outlined above. First Choice worksheets must first be converted into Lotus 1-2-3 format. For details, consult a book on PFS:First Choice (such as "Understanding PFS:First Choice," by the author of this book).

You can retrieve just part of a 1-2-3 or Professional Plan worksheet. Details about this process are contained in the Professional Write manual.

SAVING FILES

As you edit a document, the changes affect the working copy, which resides in the computer's main memory (RAM). However, because the contents of this memory are lost each time you shut off the computer, before you exit Professional Write you must save a duplicate of the working copy to a disk file in order to preserve any editing changes.

If the document you are working on is a new one, you must create a new name for the file to hold the document. On the other hand, you may be editing a document that you retrieved earlier from a disk file. In that case, you can either save the document back to the same file, or you can save it to a new file, thereby preserving the original document as well as the edited version. For long or important documents, you might also want to save an extra copy as a backup, perhaps on a separate floppy disk.

You can save a document in one of several different *formats*, or file types. These include Professional Write's Normal format, ASCII, or any of the word processor formats shown in Table 7.1. You can also encrypt a file and assign it a password. When you save a document, you can attach a file description, which can later be helpful in locating that particular file.

Table 7.1: Professional Write Will Save Files in These Formats

DCA
Microsoft Word, versions 3 and 4
MultiMate
OfficeWriter, version 6
PFS:First Choice, versions 1, 2, and 3
Professional Write, version 1
Wang PC
WordPerfect, versions 3, 4.1, 4.2, and 5.0
WordStar, versions 3 and 4

A Warning Note

Whenever you save a document, you must enter the name of the file into which a duplicate of the working copy will be written. If the name you select is the same as that of the file last retrieved into the working copy, the file is written *without any warning that the original contents are about to be overwritten*.

This is a weakness of the software, and it's one place that you need to be very careful. If you have made a mess of the working copy and you then press Ctrl-S, ↵, you will lose the original file contents and possibly a lot of work.

On the other hand, if you enter an existing file name that is different from that of the file last retrieved into the working copy, a warning message appears telling you that you are about to overwrite an existing file. You can then either go ahead with the save or abort it.

NORMAL PROFESSIONAL WRITE FORMAT

This is the format that you will usually use for saving files, unless you are planning to use the file with a different word processor or unless you want to encrypt the file for security purposes.

Alternatively, press the speed key Ctrl-S (S for save).

To save a duplicate of the working copy in normal format, begin by selecting *Save working copy* from the File/Print menu (F2), and the Save Filename dialog box appears (Figure 7.3).

The Save Filename Dialog Box

This display consists of three lines, containing various options for you to fill in. You can move back and forth between these options with the Tab and Shift-Tab keys.

The options for this dialog box are

- **Filename:** Initially, the name of the current disk drive and directory are listed here. For instance, in Figure 7.3 the directory shown is C:\MYWORK. If necessary, delete the current disk drive and/or directory names (use Ctrl-E) and enter the correct names. Then, if you know exactly which file name you plan to use, enter it right after the directory name. Otherwise, if you first want to view the contents of this directory by using the file directory, *do not* enter the file name.
- **Description:** You can enter a short summary (up to 40 characters) of the file's contents on this line.
- **File type:** For a normal Professional Write file, leave the entry as N. The other choices are

For details on how to use the file directory, see "The File Directory."

A:	ASCII file
E:	Encrypted Professional Write file
O:	Other type of file

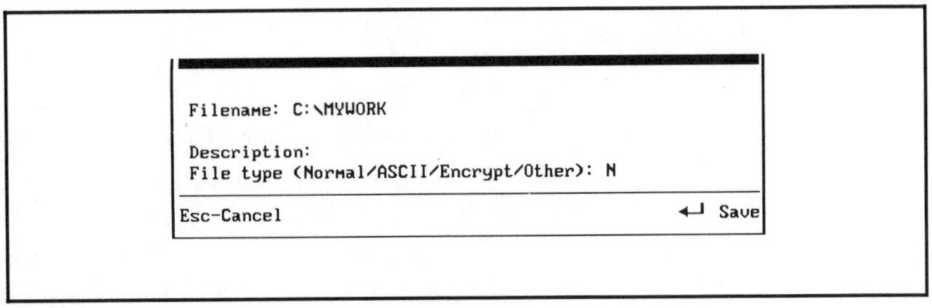

Figure 7.3: The Save Filename dialog box

After you have filled in the three entries, press ↵ to go on. If you entered a file name on the *Filename* line, a duplicate of the working copy will be written to this file. If you did not write a file name, then the file directory will appear. Select the filename you want from the file directory and then press ↵.

ENCRYPTED PROFESSIONAL WRITE FORMAT

If you are saving a file whose contents you would like to keep secure from other users, you can encrypt the file as it's being written. You also must then assign a password to the file. Subsequently, when you want to use the file, you will need to supply that same password to Professional Write. Note that you can encrypt only files that are written in Professional Write format—not files written either in ASCII or another word processor format.

Here are the steps for writing an encrypted file:

1. Select *Save working copy* from the File/Print menu (F2), or press Ctrl-S.
2. Fill in the Save Filename dialog box (Figure 7.3) as described in the previous section, "Normal Professional Write Format," with the following exception:
3. For the line *File type:*, enter **E** for Encrypt.
4. Enter a password (see below for details), press ↵, and the file will be saved.

For details on using special characters, see Chapter 2.

When entering a password, you can enter up to 20 characters (you can actually enter up to 24, but only the first 20 are saved). You can use any combination of characters from the keyboard: letters, digits, punctuation marks, etc. You can even use the special characters accessible through the Alt key.

Make sure you have either a very good memory or a secure place in which to keep the password. It's very difficult to retrieve an encrypted file without its password, unless you know an excellent hacker. Software Publishing Corporation will decrypt a file for you for a nominal charge. For more information contact SPC, 1901 Landings Drive, Mountain View, CA, 94000.

ASCII FILES

Generally, you save a file in ASCII format when you want to transmit the file either to another location via a modem, to a word processor that's not on the list in Table 7.1, or to another type of software package, such as a spreadsheet program. However, you will probably want to avoid using this type of file as much as possible because you can save only raw text and hard returns (one at the end of each line). Other information, such as text style (boldfacing, font, etc.) and page layout details, (headers and footers, page numbering, etc.) can't be included.

To copy the contents of the working copy to an ASCII file, select *Save working copy* from the File/Print menu (F2) (or press Ctrl-S). In the Save File dialog box enter **A** for *File type*. Only the text of the working copy will be saved, with a hard return at the end of each line.

OTHER WORD PROCESSOR FORMATS

To save a file in another word processor format:

1. Select *Save working copy* from the File/Print menu (F2) (or press Ctrl-S).
2. Fill in the Save File dialog box as described above, except
3. Enter **O** for the entry *File type*.
4. When you are finished, press ↵. A warning message appears, reminding you that some word processors expect document files to have a special file name extension.

5. If you forgot to include the file name extension, you can return to the Save Filename dialog box by pressing Esc. You can then add the correct extension to the file name. (If you don't know the extension, just press ↵ to continue.)
6. Select the correct file type from the File Type menu that appears (Figure 7.4).

Points to Ponder

Make sure that the converted document is scrutinized very carefully when it's eventually read into the other word processor.

As the working copy is written to the file, it's first converted into the format specified by you in step 6. Bear in mind that this conversion may not be 100% accurate. Some special information that's contained in the working copy, such as page format or text style, may have no equivalents in the other word processor. Other information may not be converted properly or in the way that you expect.

In step 5 above, if you don't know the correct file name extension for the word processor in question, just press ↵ to go on; the file will be assigned the name you selected—with no extension. When you (or somebody else) is ready to use that file with the other word processor, you can then rename the file to add the correct extension; or you may be able to get the word processor to read the file anyway.

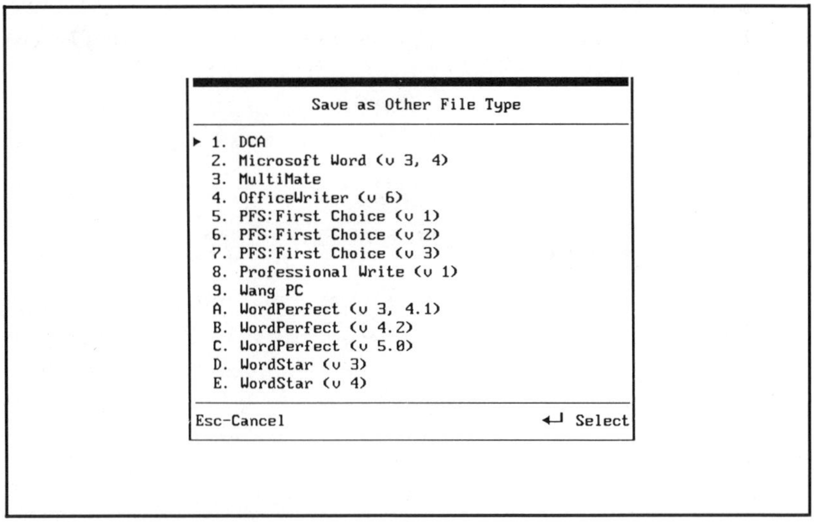

Figure 7.4: The File Type menu

MAKING BACKUPS

A backup is a simple tool for saving hours of aggravation and anxiety. When you back up a file, you make a duplicate of it either to the same disk (or directory) with a different name, or to a different disk (or directory) either with the same or a different name.

You can make a copy of a file either from within Professional Write or from the DOS prompt.

For example, suppose you want to make a backup of the file MYDOC in the directory \MYSTUFF on the hard-disk drive C. The safest course is to create the backup file on a floppy disk.

To make this backup within Professional Write:

1. Begin by making sure that the latest version of the document is in the working copy.
2. Insert a formatted floppy disk into drive A.
3. Press the speed key Ctrl-S.
4. When the Save File dialog box appears, press Ctrl-E to erase the current entry, then enter **A:MYDOC**.
5. Enter a short file description indicating that this file is a backup of the original on drive C.
6. Press ↵, and the file will be written.

This process takes only a few minutes, but developing the backup habit will eventually save you time and trouble.

DELETING FILES

When a file is no longer of any use to you it can be easily deleted from a disk. Too easily. Before deleting a file, make sure that either (1) you really don't need the file anymore, or (2) a backup of the file exists somewhere. Once a file has been deleted, there are two ways in which you can get it back:

- You own a copy of a file management program, like *Norton's Utilities*, which can be used for unerasing a file.
- You happen to know a very clever computer hacker.

Once you are sure you want to delete a file, here's how to do it:

1. Select *Delete file* from the File/Print menu (F2). When the Delete File dialog box appears, the current disk drive and directory are displayed.
2. If necessary, press Ctrl-E and then enter the names of the current disk drive and/or directory you want.

3a. If you know the name of the file you plan to delete, enter it right after the directory name. Then press ↵, and the file will be deleted. Otherwise:

3b. If you want to select the file by using the file directory, press ↵ immediately after you enter the directory name. Then select the file that you want from the file directory; finish by pressing ↵ and the file will be deleted.

For details on how to use the directory, see "The File Directory."

THE FILE DIRECTORY

Whenever you need to save, retrieve, or delete a file, you can use the file directory to help you find exactly the file that you want. In addition, the file directory is a useful tool for managing all of your files—not just those created by Professional Write.

To see how to display the file directory in a given circumstance, refer to the relevant section in this chapter. For instance, to use the file directory to help you save a file in normal Professional Write format, refer to the section "Normal Professional Write Format."

A QUICK TOUR AROUND THE FILE DIRECTORY

A typical file directory display is shown in Figure 7.5. The various components of the display are explained below, and then some of the operations that you can perform from this display are discussed.

- **Directory name:** The top line of the display indicates the name of the *current directory* whose files and subdirectories are displayed on screen. For example, in Figure 7.5 the current directory is \PWFIGS on drive C.

Directory Listing of C:\PWFIGS

Filename Ext		Date	Size	Description
▸ ..		1/01/80	0	Parent Directory
ZP1		1/01/80	1555	
ZP1	.SCR	1/01/80	8128	
ZP2	.SCR	1/01/80	8128	
ZP3	.SCR	1/01/80	8128	
ZP4	.SCR	1/01/80	8128	
ZP5	.SCR	1/01/80	8128	
ZP6	.SCR	1/01/80	8128	
ZP7	.SCR	1/01/80	8128	
ATEMP1		1/01/80	1076	Temporary client billing information
ATEMP2		1/01/80	1076	Accounts receivable for 4-1-89
ATEMP3		1/01/80	1076	Last week's laundry list
CH1		1/01/80	0	Directory
CH2		1/01/80	0	Directory
CH3		1/01/80	0	Directory
CH4		1/01/80	0	Directory

Directory or filename: ..

Get file. ↓,PgDn-More files
Esc-Cancel F1-Help F8-Sort F9-Search documents ↵ Get

Figure 7.5: A file directory display

- **File list:** The names of all files and subdirectories in the current directory are displayed starting just below the line beginning *Filename*. For each file or subdirectory, the following information is listed:
    - File name and extension
    - Date when created or last updated
    - File size (shown as number of bytes)
    - Description
- **Directory or filename:** You can enter the name of a directory and/or file on this line.
- **Keystrokes:** The bottom two lines list some of the useful keys that you can use with this display.

Notice that the file list contains three different types of entries. You can tell which is which by examining the entry in the *Description* column for each entry.

If the Entry in the DESCRIPTION Column is:	*The Entry Represents a:*
Parent Directory	Parent directory of the current directory (there is only one).
Directory	Directory (or subdirectory) under the current directory.
Anything else	An ordinary file in the current directory. If descriptive text appears here, it was entered in the Save File dialog box, when the file was saved.

Here are some of the operations that can be performed from the file directory display:

- Select a file whose name is displayed in the file list
- Display the contents of a different directory or disk drive
- Display a subset of files in a directory
- Sort the file list displayed on screen
- Look for a group of files containing a particular word or group of words.

HOW TO SELECT A FILE

After the file directory appears, you may eventually want to select a file from the list of files displayed. For instance, you may have called the file directory to help you locate a specific file that you want to retrieve into the working copy.

If you don't see the file you want, use the PgDn and PgUp keys to scroll through the entire file list.

When the file directory first appears, the top entry in the file list is highlighted. To select a file, first highlight its name by using the ↓ and ↑ keys. Notice that the name of the highlighted file also appears on the line *Directory or filename*. After you have highlighted the file, press ↵ and the file is selected.

You can also select a file by entering its name directly onto the line *Directory or filename* and then pressing ↵.

See "A Warning Note" in "Saving Files," above.

The disposition of the file that you select depends on how you call the file directory. For example, if you are in the process of saving a file and you call the file directory, then the contents of the working copy will be written to the selected file.

HOW TO DISPLAY OTHER GROUPS OF FILES

If you decide that you want to view the contents of another disk drive or directory, you can do so directly from the file directory. You can also display a subset of the files in a particular drive or directory.

To display a subset of files on the current directory, use the DOS wildcards ? and * to indicate which subset you want displayed:

- ? stands for *any single character*
- * stands for *any group of characters*

Table 7.2 lists some examples of how to use these wildcards.

To select another disk drive: Enter the name of the drive on the *Directory or filename* line and then press ↵. The list of files on that drive will appear on screen. For example, you could examine the contents of drive A by entering **A:**.

Table 7.2: Using the DOS Wildcards to Display Subsets of Files

ENTRY ON THE DIRECTORY OR FILENAME LINE	FILES DISPLAYED
.	All files
BALANCE.*	All files whose name is BALANCE, regardless of the file extension
*.SCR	All files whose extension is SCR
C*.*	All files whose name begins with C.

To select another directory: use either of the following methods:

- If the name of a directory appears in the file list, highlight it with the ↑ and ↓ keys and then press ↵.
- Enter the *full* name of the directory on the line *Directory or filename* and then press ↵.

Note that you can select the parent of the current directory by highlighting the top entry of the file list. Or you can enter .. (double period) on the *Directory or filename* line and then press ↵.

After you have selected a directory, its contents will appear in the Directory Listing, replacing the original screen display. You can then work with this directory, just as you did with the previous one.

HOW TO SORT THE DIRECTORY DISPLAY

You can have the display sorted in various ways—by file name, extension, date, or size. To create a sorted file, press the F8 key, and the Sort Order dialog box appears (Figure 7.6). Notice that there are four items listed here: file name, extension, date of last update, and file size.

You can sort the directory on any one of these items, or on any combination of items:

- If you want to sort on a single item, enter the number **1** next to it; then delete the numbers next to the other items.

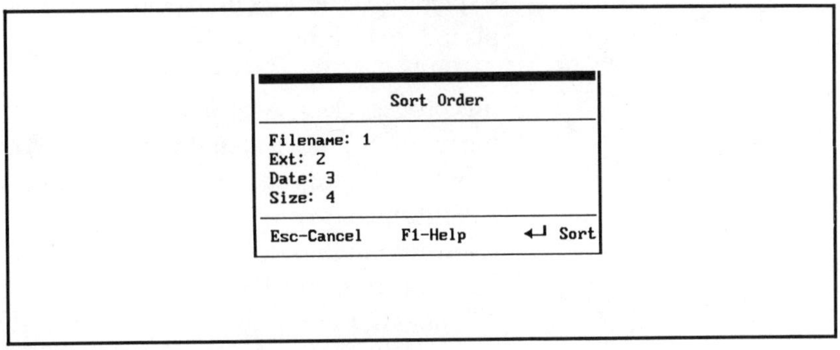

Figure 7.6: The Sort Order dialog box

- If you want to sort on several items, enter the number **1** next to the *primary sort item*, the number **2** next to the *secondary sort item*, and so on. Delete the numbers next to the items not involved in the sort.

For instance, to sort only on file name, enter the number 1 next to *Filename* in the Sort Order dialog box and delete the other three entries. As an example, the directory in Figure 7.5 is sorted by file name and extension.

How Sorting is Carried Out

All of the characters on the keyboard are arranged into a *sorting sequence*. Characters or words are alphabetized (or sorted) according to this sequence. The sorting sequence goes roughly like this:

- Blank space (the "lowest" of all the characters)
- The special characters, such as $, %, etc.
- The digits 0–9
- The letters A–Z

Notice that for purposes of sorting, digits are treated as ordinary characters, not as numbers.

When two strings of characters are compared during the sorting process, they are compared on a character-by-character basis. When a mismatch is found between two corresponding characters, the string with the lower character (according to the above sorting sequence) is considered to be the lower of the two strings and it will be placed first in the sorted list.

Table 7.3 shows several sorting examples that should help make this process clear. A couple of items in this table are worth commenting on. First, notice that the string AZZZZZZZ comes before B. This is because there is a mismatch in the very first pair of letters—A and B; and since A comes before B in the sorting sequence, AZZZZZZZ is lower than B. The fact that AZZZZZZZ has many more characters than B is quite irrelevant.

The other interesting comparison is that the *string* 15 comes before the *string* 3. Again, this is because the character 1 comes before 3 in the sorting sequence. The fact that the character 5 follows the 1 is also irrelevant. Remember: each digit is treated as a character, not a number.

Table 7.3: Sorting Examples

THIS	COMES BEFORE THIS
$	1
1	2
1	A
A	B
A	AB
AB	AC
AB	B
AZZZZZZZ	B
15	16
15	3

SEARCHING THROUGH MULTIPLE DOCUMENTS

This feature works only with files in Professional Write format.

With the Document Search feature, you can use a single operation to search automatically through a group of files for a particular word or group of words. Here's how this feature can be useful:

- Locating all the files that contain information on a particular topic.
- Looking for a file whose name you have forgotten, but whose subject matter is familiar to you.

In one pass you can search either through all the files in a directory or through a selected subset of files. You can search for a single word, a group of words, or part of a word.

For instance, suppose that you want to find a file containing a letter to Peter Rabbit. You know which directory contains the file, but you can't recall the file name. You can instruct Professional Write to search through the all the files in that directory, looking for any that contain the words *Peter Rabbit*.

As the search through the files progresses, Professional Write compiles a list of all files containing the words *Peter Rabbit*. When the search ends, a file directory is displayed, listing all files that contain *Peter Rabbit*. You can then manipulate this directory just like any other.

Searching Through an Entire Directory

Suppose you want to find all the files in a directory that contain a single word or specific group of words. Here are the steps:

1. Bring up Professional Write's directory display by selecting *Get file* from the File/Print menu (F2); when the Filename dialog box appears, enter the name of the directory and then press ↵.
2. When the directory display appears, press F9, and the Search Multiple Documents dialog box appears (Figure 7.7)
3. On the *Find* line, enter the word or words that you want to find.
4. On the *Directory* line, enter the name of the directory you want to search and then press ↵.

You can also search through selected groups of files. See "Searching through Selected Files," below.

Professional Write searches every file specified on the *Directory* line. When the search is finished, a new directory display appears. Each file in this list contains the word or words that you specified. Select the file that you want and then press ↵. That file will be loaded into the working copy, and the cursor will be positioned at the first occurrence of the group of words that you specified.

Looking for Part of a Word

For more information about using this wildcard, see "How to Find Part of a Word" in Chapter 6.

If you want to search for a word, but you don't remember its exact spelling, you can use the double-period wildcard (..) to help. Remember: This wildcard stands for *any group of characters*. For instance, suppose you want to find a particular letter that you wrote

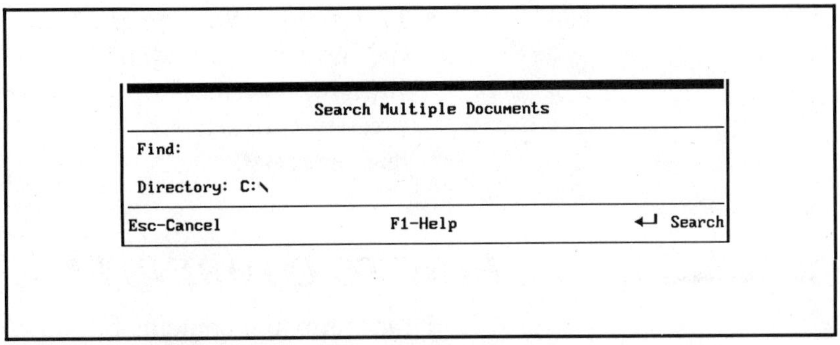

Figure 7.7: Search Multiple Documents dialog box

to someone. You know which directory contains the file, and you also remember that the first name of the person to whom you wrote is Peter. You can't recall his last name, although you are pretty sure it begins with the letter R. You can search the directory for the words *Peter R..*; the results of the search will be a list of files containing strings such as *Peter Rabbit*, *Peter R. Doyle*, *Peter Ran*, and so on.

Searching Through Selected Files

For more information about DOS wildcards, see "How to Display Other Groups of Files," above.

You can search through a selected group of files within a directory by using the DOS wildcards * and ? when you select the directory to be searched:

- ? stands for *any single character*
- * stands for *any group of characters*

For example, suppose you want to search the directory \MYWORK, but only through those files that have the extension .DOC. To do this, you would enter **\MYWORK*.DOC** on the *Directory* line in the Search Multiple Documents dialog box.

Points to Ponder

- When a word search is being carried out, multiple spaces between words are treated as a single space, both in the words that you specify and in the files being searched. For instance, *Dear   John* is treated as *Dear John*.

- Professional Write keeps a temporary list of the files found in the most recent search. You can quickly retrieve this list: Bring up the file directory, press F9, and then immediately press ↵. To retrieve another document in this list, select it and press ↵.

HOW TO COMBINE FILES

You can insert the contents of one file into the current working copy, a convenient way of combining two files. The file to be inserted can be either type of Professional Write file (normal or encrypted), or it can be an ASCII file.

The margins and fonts of an inserted file are handled in the following way:

- If the inserted file is in Professional Write format, the left and right margins, as well as the fonts of the inserted text, are preserved when the text is inserted into the working copy.
- If the inserted file is in ASCII format, the left margin is generally set to the current margin. The right margin is set to that of the longest line, provided that it falls within Professional Write's maximum of 250. In addition, the font of the inserted text is set to the regular font of the working copy.
- If the right margin of a line being inserted exceeds 250, it's reset to 250 and the remainder is wrapped to the next line.

Suppose that you want to insert document B somewhere into document A. Here's how to do it:

1. Retrieve document A into the working copy.
2. Move the cursor to the spot where document B is to be inserted. This must be either a blank line or the beginning of an existing line.
3. Select *Insert file* from the File/Print menu (F2) and enter the name of the file to be inserted.

When the file is inserted, text is automatically repositioned within the working copy to make room for it.

If you want to combine a document that's in Professional Write format (document A) with a document that's in another word processor format (document B), you first need to convert document B into Professional Write format, as follows:

1. Begin by erasing the working copy.
2. Retrieve document B into the working copy.
3. Save the working copy to a new file (call it *file C*) in Professional Write normal format.
4. Retrieve document A into the working copy.
5. Insert document C, following the procedure described earlier.

8

An Introduction to Fonts and Printers

WHAT IS A FONT?

The term *font* refers to certain characreristics shared by a group of characters. When we say that a character is printed or displayed in a particular font, we are describing the exact nature of that character—size, shape, and so on.

You can greatly improve the appearance of a document by using different fonts. The amount of flexibility that you have depends primarily on the capabilities of your printer. Some laser printers offer virtually unlimited font selections. Many dot-matrix printers contain a modest variety of built-in fonts, while others offer hardly any at all.

The definitions of four terms that are frequently used in connection with printed text will help to clarify exactly what a font is. These terms are *typeface*, *size*, *style*, and *orientation*.

TYPEFACE

Typeface refers to the general features that apply to a family of characters. There are several hundred different typefaces, and each has its particular applications. For example, the *Times Roman* typeface is frequently used for the text in books because experience has shown that large quantities of this text are relatively comfortable on the human eye.

Figure 8.1 shows eight different typefaces. As you can see, there are many differences between them—some obvious and others quite subtle.

Monospaced and Proportionally-Spaced Typefaces

Some typefaces are *monospaced*, meaning that each character occupies the same amount of horizontal space. These typefaces are rather dull and uninteresting, but unfortunately they are the only ones available on some printers. However, a monospaced typeface can be very useful when printing columns of numbers because all of the digits line up nicely. The Courier typeface is monospaced (see Figure 8.1).

Other typefaces are *proportionally spaced*, meaning that each character takes up only as much horizontal space as it requires. You can

This is Times Roman, a common typeface

This is Helvetica, a sans-serif typeface

This is Courier, built into many laser printers

This is Line Printer, also built into some laser printers

This is Futura, a very spiffy typeface

This is Dom Casual

This typeface is called Charter... somewhat more sophisticated than Times Roman

This is called Provence

Figure 8.1: Each typeface has its own distinguishing features

read a page of proportionally spaced text much easier than one consisting of monospaced characters, primarily because there is less white space between characters. Most of the typefaces shown in Figure 8.1 are proportionally spaced.

Serif and Sans-Serif Typefaces

Another distinguishing characteristic of a typeface is whether or not it has *serifs*, the tiny little horizontal and vertical lines at the very ends of the various parts of each letter. For example, the Helvetica typeface shown in Figure 8.1 is a *sans-serif* typeface (that is, it has no serifs). On the other hand, Times Roman is a popular serif typeface. Compare, for instance, the letter T in the examples of Helvetica and Times Roman typefaces shown in Figure 8.1.

Sans-serif typefaces have many uses. For example, large-size sans-serif typefaces are often used for titles and column headings. On the other hand, a large amount of sans-serif text is more difficult to read than the equivalent text in a serif typeface.

TYPE SIZE

The size of a group of characters is as important as any other single feature. Character size is most often measured in terms of *points*, and there are 72 points in an inch. Thus when we refer to 12-point text, we mean the following: If you print a line containing characters in that size, then the amount of vertical space occupied by that line will be 12 points, or one-sixth of an inch (see Figure 8.2). Most of the examples in Figure 8.1 are shown in 12-point.

As a point of reference, many books are often printed in 10-point text. This size is large enough to be read comfortably by most people, yet small enough so that a reasonable amount of text fits on a single page.

Pitch

Type size is also sometimes measured in terms of its *pitch*, which is the number of characters per inch. The *draft* mode for nearly all printers is a 10-pitch font, or 10 characters per inch. For a proportionally-spaced font, the pitch is also said to be *proportional*.

TEXT STYLE

The term *style* refers to variations within a particular typeface. The most common styles for enhancing text are *boldface*, *italic*, and *bold-italic*. The absence of any modifying style, such as boldface or italics, is referred to as *normal* style. There are many other styles as well, but these are much less commonly used. Two examples are *inverse* (white letters on a black background) and *hollow* (the letters are black outlines with white interiors).

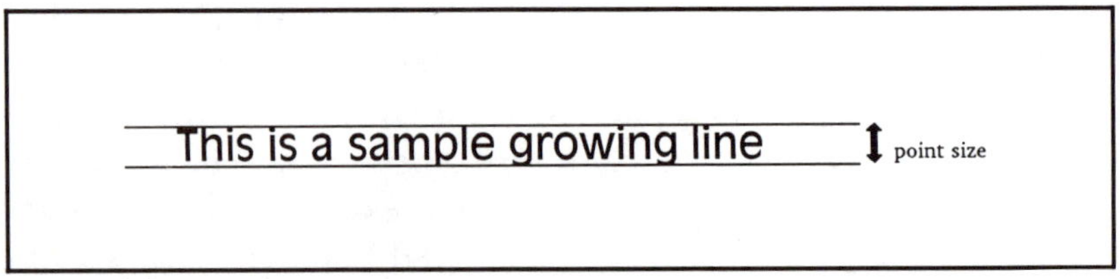

Figure 8.2: Point size is the vertical space occupied by the letters of a typeface

ORIENTATION

Some printers can print in either of two orientations: *Portrait* or *Landscape* (see Figures 8.3 and 8.4). By far the more common orientation is Portrait, and all printers can output in this mode. Remember: For most printers, each character is printed as a series of dots, so in principle one orientation is as easy to output as another. Your printer simply has to have the necessary built-in information to be able to

Martin's Coins
1234 Fifth Ave.
Oakland, CA

September 12, 1888

Gompers Stagecoaches
40 Austin Way
Sacramento, CA

Dear Sirs:

Many thanks for the gold shipment. It arrived intact, we are happy to say, and it tallied to the nearest gram.

We appreciate the care and security you have attached to your shipments, and we look forward to many more pleasant associations with your firm.

Sincerely,

Samuel Martin, Esq.

Figure 8.3: Portrait orientation

<u>SEMI-ANNUAL SALES FIGURES</u>
(thousands of dollars)

	Terminals	Motherboards	Monitors	Keyboards	Hard Disks	Add-ins	Software
January	45	82	25	18	77	195	204
February	37	78	14	15	89	205	155
March	51	92	33	21	94	188	242
April	39	98	42	18	81	237	198
May	48	89	19	26	88	222	266
June	62	72	29	35	61	159	187

Figure 8.4: Landscape orientation

print in Landscape mode, but some printers (many dot-matrix printers, in particular) just don't have it. Daisy-wheel printers are generally limited to the Portrait orientation.

Whenever any reference in this book is made to a typeface, you can assume that the orientation is Portrait, unless specifically stated otherwise.

FONT DEFINED

Now that the various ways of describing any group of characters have been introduced, the term *font* can be defined: *A font is a particular combination of typeface, size, style, and orientation.*

To specify a font completely, the name of the typeface and the style, size, and orientation must be included. If the style is not specified, it's assumed to be *normal*. If the orientation is not specified, it's assumed to be Portrait.

For example, Times Roman 12-point Italic is a particular font: The typeface is Times Roman, the size is 12 points, the style is Italic, and the orientation is taken to be Portrait.

Frequently, the term *font* is misused as a synonym for *typeface*. For example, many programs display a "font" menu, but the menu actually shows a list of typeface names. If you are aware of this incorrect usage, you shouldn't have any difficulty with the terminology; you must simply decide whether an author really means *font* or *typeface*!

CHARACTER SETS

A *character set*, sometimes called a *symbol set*, refers to the specific range of characters that is available to you when you use a particular font. For example, when using a dot-matrix printer, you are limited to the character set built into the printer for that font.

Suppose you purchase a font cartridge for a laser printer, which may contain a few dozen fonts. For each of these fonts, you will be limited to the particular character set built into the cartridge for that font.

Each character set is designed for a specific purpose. For example, many of the fonts marketed by commercial sources are available in the character set called USASCII, which consists of the characters most often used in ordinary word processing. They are:

- Letters: A–Z *(both uppercase and lowercase)*
- Digits: 0–9
- Special characters: All of those available on a standard keyboard (?, ", and so on).

Some character sets contain characters specific to a particular language. For example, Hewlett-Packard's French character set contains the character é, while the German character set includes Ä. Other character sets contain specialized symbols. For instance, Hewlett-Packard's Math character set contains many Greek characters, as well as other special mathematical symbols such as ± and ≈.

Whenever you decide to acquire a new set of fonts from a particular vendor, you should make sure that the set includes all of the characters that you plan to use.

PRINTER CAPABILITIES AND LIMITATIONS

Professional Write can output to a large variety of dot-matrix, daisy-wheel and laser printers. Because printing is a main element in producing good-looking documents, it's useful to be aware of the differences between various types of printers. Most important of all, you need to understand what you can expect from your own particular printer, as well as its limitations.

PRINT QUALITY

All printers (except daisy-wheel types) have one thing in common: They generate their output by placing dots of ink on the page. Your particular printer has certain built-in limitations, and if you understand these, you can work toward achieving the best possible output.

The quality of a printer's output is determined by three principal factors:

- The number of dots printed per linear inch, called the *resolution* of the printer.
- The amount and quality of ink placed in each dot, which helps to determine the *saturation* of the images on the page.
- The *accuracy* with which the printer places the dots on the page.

Different printers have different capabilities, of course, but as a general rule, laser printers perform better than dot-matrix printers in all three areas.

RESOLUTION AND DOTS

Most laser printers, as well as many dot-matrix printers, print approximately 300 dots per inch. However, the accuracy with which these dots are placed on the page is as important as the resolution itself.

With laser printers, each dot is individually and accurately positioned electronically, which gives laser-printed text and graphics their sharp look. For dot-matrix printers, the accuracy of dot placement is determined by the mechanical positioning of bulky objects like the paper roller and print head. Because of the difficulty of positioning these objects both rapidly and accurately, dot-matrix output is generally far less clear than that from laser printers. In addition, the quality of print varies tremendously among dot-matrix printers, even those of the same make and model, because it's highly dependent on a variety of mechanical factors.

There are two major types of dot-matrix printers: 9-pin and 24-pin. Without getting too technical, the more pins your printer has, the better its resolution will be. Most nine-pin printers can't print with a very high resolution, and generally they produce output of only poor-to-medium quality.

Keep in mind that even though a 24-pin printer may supposedly have a resolution of as much as 360 dots per inch, there will always be some error in the positioning of the dots on the printed page, due to mechanical limitations. It would be unrealistic, therefore, to expect such a printer to have the same degree of print quality as the average laser printer. However, if you have a fairly recent vintage 24-pin printer, it may be able to generate quality that is sufficient for your desktop-publishing needs.

The amount of ink placed into each dot is another important factor in how the final printout appears. Laser printers generally are much better than dot-matrix printers at delivering ink to the page. Moreover, the amount of ink delivered per dot remains relatively constant throughout the life of a laser printer toner cartridge, so you can generally expect uniformly high print quality from a laser printer.

Dot-matrix printer ribbons start to deteriorate from the beginning of their life, meaning that not only is the initial print quality inferior to that of laser printers, but also the quality gradually declines as the ribbon wears out.

GETTING THE MOST FROM YOUR PRINTER

If you are not satisfied with the output quality of your printer, a few simple printer adjustments may make a considerable difference.

Dot-matrix printers are mechanically quite reliable. Nevertheless, you can adjust various mechanical factors to optimize the print quality from these printers in several ways.

The ribbon in a printer wears out gradually, just as an automobile gradually gets out of tune—so slowly that you may not notice it until the car fails to start. One of the easiest ways to improve the print contrast is to use only the highest quality ribbon for final printing of a document. Often, carbon-based, one-pass-only ribbons produce the darkest images. A good strategy is to use a new ribbon for the final printing of documents and then remove that ribbon and save it, using other ribbons for the rest of your work.

Another tactic that can sometimes improve the printout clarity is to change the way paper is fed through. Many printers have both friction and tractor feed. Try using each one in turn to determine whether either produces better output. The reason that this ploy may work is that even the slightest amount of paper slippage during feed can greatly reduce the sharpness of the printer; in some cases, one type of feed may cause much less slippage than the other.

If you're using continuous-feed paper, the weight of the paper hanging below the printer may cause a small amount of slippage in the printer, leading to loss of print clarity. You might try feeding sheets one at a time to reduce this slippage when generating a final printout.

FONTS AND DOT-MATRIX PRINTERS

In many ways it is much easier to use a dot-matrix printer instead of a laser printer because you don't have to be concerned with soft fonts, font cartridges, and other confusing issues. On the other hand, the print quality of a dot-matrix printer is not as crisp and clear as that of a laser printer, nor do you have the variety of fonts that are available with a laser printer.

Each dot-matrix printer comes with a set of built-in fonts; you can print only with these fonts on that printer. If your printer is on Professional Write's list (which you can see in the Setup program), then you can probably use all of the fonts that are built into the printer. The staff of Software Publishing have done an excellent job of researching these printers, and they have incorporated into Professional Write the various commands necessary for using the different fonts with these printers.

When you want to use one of the built-in fonts for your printer, you simply select that font from Professional Write's Font menu. The correct commands for printing text in that font are then sent to the printer by Professional Write.

Some printers come with hardly any choice of fonts, while others are equipped with dozens. For example, Table 8.1 lists the built-in fonts for the Epson LQ-2550, one of the currently popular 24- pin printers. You can assign any of these fonts to text within a document.

FONTS AND LASER PRINTERS

Laser printers are extremely versatile instruments. Besides being able to print high quality graphics, they are also capable of printing a wide variety of fonts.

Table 8.1: Built-in Fonts for the Epson LQ-2550 Dot-Matrix Printer

FONT	POINTS	PITCH[1]	STYLES[2]
Roman	12	10,12,15,prop.[3]	N,B,I
Sans Serif	12	10,12,15,prop.	N,B,I
Courier	12	10,12,15	N,B,I
Prestige	12	10,12,15	N,B,I
Script	12	15	N,B,I
Double Wide	12	5	N,B,I,BI
Double High	14	10	N,B,I,BI

[1] number of characters per inch
[2] **N:** Normal; **B:** Boldface; **I:** Italics, **BI:** Bold italics
[3] proportionally-spaced font

Before a laser printer can print text in a particular font, it must have access to that font, which can be gained in one of three ways:

- The font is built into the printer's permanent memory.
- The font is contained in a font cartridge plugged into the printer.
- The font is downloaded from a soft font file on your computer's hard disk into the printer's (non-permanent) memory (RAM).

When using Professional Write, you always have access both to the printer's built-in fonts and also to those contained in any font cartridges plugged into the printer. In addition, you also have access to as many downloaded soft fonts as will fit in the printer's RAM *provided* these fonts are on Professional Write's font list, a topic covered in more detail later on.

In a single document, you can use fonts from all three sources: built-in, cartridge, and soft fonts.

For information about using fonts within a document, see Chapter 9.

BUILT-IN FONTS

A laser printer generally comes with a number of *built-in fonts* that reside in the printer's permanent, read-only memory (ROM). You can use any of these fonts when printing a document without much difficulty: As you are building a document, simply assign one or more of these printer fonts to the various bits and pieces of your text. Then, when you have finished, send the document to the printer.

A few laser printers come with a wide variety of built-in fonts, in particular, those printers that are PostScript compatible, such as the Apple LaserWriter + and the QMS PS 800 + series. The font selection for these printers is more than adequate for just about any type of document you might care to generate.

However, the selection of built-in fonts for most other laser printers is very limited. If you restrict yourself to these fonts, your documents will look as dull as dishwater. For instance, the HP LaserJet II has only two built-in typefaces: Courier and Line Printer, each of which is available in a single type size. Both of these typefaces are monospaced, and while they do have some uses, in general they are not well suited for producing attractive documents.

FONT CARTRIDGES

With many laser printers, you can use different *font cartridges*. For instance, there are nearly two dozen different font cartridges available for the HP LaserJet II. Each of these cartridges contains its own particular selection of fonts. When you insert a cartridge into the printer, the fonts built into that cartridge become available to the printer. Some printers are equipped with two slots, allowing two different font cartridges to be used at the same time, thus increasing the number of fonts at your disposal.

Font cartridges are very handy because you can gain instant access to a different set of fonts simply by replacing one cartridge with another. On the other hand, font cartridges are not inexpensive, and to acquire a sizeable array of fonts can cost a great deal of money.

Professional Write can be installed to use either one or two font cartridges, depending on the particular printer. To use a font cartridge with Professional Write, you need to go through a three-step process:

- First, you must decide on which fonts you want to use.
- Plug the appropriate font cartridge(s) into your printer.
- Enter *Setup* from the Main menu and then select the correct cartridge(s) for your printer.

See Appendix A for details on installing Professional Write for a printer cartridge.

After you have installed a cartridge with the Setup program, you can assign any of the fonts in that cartridge to the text of the documents you create.

SOFT FONTS

A *soft font*, also known as a *font file*, is a file that resides on your hard disk. It contains all of the information about a particular font. Some vendors, such as Hewlett-Packard, market soft fonts as groups, or *font sets*, which come on one or more floppy disks. Each font set contains a collection of related font files—usually one or two typefaces in various sizes and styles. For example, the Hewlett-Packard 33411AC font set contains soft fonts for two different typefaces: Times Roman and Helvetica. Sizes range from 6 to 30 points, and type styles include normal, bold, and italic. Both Portrait and Landscape modes are included.

For more information, see "Hewlett-Packard Fonts" and "Other Font Sources" in this chapter.

Professional Write is specifically designed to use either soft fonts marketed by Hewlett-Packard or soft fonts that are HP-compatible. When you use the Setup program, you select which font set (referred to by the Setup program as a *soft font family*) you want to use. You can use only one font set at a time.

When you select a particular font set with the Setup program, you are restricting yourself to those fonts available in that set. For example, suppose you select the Hewlett-Packard font set called AC-Times Roman & Helvetica Base Set. You can then use any of the fonts shown in Table 8.2. These fonts can be either those marketed by Hewlett-Packard, or any HP-compatible fonts from other vendors.

Table 8.2: Fonts Available with the AC-Times Roman and Helvetica Base Set

TYPEFACE	POINT SIZES	STYLES[1]	ORIENTATIONS[2]
Courier	12	N,B	P,L
Line Printer	8.5	N	P,L
Times Roman	6,8,10,12,14	N,B,I	P,L
"	18,24,30	B	P,L
Helvetica	6,8,10,12,14	N,B,I	P,L
"	18,24,30	B	P,L

[1]N = Normal, B = Bold, I = Italics
[2]P = Portrait, L = Landscape

See Appendix A for details on using Setup to install Professional Write for a set of soft fonts.

With some products, you create the font files directly from a font generator (see "Other Font Sources," below).

How to Use Soft Fonts

Here are the general steps for using a set of soft fonts:

- Enter Professional Write's Setup program from the Main menu.
- Select the font set (that is, the soft font family) you want to use.
- From DOS, create a separate font directory on your hard disk for holding soft fonts.
- Onto this font directory, copy the soft font files that correspond to the font set you selected in Setup.
- If the soft fonts are supplied by a vendor *other than* Hewlett-Packard, make sure that the name of each font file is *exactly the same* as those of the corresponding Hewlett-Packard soft fonts because Professional Write recognizes only Hewlett-Packard font file names. If necessary, rename the font files to the corresponding HP font file names (see "Soft Font File Name Conventions," below).

After you have completed these steps, you can use any of the fonts contained in the soft font family you selected.

COMMERCIAL SOURCES OF SOFT FONTS

Hewlett-Packard Fonts

Professional Write has been written specifically to accommodate font files marketed by Hewlett-Packard, which offers a wide variety of soft font disk sets. Each disk set contains a group of related fonts (see Table 8.2 for an example). To use these fonts, simply copy them into the font directory on your hard disk and then select that font set from the Setup program, as described above. The quality of Hewlett-Packard soft fonts is first-rate, a standard by which other products are measured. Using these fonts with a laser printer, you'll get the best possible quality for printed text.

All of Hewlett-Packard soft font sets are widely available, and you can also obtain a catalog describing all of the available font sets (as well as font cartridges). The company maintains the following toll-free number for ordering either the catalog or font sets: 1-800-752-0900.

Other Font Sources

Many vendors market soft fonts that are HP-compatible. There is a wide range in both quality of print output and price. Before purchasing one of these products, make sure you see a sample of the printed output; the quality of some products is very good, while that of others is mediocre. You can find out about many of these products by reading the advertisements in national computer magazines, such as *Publish!*, *PC Magazine*, and *PC World*.

One of the most versatile of the soft font products currently available is called Glyphix, which is marketed by Swfte Company. Unlike HP font sets, the Glyphix software comes with a font generator, which is an easy-to-use menu-driven program that allows you to select exactly which fonts you want. You select a typeface, then the sizes, styles, and orientations you would like, and the font generator makes the font files.

See "How to Use Soft Fonts," above.

These font files are completely compatible with HP soft font files, but they have different file names from their HP counterparts. In order to use them with Professional Write, you must rename them to the equivalent HP file names. The following section, "Soft Font File Name Conventions," describes how to name font files.

After you have renamed the font files, you can select and use them just as you would use HP soft fonts.

The Glyphix software is available from the following source:

Swfte

Box 219

Rockland, DE 19732

(1-302) 429-8434

SOFT FONT FILE NAME CONVENTIONS

In order to use an HP-compatible soft font file, it must be renamed to the equivalent Hewlett-Packard soft font file name. To do this, you need to know what the corresponding HP file names are. Figure 8.5 shows the naming convention for HP soft font file names. Note that the first two characters of the name are a code for the typeface for that font. The most common codes are **TR** and **HV** for Times Roman and Helvetica.

As an example, suppose that you generated an HP-compatible soft font file for Helvetica 15 Point Bold, in Landscape orientation. To use this with Professional Write, you would rename it, following the conventions shown in Figure 8.5, to HV150BPN.USL. Notice that the "PN" part of the file name is always the same.

DOWNLOADING SOFT FONTS

Before your printer can output text in a particular soft font, that soft font must be *downloaded* from your computer to the printer's memory. The reason is that when you first turn on the printer, the information about that soft font is stored in the font file on your hard disk—*but not in the printer's memory*. When you download a soft font you are essentially copying the font information into the printer's memory.

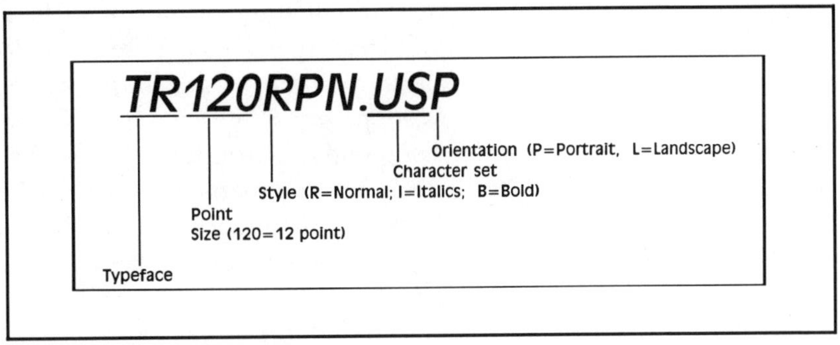

Figure 8.5: Soft font file name conventions

Once a soft font has been downloaded to the printer, the information remains there until one of the following occurs:

- The printer is turned off, which destroys all information in the printer's memory;
- The memory is cleared, either by pushing one of the buttons on the front control panel of the printer, or by sending a suitable "clear memory" instruction from the computer;
- The font is removed from memory to make room for another font. This will also require a suitable instruction from the computer.

Soft fonts are downloaded to the printer as part of a Professional Write print job. That is, when you print a document, one of the print instructions you supply to Professional Write is whether or not to download the appropriate fonts before printing the document. If you know that the soft fonts for that document have already been downloaded, you can instruct the software not to download the fonts again.

For example, suppose you have just turned your printer on and you want to print a document that uses three soft fonts, call them A, B, and C. Because the printer's memory will be blank (since you just turned it on), instruct Professional Write to download the soft fonts A, B, and C before printing the document.

To carry this one step further, suppose that later on you want to print another document that contains the soft fonts B and C. If you have not turned off the printer since the first document was printed, you would tell Professional Write not to download the soft fonts, inasmuch as they already reside in the printer's memory.

Now suppose that later in the same day you decide to print a document containing the soft fonts B and D (the printer still hasn't been turned off, and its memory contains the soft fonts A, B, and C). When you print this document, Professional Write will need to download the soft fonts first because font D isn't in the printer's memory.

HOW MANY FONTS SHOULD YOU USE?

For more information, see "Soft Fonts" in this chapter.

When you discover the world of soft fonts, you can easily develop strong delusions of grandeur regarding the design possibilities at your fingertips. When I first acquired a laser printer, I soon began to lust after every soft font that was available on the market.

It is true that there are an enormous number of fonts on the commercial market—literally tens of thousands, encompassing a wide range of different designs. And it is also true that if you have the inclination and ability, you can create beautiful documents by using a wide variety of fonts for different purposes.

Unfortunately, everything worthwhile in life has its price, and soft fonts are no exception. For one thing, fonts cost money, and you can spend a great deal acquiring a good library of soft fonts. However, that's only the up-front cost; an even greater expense lurks close by: hard-disk and printer memory requirements.

HARD-DISK REQUIREMENTS

Soft font files take up hard-disk space, and you can easily fill up a reasonably-sized hard disk just with font files! (As an aside, don't even consider using a laser printer if your computer doesn't have a hard disk—you'll spend all your time swapping floppy disks containing font files.)

Table 8.3 lists disk storage requirements for various font files. These figures are not exact, because files supplied by different publishers vary somewhat in size, but they are close, certainly to within 5 or 10 percent. It's important to note that each entry in the table is for a *single font*, that is, a specific combination of typeface, point size, orientation, and style.

To appreciate these figures, suppose that you want to store the following set of fonts:

- Number of typefaces: 5
- Point sizes for each typeface: 10, 12, 18, 24, 30, and 48
- Orientation: both Portrait and Landscape
- Styles: Normal, Bold, and Italic

A little arithmetic reveals that these files will require about 21 megabytes of disk space! If you have a 20-megabyte hard disk, you have a problem. If you you are lucky enough to have a 40-megabyte disk, you still have a problem, because the disk is probably full of programs and various data files, and you'll have difficulty finding 21 megabytes of free space.

LASER PRINTER MEMORY REQUIREMENTS

In order for a laser printer to generate text in a particular font, that font file must first be downloaded into the printer's memory. Most

***Table** 8.3:* Hard-Disk Space Requirements for Soft Font Files

POINT SIZE	APPROXIMATE REQUIRED DISK SPACE (BYTES)
10	23,000
12	30,000
18	58,000
24	98,000
30	142,000
48	381,000

laser printers come equipped with enough memory to contain several font files—just enough to make you want to purchase more memory.

For example, a Hewlett-Packard LaserJet II comes equipped with 512K of RAM. Some of this memory is used by the printer itself for control purposes, but most of it is available for font files or graphics.

If you look at Table 8.3, you'll see that several modest-sized font files can fit into 512K. For instance, you could easily load in font sizes of both 12 and 18 points, in Normal, Bold, and Italic styles. However, you can't load in even two fonts in 48-point size, or even one 48-point and one 30-point font.

So because of printer memory limitations, even if you have a gigantic hard disk filled to the brim with jillions of soft font files, you'll be able to use only a very small number of them for any particular print job.

GETTING REASONABLE

All of this may seem like a dismal assessment of the worth of soft fonts, but actually they are a wonderful tool, and you can make good use of a laser printer by staying within the bounds of reason.

If you want to build a large font library, you can do so without totally clogging up your hard disk: Leave on the disk only those fonts you plan to use most regularly, and store the remaining font files on floppy disks. Then, whenever you need a special font, you can place it temporarily onto your hard disk, only for as long as it's needed.

With respect to laser printer memory limitations, many of the newer laser printers have slots into which you can insert memory boards. For instance, you can increase the total memory capacity of the LaserJet II to somewhat more that 2 megabytes. This gives you the ability to load into the printer as many font files as you could possibly use. The catch is that memory boards are expensive—typically costing between $500 and $1,000.

In actual practice, most computer users eventually settle in to using a few of their favorite fonts and leave the rest of them for professional graphic artists. In fact, you can produce beautifully designed documents with only a handful of well-chosen fonts.

A Sample Font Array

As a point of reference, here are the font files that I use for nearly all of my own document production:

- Charter (a variation of Times Roman): 8, 10, 12, and Point; Normal, Italics, and Bold; Portrait and Landscape
- Helvetica: 8, 10, and 12, and 15 Point; Normal, Italics, and Bold; Portrait and Landscape
- Provence (an elegant serif typeface): 8, 10, 12, 15, 20, 30, and 48 Point; Normal and Italics, Portrait
- I also keep a couple of large-size font files (30 and 48 points) for large headlines and titles.

9

Enhancing Your Documents with Multiple Fonts

YOU CAN MAKE USE OF DIFFERENT FONTS TO enhance the appearance of a document in many ways. For example, you can make a title or heading stand out by using a large font size, perhaps in boldface. You might select a small font size for special notes or for superscripts. Other specialized fonts can be used for various dramatic effects.

Several different fonts can be used within a single document, provided that all of the following are true:

- Your printer can output the fonts you want to use.
- You have used the Setup program to install Professional Write both for your printer and for the fonts you want.
- Either the fonts are built into the printer or you can supply these fonts to your printer with a font cartridge or from a group of soft font files.

For more information about types of fonts, see Chapter 8.

THE REGULAR FONT

If you add text to a line that already contains text, the font of the surrounding characters will be assigned to the new text.

Whenever you enter text on a new line in a document, the *regular font* then in effect is assigned to that text. The regular font is chosen when you use the Setup program to install Professional Write for your printer. If your printer supports multiple fonts, you must select the regular font as part of the installation process. If your printer does not support multiple fonts, then the regular font is whatever the printer uses for output.

When the Edit screen is displayed, the font currently in use is shown on the Message line (Figure 9.1). For instance, when the Edit screen displays a blank working copy, the regular font is shown (the one selected by you during Setup).

In Figure 9.1 the regular font is shown as *TmsRmn L 12*. This probably looks a little cryptic, but it translates as follows: the first part of the font name refers to the typeface, which in this case is *TmsRmn*, or Times Roman. The next letter stands for the orientation, which in this case is *L* for Landscape. Finally, the numerical part stands for the point size, 12 points in this example.

When you create a document, the regular font *then in effect in Professional Write* is assigned as the regular font for that document, and this

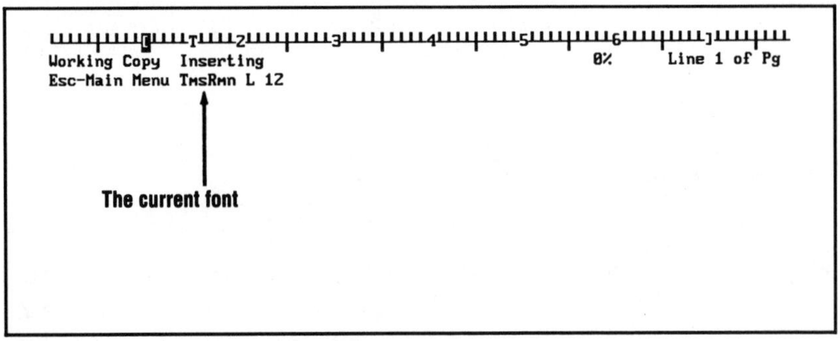

Figure 9.1: The current font is shown on the Message line

doesn't change unless you specifically assign a new regular font to the document.

CHANGING THE REGULAR FONT

For information about installing Professional Write for your printer, see Appendix A.

If you like, you can change the regular font for a document by temporarily changing the regular font currently in effect, as follows:

1. Retrieve the document into the working copy.
2. Exit to the Main menu by pressing Esc.
3. Select *Setup* from the menu.
4. Change the regular font to the new font you want (see Appendix A for details), and then exit to the Main menu.
5. Redisplay the document by selecting *Create/Edit* from the Main menu.
6. Save the document, and information about the new regular font will be saved as well.
7. Reenter setup and change the regular font back to the original font.

When a new regular font is assigned to a document, there are several implications. First of all, the new regular font is assigned to all text that was originally assigned the old regular font. Also, any new text that's entered into the document is automatically assigned the new regular font. Finally, text that's assigned any font other than the regular font is unaffected.

ASSIGNING A DIFFERENT FONT TO TEXT

The fonts currently supported by your printer are assigned during Setup. For more information, see Chapter 8 and also Appendix A.

You can assign any currently supported font to any selected block of text within a document. To assign a new font, first select the text you want and then assign that font to the block.

Notice that the phrase *currently supported fonts* does not imply that these are the only fonts that can be output by your printer. This term simply refers to those fonts for which Professional Write is currently set up.

When the cursor is placed on any character, the font assigned to it is displayed on the Message line. If that font is not the regular font for that document, the character is boldfaced on the screen because the screen cannot display different fonts; the best it can do is to boldface the character, indicating that there is something special about the font (or perhaps the style) of that character. To get a rough idea of how the different fonts will actually appear when printed, you can use the Preview feature.

Example

To understand how to change the font of selected text, consider the text shown in Figure 9.2. You can make the title stand out by increasing its size to 18 points (to contrast with the rest of the text, which is 12 points):

1. Select the heading as a text block and then press F10.
2. When the Text Block Operations menu appears, select *Change font or size*, and the Font menu appears, as shown in Figure 9.3.
3. Select the font you want from this menu: Use the PgUp, PgDn, and cursor keys to highlight the font. In this case, use the PgDn key to display additional fonts and then select the font labeled *AC-TmsRmn 18 Point.*
4. Press ↵ and that font will be assigned to the text block.

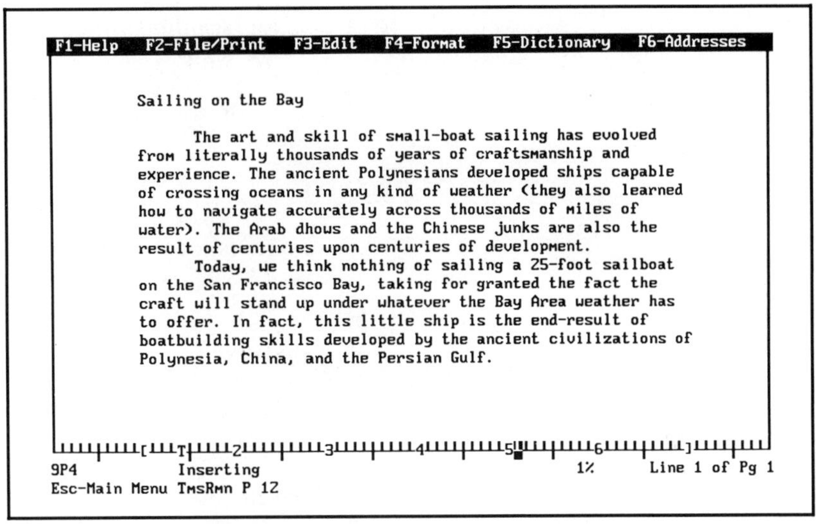

Figure 9.2: This document can be enhanced by increasing the size of the title

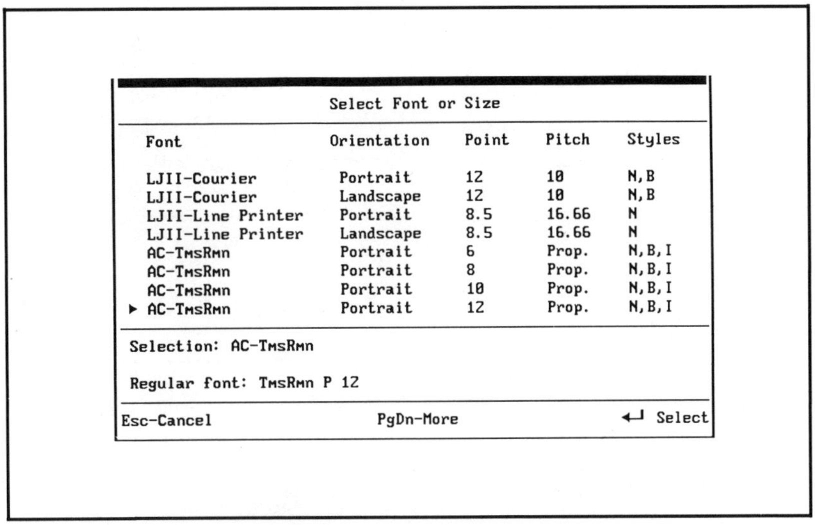

Figure 9.3: Select the font you want from this menu

Here's how to use the Preview feature to see how the page will actually appear when printed:

1. Press Ctrl-PrtSc and after a few seconds the full-page display of the document will appear.

2. To display a magnified view of the page, press Alt-V (see Figure 9.4). Use the PgDn and PgUp keys to scroll.
3. To return to the normal Edit menu, press Esc.

THE FONT MENU

The Font menu (as shown in Figure 9.3) displays all of the fonts currently supported by your printer. In addition, the regular font is displayed at the bottom of the screen.

For each font displayed on the Font menu, the following information is included:

- Name of the typeface
- The source of the font. This is the prefix attached to each typeface name. In Figure 9.3, the prefix *AC* refers to the name of the soft font family, while *LJII* means that a font is built into the LaserJet II printer. As an example, a font named *AC-TmsRmn* means that (1) the source of this font is the soft font family named AC, and (2) the typeface is Times Roman.
- Orientation: Either Portrait or Landscape
- Point size
- Pitch
- Styles: Normal, Boldface, or Italics

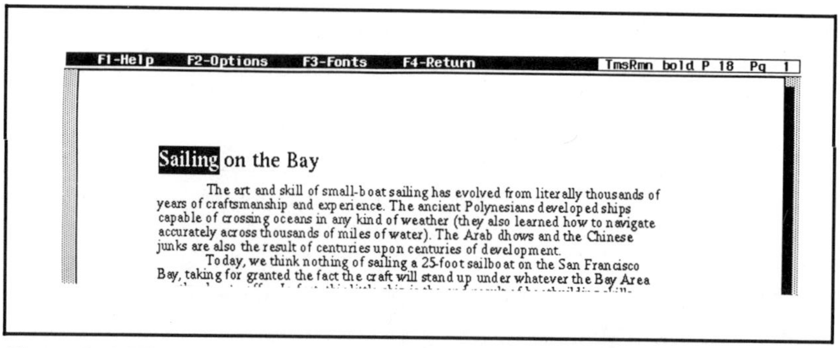

Figure 9.4: The Preview feature shows how different fonts will appear when printed

Some fonts are available in all three styles, while others are not. For instance, the font entry third down from the top in Figure 9.3 is available only in normal style, not in boldface or italics.

DECIDING WHICH FONTS YOU CAN USE

When you work on a document, there is usually a selection of fonts from which you can choose. It is useful for you to know how to determine which fonts are available.

LISTING THE CURRENTLY SUPPORTED FONTS

When you use the Setup program, you install Professional Write for your particular printer. As part of this process, you also select which cartridges or soft font family are to be used. *These selections, along with the printer's built-in fonts, determine which fonts are currently supported by your printer*. Remember: The term *currently supported* refers to those fonts for which Professional Write is currently set up.

Professional Write's Font menu lists these currently supported fonts. Whenever you assign a new font to a block, this menu appears (see "Assigning a Different Font to Text," above). You can also display the Font menu at any time, so that you can plan what fonts you may want to use:

1. Enter the Preview mode by pressing Ctrl-PrtSc.
2. Select *List available fonts* from the Fonts menu (F3).

You can scroll through this menu in the normal way. When you are finished, press Esc twice to return to the Edit menu.

LISTING THE FONTS IN A DOCUMENT

You can display a list of all fonts used in the current document. This display can be helpful in several ways. For example, if you know which fonts are in a document, you can estimate whether your laser printer's memory can accommodate all of the required soft fonts.

You can display the fonts used in the current document either from the Preview feature or from the Print Options menu. To display the font list from the Preview display, enter the Preview mode by pressing Ctrl-PrtSc and then select *List fonts in document* from the Fonts menu (F3). If the the Print Options menu happens to be displayed on the screen, you can display the font list directly by pressing F8.

CHECKING FOR UNSUPPORTED FONTS

An unsupported font is one for which Professional Write is not currently set up. You may have one or more unsupported fonts in a document, usually because Professional Write was installed for another printer setup when the document was originally created. For instance, you might have set up the program for Font Cartridge C when the document was created, but since then you have reinstalled Professional Write for Font Cartridge E, which has an entirely different set of fonts.

In some cases, you can tell if a font is currently unsupported: Place the cursor on the character in question and then look at the font name on the Message line. Sometimes an asterisk will precede the font name, indicating that the font is unsupported. However, although the asterisk *should* always appear for an unsupported font (according to the documentation for the software) it doesn't always do so.

Here's the best way to see if your document contains any unsupported fonts:

1. Display the list of fonts in the document, using the steps described earlier.
2. Make a written note of these fonts.
3. Display a list of the fonts currently supported, using the steps described earlier.

Any font that is used in your document but is not on the list of currently supported fonts is an unsupported font.

If you try to print a document with an unsupported font, the printer will substitute an available font for it. This substitution may or may not be acceptable, depending on what fonts are currently supported by the printer.

HOW TO ELIMINATE UNSUPPORTED FONTS

If you find that your document contains an unsupported font, you'll probably want to eliminate it. There are two avenues of attack open to you:

- Reinstall Professional Write so that it supports these fonts.
- Change the unsupported font to one currently supported.

If you want to replace all occurrences of an unsupported font to a font that's currently supported, you'll discover that trying to do it in the Edit screen is virtually impossible. However, there is a convenient way you can do so using the Preview feature. Chapter 12, "Previewing a Document," will explain this technique in detail.

ABOUT BOLDFACING AND ITALICS

Boldfacing and italics are handled differently by dot-matrix and laser printers. The following discussion applies primarily to laser printers, although it may apply to a few dot-matrix printers as well.

Boldfacing and italics are two different *styles* associated with a typeface. When you select a particular font from a font menu like the one shown in Figure 9.3, you may or may not be able to use boldfacing or italics with that selection. To find out, look at the far right column: It indicates which styles (Normal, Boldface, and Italics) are available for that selection of typeface and size.

For example, suppose you select *TmsRmn 12 Point* from the menu in Figure 9.3. The entry in the menu shows you that this font is available in three styles: Normal, Boldface, and Italics. Actually, the column labeled *Font* in the menu is misleading; it should be labeled something like *Font group* because when you select *TmsRmn 12 Point* you are actually selecting the following three fonts for Times Roman 12 Point:

Times Roman 12 Point Normal

Times Roman 12 Point Bold

Times Roman 12 Point Italics

This means that any text that you assign the Times Roman 12 Point font can also be assigned either boldface or italics style. However, you can't assign both styles to the same text, because there is no corresponding font.

Just to add confusion, consider the font menu shown in Figure 9.5, which is a continuation of the menu shown in Figure 9.3. The second item in the font list is labeled *TmsRmn bold*. Also, notice that the only style listed in the *Styles* column is Boldface. This means that the actual typeface is Times Roman, but because this size (18 points) is available only in boldface, the typeface is called Times Roman Bold.

If you assign a style that's not available to a group of characters, it's simply ignored by the printer. For instance, suppose you assign the Times Roman Bold 18 Point font to a word. Furthermore, suppose you then select *Italics* as the style for this word. On the Edit screen the bottom line will indicate that this word is italicized. However, when the word is printed it will not be italicized because there is no corresponding font available.

SPECIAL CONSIDERATIONS WHEN USING MULTIPLE FONTS

LEAVING ENOUGH SPACE FOR LARGE FONTS

Leave blank lines above large font text to prevent overlapping.

If you use large fonts in a document, you may find that the text on adjacent lines overlaps (see Figure 9.6, for example). Because Professional Write was originally developed to handle only one font size, the software is not well equipped to deal with this problem. In fact, there is only one way to handle overlapping: Leave one or more blank lines above each line containing a large font. This works reasonably well, but you don't have any control over line spacing—something that's really useful when working with different font sizes.

Note that the total number of lines per page doesn't change to accommodate large fonts; each line containing a large font still counts as a single line.

Select Font or Size

Font	Orientation	Point	Pitch	Styles
▸ AC-TmsRmn	Portrait	14	Prop.	N,B,I
AC-TmsRmn bold	Portrait	18	Prop.	B
AC-TmsRmn Bold	Portrait	24	Prop.	B
AC-TmsRmn Bold	Portrait	30	Prop.	B
AC-TmsRmn	Landscape	6	Prop.	N,B,I
AC-TmsRmn	Landscape	8	Prop.	N,B,I
AC-TmsRmn	Landscape	10	Prop.	N,B,I
AC-TmsRmn	Landscape	12	Prop.	N,B,I

Selection: AC-TmsRmn

Regular font: TmsRmn P 12

Esc-Cancel PgUp,PgDn-More ↵ Select

Figure 9.5: A continuation of the menu shown in Figure 9.3

Sailing on the Bay

The art and skill of small-boat sailing has evolved from literally thousands of years of craftsmanship and experience. The ancient Polynesians developed ships capable of crossing oceans in any kind of weather (they also learned how to navigate accurately across thousands of miles of water). The Arab dhows and the Chinese junks are also the result of centuries upon centuries of development.

More About the Bay

Today, we think nothing of sailing a 25-foot sailboat on the San Francisco Bay, taking for granted the fact the craft will stand up under whatever the Bay Area weather has to offer. In fact, this little ship is the end-result of boatbuilding skills developed by the ancient civilizations of Polynesia, China, and the Persian Gulf.

Figure 9.6: Large fonts can cause line overlap

LINE DRAWING

For more information about line drawing, see Chapter 11.

Unfortunately, one thing you can't do when using proportionally-spaced typefaces is to draw lines or boxes. Basically, here's the reason: When you build a line of proportionally-spaced text, the line could be any length. To draw a box around one or more lines of different lengths would require a fair amount of intelligence built into the word processor in order to determine where to place the right-most line of the box. Professional Write doesn't possess this capability (nor do most other word processors). As a result, you can't use Professional Write's line and box drawing feature to enclose any text that's in a proportional font.

To use the line drawing feature, select a monospaced font for the text to be enclosed.

WORKING WITH COLUMNS

You can create columns of either text or numbers using various fonts. However, when either mixing different fonts or using proportionally-spaced fonts in columns, you must use tab settings to align the columns.

For example, suppose you want to generate a page of text columns like those shown in Figure 9.7, and you want the text to be in a proportional font, such as Times Roman 12 Point. Here is the easiest way to accomplish this:

1. Create typewriter tab settings at the starting positions of each column.
2. Enter the text, using the Tab key to move from one column to the next.
3. Make sure to end each line with a hard return by pressing the ↵ key.
4. When you begin the printing process, select *Font Format* as one of the print styles in the Print Options dialog box.

SALEPEOPLE OF THE MONTH

	1988	1989
January	J. Parker	L. Abrams
February	W. Ruby	F. Smithers
March	R. Jensen	Z. Mostel
April	G. Litton	C. Schwamberger
May	E. Kimmel	P. Pastina
June	C. Howell	S. Howell

***Figure** 9.7:* You can line up columns of proportionally spaced text

If you want to shift columns of preexisting text and still have the printed columns line up, you will need to do a bit of fiddling. For details, see "How to Use Tabs" in Chapter 5.

When working with columns of numbers, follow the four steps listed above, but use decimal tabs instead of typewriter tabs.

IMPORTANT POINTS TO REMEMBER ABOUT FONTS

Here is a checklist of things to keep in mind when you are creating a document with multiple fonts:

- Make sure that the fonts used in your document are currently supported: see "Listing the Currently Supported Fonts" and "Checking for Unsupported Fonts" in this chapter.
- If your document uses one or more soft fonts, make sure that these soft font files exist in the soft font directory. For information about soft font files, see "Soft Fonts" in Chapter 8.
- You can see how the printed document will appear by using the Preview feature. See Chapter 12 for details.
- When using proportional fonts, make sure that before printing you select *Font Format* as one of the print styles in the Print Options dialog box. This is absolutely necessary to ensure that (1) text lines wrap properly, and (2) columns line up properly on the corresponding tab settings.

10 Printing Your Document

GETTING STARTED

Before printing a document, here is a short check list that you may want to go over in order to avoid certain pitfalls:

See Appendix A for details on using the Setup program.

- Make sure that you have correctly set up Professional Write for your particular printer. This includes not only selecting the correct printer itself but also the correct printer port. If you are using a laser printer, you may also select either one or two cartridges, a soft font family, or both.
- Be sure that all of the fonts and styles that you have included in your document are accessible to your printer—either as built-in fonts, cartridge fonts, or soft fonts.
- You must load the document to be printed into the working copy.

Before printing a document, you may want to use Professional Write's Preview feature to see how the document will appear when printed. To preview a document, press Ctrl-PrtSc. For details about using this feature, see Chapter 12.

You can also use the speed key Ctrl-O to initiate printing.

To begin the printing process, select *Print working copy* from the File/Print menu (F2), and the Print Options dialog box will appear (Figure 10.1). The options offered you here are discussed in the following section, "The Print Options Dialog Box."

After you have filled in the various entries in the Print Options dialox box, press ↵ and the printing will begin. To interrupt printing at any time, press Esc. You can then either terminate printing by pressing Esc a second time or continue with the printing by pressing the ↵ key.

Note that when you instruct Professional Write to interrupt the output process, the printer may seem to be ignoring you by continuing to print. This can occur if:

- The printer has a print buffer, and several pages have already been transmitted there from your computer.
- Your computer has a print spooler that has its own print buffer. Output sent to this buffer from Professional Write will be sent to the printer, regardless of any instructions you give to Professional Write.

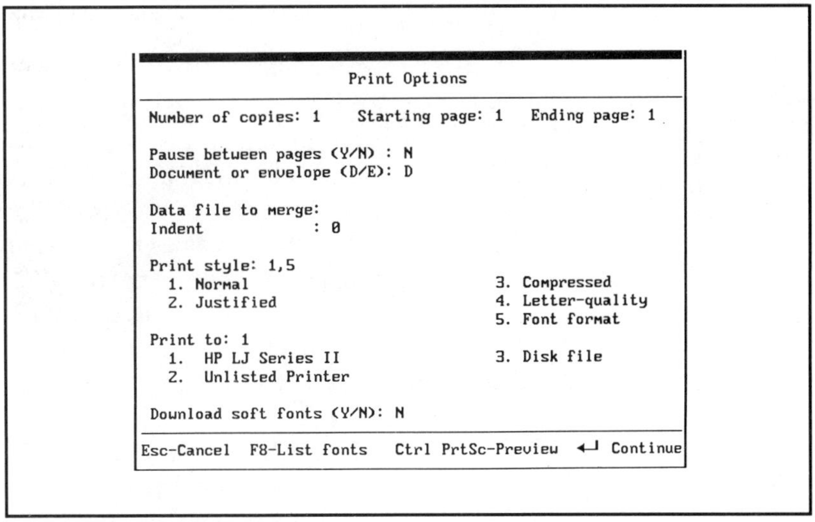

Figure 10.1: Select your print options from this menu

THE PRINT OPTIONS DIALOG BOX

With the options in this dialog box you can control many aspects of your printing. As you work your way through these options, keep in mind that

- You can move from one option to another by pressing Tab or Shift-Tab.
- To change the value of an option, first delete the current value by pressing Ctrl-E. Then enter the new value.
- After you have filled in all the entries you need, press ↵ and printing will begin.

NUMBER OF COPIES

Enter the number of copies of the document you want printed. If you want multiple copies it is usually much faster to enter the number of copies you want rather than go through the entire print process several times.

STARTING AND ENDING PAGES

Page numbers on the screen may have no relationship to the actual number of pages printed.

If you don't change the values initially displayed for the Starting and Ending page options, the entire document will be printed. However, you can print only part of a document by filling in the appropriate page numbers for these entries. The values you enter here must correspond to the count of the *actual physical pages* that are printed. Notice that initially the values for *Starting Page* and *Ending Page* correspond to the first and last pages of your document, *as measured by the page counter at the bottom right-hand corner of your edit screen.*

The page numbers shown at the bottom of the screen may have no relationship to the actual count of printed pages. For instance, consider the page shown in Figure 10.2. According to the page counter on the Status line, the screen is displaying the contents of a single page.

However, there are three *NEW PAGE* commands in the text, and each of these will generate a page break, that is, begin a new page. Consequently, what you see in Figure 10.2 will actually be printed on four pages.

To print only the first two of these pages, you would enter the numbers **1** and **2** for *Starting page* and *Ending page*.

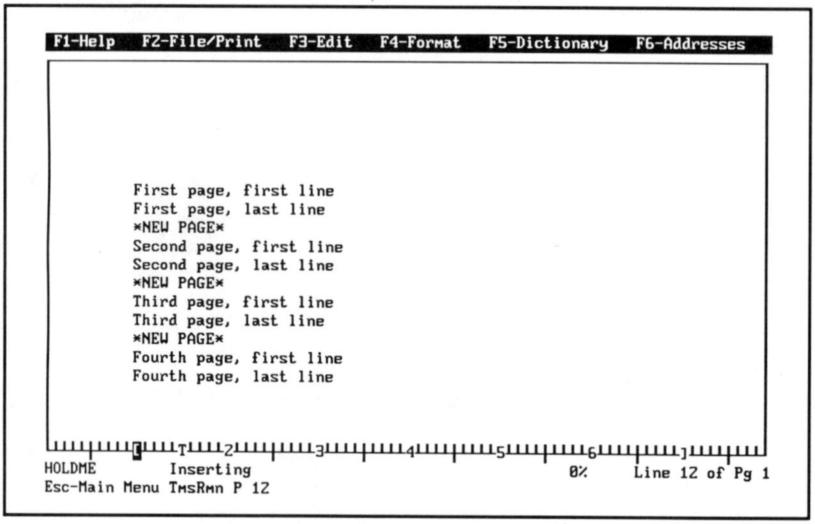

Figure 10.2: This screen will print as four separate pages

There are other reasons why the physical page count may bear no relationship to page numbers appearing on the screen. For instance, if you include page numbers in either a header or footer (which are displayed on the screen), they may be different from the page count of printed pages. Or, if your document has a cover page, you may have started the page count with the number 1 on the second printed page.

One way to determine the relationship between what you see on the screen and the actual physical page numbers is to use the Preview feature. In most cases, the page number that is displayed here corresponds to the physical page that will be printed. Figure 10.3 shows a preview of the first page to be printed from the screen shown in Figure 10.2.

PAUSE BETWEEN PAGES

If you select **Y** for this option, Professional Write will pause before printing each page, giving you time to feed individual pages to the printer.

This option is particularly useful when you are using a printer that doesn't have an automatic single-sheet feeder. For instance, suppose you have a dot-matrix printer that normally uses continuous-feed paper, but you want to print a letter on individual letterhead paper. Selecting **Y** for this option will allow you to do so.

Most laser printers feed single sheets automatically, so that you would normally select **N** for this option. However, some laser printers, such as the LaserJet II, also have a special slot for inserting

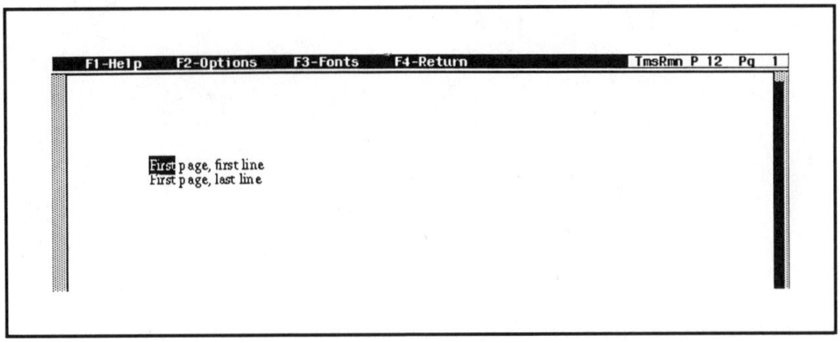

Figure 10.3: The Preview screen: the page number at the top right represents the actual physical page count

individual sheets, such as letterhead. To control sheet feeding manually in this situation, enter **Y** for this option.

DOCUMENT OR ENVELOPE

This option specifies what type of printing is being done. Normally, you will be printing ordinary documents, corresponding to a value of **D** for this option. If you are printing an envelope, set this option to **E**. For more details, see "Printing Envelopes," below.

DATA FILE TO MERGE

If you are printing form letters, fill in the name of the data file here. Include the complete pathname of the file and also the disk drive, if necessary. For information on creating form letters, see Chapter 14. If you are not printing form letters, leave this option blank.

INDENT

If you enter a number for this option, it is saved along with the working copy.

You can indent your entire document to the right by entering a value here. The number you enter will be interpreted by most printers as tenths of an inch. For instance, entering the number **5** will shift every line in the document by one-half inch. You may need to experiment with this option to find the value that produces the best looking pages for your printer.

PRINT STYLE

This option can be used to control various aspects of your printed document. They include:

- Normal or full justification
- Selecting different quality output fonts
- Adjusting for proper line breaks when proportional fonts are used.

You can select more than one style for this option. For instance, to select both Normal and Font Format styles, enter **1,5**.

Justified

If you select *Normal* style, your document will be printed with a ragged right margin. If you select *Justified*, lines will be fully justified—that is, the right margin will be even.

Full justification is accomplished by adding extra spaces between words. Generally, this leads to excessive white space on the page, making it more difficult to read. For example, Figures 10.4 and 10.5 show the same document, with and without full justification. If you examine these two figures, you can see that the fully-justified page has more open space, which is generally found to be distracting.

Compressed and Letter-Quality

Generally, selecting either *Compressed* or *Letter-quality* will have no effect on the output from a laser printer. These options are used for controlling the print style on dot-matrix printers.

Sailing on the Bay

The art and skill of small-boat sailing has evolved from literally thousands of years of craftsmanship and experience. The ancient Polynesians developed ships capable of crossing oceans in any kind of weather (they also learned how to navigate accurately across thousands of miles of water). The Arab dhows and the Chinese junks are also the result of centuries upon centuries of development.

Today, we think nothing of sailing a 25-foot sailboat on the San Francisco Bay, taking for granted the fact the craft will stand up under whatever the Bay Area weather has to offer. In fact, this little ship is the end-result of boatbuilding skills developed by the ancient civilizations of Polynesia, China, and the Persian Gulf.

Figure 10.4: A document without full justification

Sailing on the Bay

The art and skill of small-boat sailing has evolved from literally thousands of years of craftsmanship and experience. The ancient Polynesians developed ships capable of crossing oceans in any kind of weather (they also learned how to navigate accurately across thousands of miles of water). The Arab dhows and the Chinese junks are also the result of centuries upon centuries of development.

Today, we think nothing of sailing a 25-foot sailboat on the San Francisco Bay, taking for granted the fact the craft will stand up under whatever the Bay Area weather has to offer. In fact, this little ship is the end-result of boatbuilding skills developed by the ancient civilizations of Polynesia, China, and the Persian Gulf.

Figure 10.5: The same document shown in Figure 10.4 with full justification

Some dot-matrix printers can print in *compressed* mode, which means that more characters per inch are printed. In addition, many dot-matrix printers can output text in more than one print quality, such as *draft* and *letter-quality*. You may want to experiment with your printer, trying both *Compressed* and *Letter-quality*. When you select either *Compressed* or *Letter-quality*, any boldfacing, underlining, or other text styles that you have included in your document will still be included in the printed output.

If you select either *Compressed* or *Letter-quality*, the entire document will be printed in that style. If you want to print only part of a document in compressed mode, for example, you may be able to do so by one of two methods:

- If your printer supports different fonts, you may be able to assign a compressed font (that is, a larger pitch) to selected text blocks.
- You can enter printer codes at selected places in your document. For example, to print a particular paragraph in compressed mode, you would precede the paragraph with a special printer code to turn on compressed mode. Then, end the paragraph with another printer code to return to the normal print mode.

See "Sending Special Instructions to Your Printer," below.

When you select either of these print styles, you can't also select the Font Format print style (see below) to correct the line breaks.

If you select either *Compressed* or *Letter-quality*, you may find that the lines are shorter than they could be (that is, the right margin is too large) because of the reduced size of the individual characters. You can solve this problem by increasing the right margin of the document.

For example, suppose that for a particular printer compressed mode prints 130 characters per line. You could change the right margin from 70 (normal value) to something like 115 or 120 and then try printing the document or using the Preview mode. With a little bit of fiddling, you can find the best values for the left and right margins.

Font Format

Select this style for any proportionally-spaced font.

This style is a particularly important one because it must be used when your document contains any proportionally-spaced fonts. It can also be used effectively when the regular font is monospaced at a pitch other than 10 characters per inch.

The *Font Format* style has two main uses:

- During printing, it creates line breaks as close as possible to the right margin.
- It forces printed text to line up with tab settings.

To illustrate how the Font Format print style works, consider the working copy shown in Figure 10.6. Printed on a laser printer, using the font Times Roman 12 point (which is a proportional font), but *without* the *Font Format* style, the document will look like that shown in Figure 10.7. Notice that the line breaks on the printed page are exactly the same as those shown on the screen, but as a result the printed page has several inches of right margin.

On the other hand, if the same document is printed with the *Font Format* style selected, the result is shown in Figure 10.4. Here, the page has been properly reformatted, so that each line is extended as close as possible to the right margin.

See "How to Use Tabs" in Chapter 5.

A similar result occurs if you try to use proportional fonts with columns of text or numbers: unless you select *Font Format* as a print style, the columns will not line up properly.

Because the *Font Format* style changes the line breaks, the page breaks of the printed document will usually not be the same as those

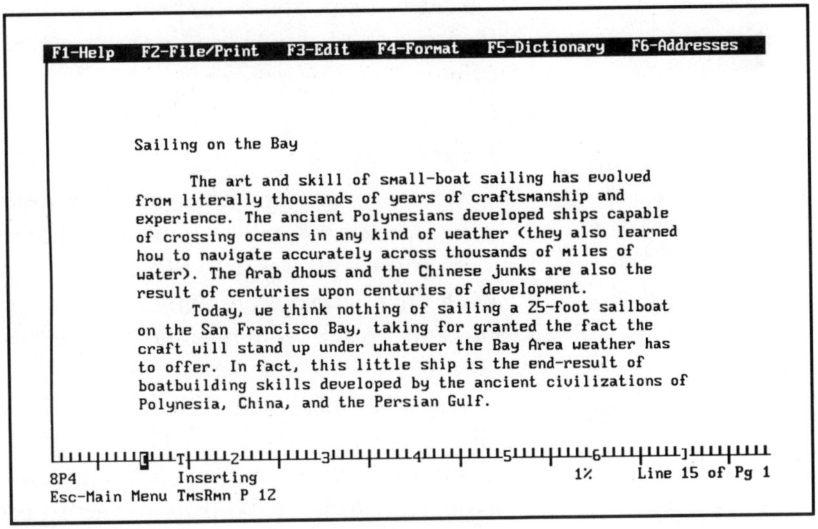

Figure 10.6: A document in the working copy

Sailing on the Bay

The art and skill of small-boat sailing has evolved from literally thousands of years of craftsmanship and experience. The ancient Polynesians developed ships capable of crossing oceans in any kind of weather (they also learned how to navigate accurately across thousands of miles of water). The Arab dhows and the Chinese junks are also the result of centuries upon centuries of development.

Today, we think nothing of sailing a 25-foot sailboat on the San Francisco Bay, taking for granted the fact the craft will stand up under whatever the Bay Area weather has to offer. In fact, this little ship is the end-result of boatbuilding skills developed by the ancient civilizations of Polynesia, China, and the Persian Gulf.

Figure 10.7: Printing a document with a proportional font, but without using the *Font Format* print style

shown on the Edit screen (a page break appears as a double horizontal line across the entire screen). This is another reason why the page numbers appearing on the screen may not correspond to the actual printed pages (see "Starting and Ending Pages," above).

For more information, see "Joining Documents at Print Time," below.

If you are joining two or more documents at print time, you can't use *Font Format* because this print style is ignored when the joined document is printed.

One last note about this print style: It has no effect when you select Printer 2 (see below) because you can't select alternate fonts with this printer.

Print to

See "Outputting to a Disk File," below, for additional details.

When you set up Professional Write for your computer system, you can select two different printers. For example, you can have both a dot-matrix printer and a laser printer attached to your computer. With the *Print to* option, you can print to either of these printers. (Or you can "print" to a disk file, a topic covered in detail later in this chapter.)

One of Professional Write's limitations is that you cannot assign alternate fonts to Printer 2. Therefore, if you are using a laser printer or some other type that supports alternate fonts, this printer must be assigned as Printer 1 during the setup process (see Appendix A for details about setting up Professional Write for your printers).

Because of this limitation, there doesn't seem to be much of an argument for bothering to set up Professional Write for a second printer. However, it's always possible that you may find a reason to use the *Printer 2* option, even with its severe limitations.

DOWNLOAD SOFT FONTS

For more information about soft fonts, see Chapter 8.

When you send a document containing various fonts to a laser printer, all of those fonts must already be known to the printer—either in the printer's permanent memory, in one of it's plug-in font cartridges, or in its RAM. If any of the fonts used in a document are soft fonts, then those fonts must be **downloaded to the printer's RAM before the document is printed**.

If your document contains one or more soft fonts that have not yet been downloaded, select **Y** for this option. On the other hand, if you know that the printer's RAM contains all of the required soft fonts, select **N**.

If you select **Y** for this option, then when you eventually press ↵ to begin printing, every soft font specified in your document will be downloaded, *even if the font has been previously downloaded*. As the fonts are being downloaded, an informative message will appear on screen to let you know that something constructive is happening; downloading can take several minutes, and you might begin to wonder what was going on.

LIST FONTS

You can use the *List Fonts* key (F8) to display a list of every font used in the current document. Figure 10.8 shows an example of this display, in which the current document contains two fonts: Times Roman 18 point Bold, and Times Roman 12 point Normal.

This display can help you decide whether or not you need to download any fonts to your laser printer before printing the document.

If an asterisk appears next to a font name in this display, then that font is not currently supported by your printer. This might occur if you have used the Setup program to change printers after the current

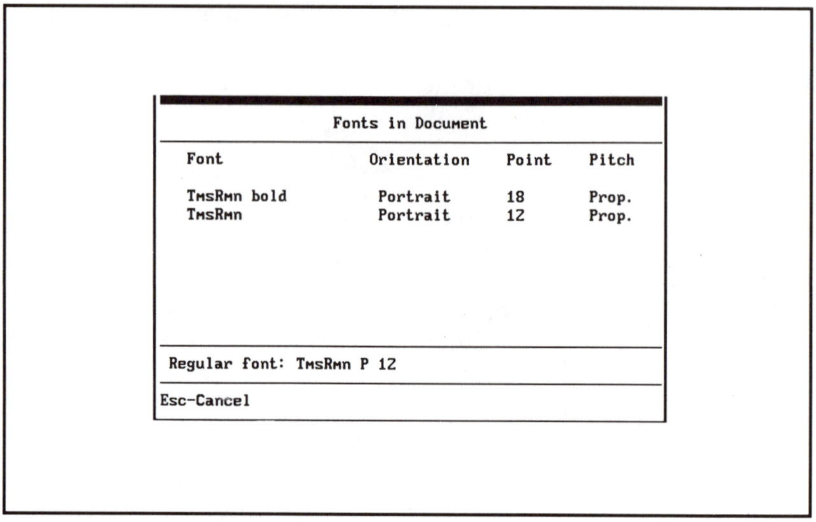

Figure 10.8: A list of the fonts in the current document

document was created. If you find one or more unsupported fonts, you must do one of the following:

- Replace it with a font that's supported by your printer, or
- Use the Setup program to change the printer options to support the fonts.

Note that a font may not be currently supported by your printer, and yet the font is not marked by an asterisk in the font display generated by pressing F8. Generally, a font is marked with an asterisk if it is incompatible with the printer currently selected as Printer 1.

Preview

For details, see Chapter 12.

You can get a preview of your document by pressing the *Preview* key (Ctrl-PrtSc) while the Print Options dialog box is displayed. You thus have an opportunity to make various selections from the Print Options box and then immediately see their effect on the document's appearance.

OUTPUTTING TO A DISK FILE

If you like, you can have your print output directed to a disk file rather than to a printer. This file will be in ASCII format, but all of the page layout features are preserved, such as margins, headers, and footers. However, information about type styles and fonts is lost.

You might want to direct a document to a disk file for subsequent "quick-and-dirty" output to a remote printer; because the basic page layout information is intact, the output will look reasonably good.

To output a document to a disk file:

1. Bring up the Print Options dialog box either by selecting *Print working copy* from the File/Print menu (F2), or pressing the speed key Ctrl-O.
2. Enter **3** for the *Print to* option in the Print Options dialog box and then press ↵. The Save Filename dialog box appears (Figure 10.9).
3. On the *Filename:* line, enter the name of the file to which the output is to be written. Include the name of the directory, including its full pathname. If you are writing to a floppy disk, enter the name of the disk drive before the file name.

Points to Ponder

When outputting to a disk file, you must enter a file name as well as a disk drive and/or directory. That is, you can't access the file directory from this part of Professional Write.

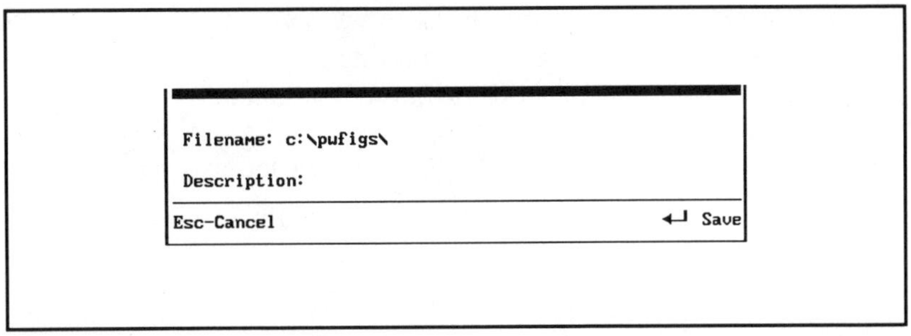

Figure 10.9: Enter the name of the file to which the output is to be written

Since the output file is in ASCII format, the *Print styles* options have no effect because all font information is lost when the file is created. On the other hand, line breaks will appear in this file exactly as they appear on the Edit screen.

PRINTING ENVELOPES

Professional Write contains a very clever mechanism that allows you to print the inside address of a letter onto an envelope with practically no effort. This is one of the slickest methods I have ever seen, and it beats any of the higher-priced word processors hands down.

To make this method work, your letter must conform to one of the styles shown in Figure 10.10. Here are the details:

- If the date is entered on the left side of the page, it must begin exactly at the left margin.
- The inside address must also be entered exactly at the left margin.
- At least one blank line must come immediately after the inside address.
- The first line of the inside address *must not* end with a digit. Otherwise, that line will be interpreted as a date by Professional Write, and it will be skipped.

None of these rules contradicts any standard practices for writing letters. Just make sure that you leave a blank line after the inside address, start the address (and, if you wish, the date) at the left margin, and you will generally conform to the rules without needing to think about them.

To print an envelope:

1. Retrieve the letter you are going to use into the working copy.
2. Make sure that it conforms to one of the styles shown in Figure 10.10.
3. Select *Print working copy* from the File/Print menu (F2), or press Ctrl-O.

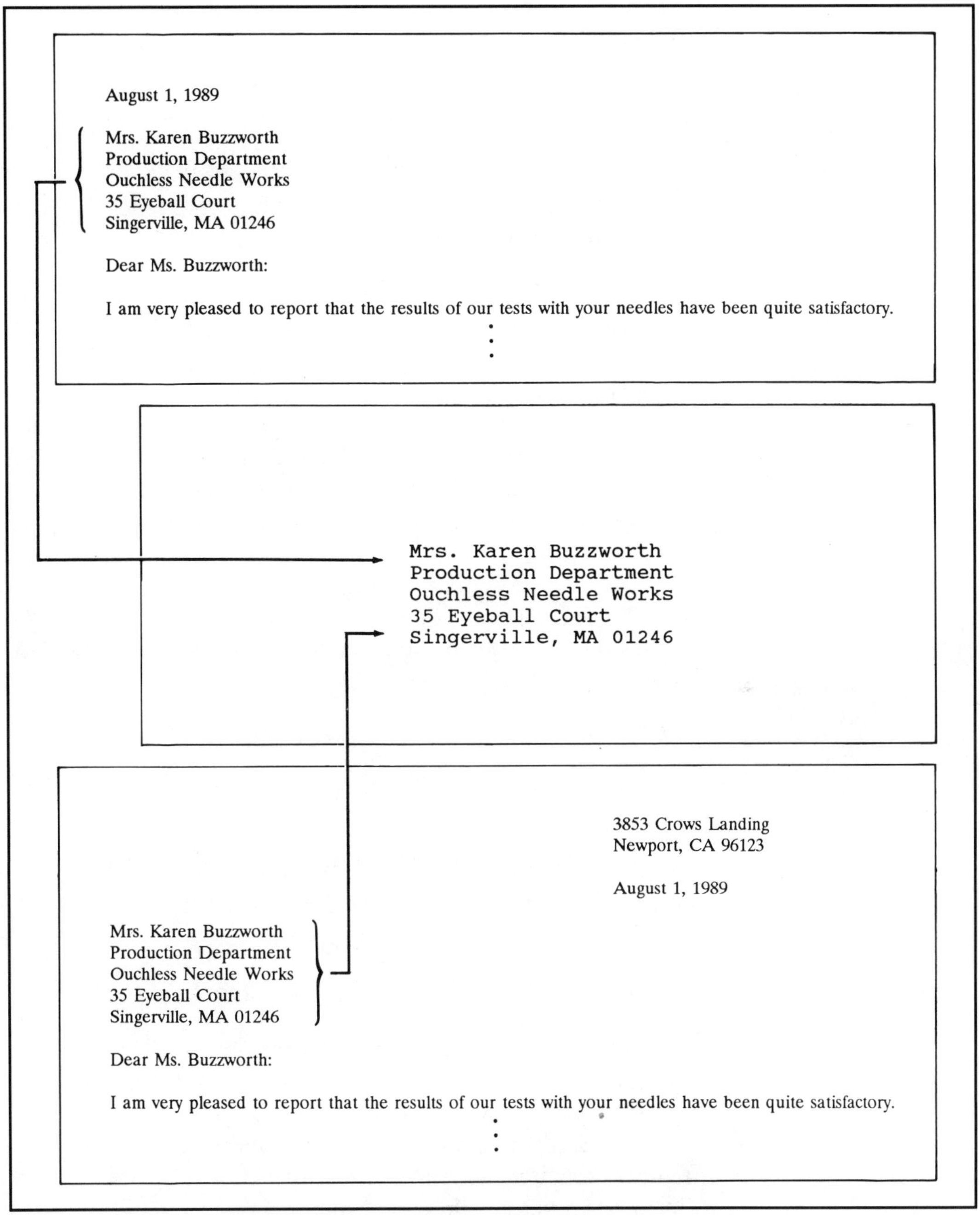

August 1, 1989

Mrs. Karen Buzzworth
Production Department
Ouchless Needle Works
35 Eyeball Court
Singerville, MA 01246

Dear Ms. Buzzworth:

I am very pleased to report that the results of our tests with your needles have been quite satisfactory.

⋮

```
Mrs. Karen Buzzworth
Production Department
Ouchless Needle Works
35 Eyeball Court
Singerville, MA 01246
```

3853 Crows Landing
Newport, CA 96123

August 1, 1989

Mrs. Karen Buzzworth
Production Department
Ouchless Needle Works
35 Eyeball Court
Singerville, MA 01246

Dear Ms. Buzzworth:

I am very pleased to report that the results of our tests with your needles have been quite satisfactory.

⋮

Figure 10.10: Either of these letter styles can be used for printing an envelope

4. Enter **E** for the *Document or envelope* option in the Print Options dialog box.
5. If you are using a dot-matrix printer, select either *Normal*, *Compressed*, or *Letter-quality* for the *Print style* option.
6. Insert a blank envelope into your printer.
7. Press ↵ and the inside address of your letter will be printed on the envelope.

When the envelope is printed, the address is printed in whatever font was assigned to it in the letter—if possible. Otherwise, the best possible alternative will be automatically selected.

For example, many laser printers require that you insert an envelope sideways. This means that the printer must print the address in landscape orientation. Professional Write handles this by selecting the best possible landscape font that exists in the printer. For example, if the regular font for a letter is Times Roman 12 point Portrait, and if the Times Roman 12 point Landscape font has already been downloaded, then that landscape font will automatically be used for printing envelopes.

Once a landscape font has been downloaded, you don't need to assign it to addresses to be printed. Professional Write will automatically do so.

If you need to download a landscape font for printing one or more envelopes, here's one way to do it:

1. Retrieve a letter into the working copy.
2. Assign the landscape font you plan to use to the inside address of the letter.
3. Press Ctrl-O to display the Print Options dialog box.
4. Enter **Y** for *Download soft fonts*.
5. Press ↵ to begin printing the first envelope.
6. Return the address to its original font.

The landscape font you select for the address will be downloaded to the printer and then used for printing the address. For subsequent letters, steps 2, 4, and 6 can be omitted.

If you don't download a landscape font to the laser printer, one of the printer's built-in landscape fonts will be automatically selected. The print quality of these built-in fonts may not be the greatest, but the whole process is so smooth that you won't want to complain (especially if you have had any experience trying to force a dot-matrix printer to print an envelope).

When printing an envelope on a dot-matrix printer, the address will be printed with whatever font was assigned to that address in the letter.

To save money, use envelope-sized sheets of scratch paper when experimenting.

Generally, an address is printed somewhere near the middle of the envelope. If you want to move the address farther to the right, redisplay the Print Options dialog box and then enter a value for *Indent*. For instance, to shift the address one inch to the right, enter the value **10**.

If you want to move the address up or down and you are using a dot-matrix printer, you can fiddle with the initial position of the envelope in the printer. For laser printers, you may not be able to adjust the vertical position of the printed address.

JOINING DOCUMENTS AT PRINT TIME

You can combine two or more separate documents as they are being printed. For example, you might want to do this if you had created a document that was too large to fit into the computer's memory and you needed to create it piecemeal, storing it in several different files. Or, you might want to combine a document you had created with one generated by another software package.

To join one document to another at print time, first retrieve into the working copy the main document to be printed. Before printing it, include in this document a *JOIN* instruction for each other document to be printed along with the working copy. Place each *JOIN* instruction exactly where you want the text from the joined file to be inserted.

WHAT TYPES OF FILES CAN BE JOINED

When printing the working copy, you can join any of the following types of files:

- An ASCII file
- A normal file generated by Professional Write, but not an encrypted file

- A worksheet printed to a disk file, generated by any of the following software products: Lotus 1-2-3, Professional Plan, PFS:First Choice, or PFS:Plan.

Note that you can join *any* file that is in ASCII format. This gives you a good deal of flexibility in the types of files that can be joined. For example, suppose you want to include as part of a Professional Write document a report generated by some type of database package. You can do this provided that the package can output its report to a disk file in ASCII format. The same is true for any type of software package—word processors, spreadsheets, and so on.

HOW TO USE THE *JOIN* COMMAND

You must include the disk drive and pathname, unless they are the same as the data directory defined in the Setup program.

To join the file *filename* to the document in the working copy when printed, insert the following command at the place in the working copy where you want the joined file to be printed: ***JOIN** *filename** or ***J** *filename**. Each join command should be on a separate line, starting at the left margin. Here, *filename* must include the complete file name, including the disk drive and pathname. Enter this command exactly as shown, with no spaces except between the word JOIN and the file name.

Points to Ponder

When a file is joined to the printout of the working copy, page numbering continues normally, including the pages of joined text. In addition, any header or footer defined for the working copy is applied to all pages of the joined text.

You can include as many *JOIN* commands as you want in the working copy. Place each command exactly where you want the joined file to be printed.

If you are joining another Professional Write document to the working copy, the fonts and styles of that document are preserved. Tabs and left and right margins are also preserved. However, the page length is set to that of the working copy.

When a joined file is printed, a blank line is inserted at the beginning and the end of the joined text.

You can't use the Preview feature to see the results of a *JOIN* command; Preview simply displays the command itself, rather than the joined documents. You must print the document to determine whether the documents have been joined the way you want.

In some circumstances, you may find problems with the line spacing or pagination of the printed output. For example, there may be large gaps before or after the printout of the joined file. Here are some suggestions for solving this type of problem:

- If you are using a laser printer, make sure that the page length is set to its proper value (on most laser printers, this is 60 lines per page).
- If the file to be joined is in Professional Write format, retrieve it into the working copy and set its page length either to zero or to the same value as that of the file to which it is to be joined.

*LIMITATIONS WHEN USING THE *JOIN* COMMAND*

There are several restrictions to follow when you join files at print time. First of all, you can't include a *JOIN* command in a file to be joined. (This would be a cute way to chain files together at print time, but unfortunately it won't work.) Similarly, you can't include any of the following commands within a file to be joined:

NEW PAGE	*GRAPH*
JUSTIFY	*CENTER*
PRINTER	*RIGHT*
FORMAT	

One of the most serious limitations imposed on joined files is the following: If you select the *Font format* print style in the Print Options dialog box, it has no effect on a joined file. The real significance of this is that *you can't use a proportional font in a joined file*. The reason is that unless the *Font format* style is turned on, line breaks are not correct for proportional font text. If you are used to printing high quality text on a laser printer, this is a severe limitation.

To get around this problem, you can simply avoid using the *JOIN* command when you want to print files with proportional fonts. The most direct approach is to print each file separately but set the page numbers to run consecutively. For example, if the first document ends with page 25, create a header or footer for the second document that matches the header or footer of the working copy and set the starting page number to 26.

PRINTING GRAPHS WITH YOUR DOCUMENT

Graphics can make an enormous difference in the impact of a printed page (see Figure 10.11, for example).

When you print a document, you can include a graph that's on a separate file. Graph files generated by any of the following products can be printed as part of your document:

- PFS:First Choice (Professional Write format)
- PFS:First Graphics (Professional Write format)
- PFS:Graph, Version B (printed to a disk file)
- Professional Plan (Professional Write format)
- Harvard Graphics (picture file)
- Harvard Presentation Graphics (PFS:WRITE format)

To include a graph contained in the file *filename*, use the following command: ***GRAPH** *filename** or ***G** *filename**.

Here, *filename* must include the complete file name, including the disk drive and pathname. Enter this command exactly as shown, with no spaces except between the word GRAPH and the file name. Include the disk drive and pathname, unless they are the same as the data directory defined in the Setup program.

SEMI-ANNUAL SALES REPORT

The last six months have shown a somewhat puzzling trend. Even though we have doubled everybody's salary and included other fringe benefits, the sales are not what we would like.

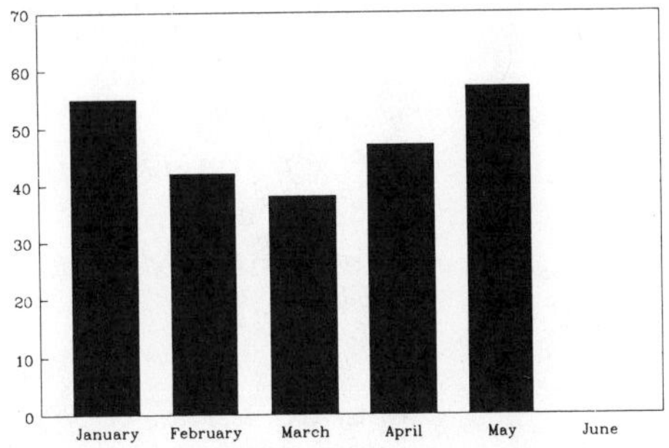

To encourage more aggressiveness on the part of the sales staff, the Board of Trustees has voted **another 50% salary increase** across the board. Let's hope this generates increased sales in the coming months!

Figure 10.11: Graphics can enhance a page

You can include as many graphs as you wish in a single document. Use a separate *GRAPH* command at the exact position where each graph is to be printed. Each *GRAPH* command should be entered flush left on a blank line.

Points to Ponder

Text in the document is automatically pushed down to make space for each graph. If necessary, a page break will be created if there is not enough room on the current page for the graph.

The Preview feature won't display a graph that will be printed with a document. However, it does leave an amount of blank space equal to what will be taken up by the graph when printed.

SENDING SPECIAL INSTRUCTIONS TO YOUR PRINTER

You will probably find that Professional Write supports most, if not all, of the fonts and styles for your printer. Occasionally, however, you may find it necessary to send special instructions, or commands, to your printer from within a document, for example, if your printer has one or more special print styles or fonts that are not supported by Professional Write. You can also use printer commands to control various features that may not be otherwise accessible through Professional Write.

When you use printer commands, you will need to have access to the list of codes accepted by your printer. These are usually included in the Printer Manual that accompanies the software.

The form of a printer command is: ***PRINTER** *code1, code2,...** or ***P** *code1, code2,...**. Each of the codes, *code1*, *code2*, etc., represents a separate *decimal* code; you can include up to 20 codes in a single *PRINTER* command.

Example

Suppose you are using an NEC Pinwriter 2200 dot-matrix printer. You want to instruct the printer to begin printing in the condensed mode of 15 characters per inch. The command to do this is (27,103). To send this command to the printer, you would include the following in your text, immediately before the text to be printed in condensed mode:

```
*PRINTER 27,103*
```

Similarly, the printer command to resume printing at 10 characters per inch print is

```
*PRINTER 27,80*
```

You would include this command at that point in the text where normal printing was to resume.

Figure 10.12 shows how you would use the printer commands to generate a line in compressed mode, then return to the normal font. Figure 10.13 shows the printed output. Notice that each *PRINTER* command generates a blank line. To eliminate these, begin entering your text immediately after each command, that is, on the same line. In fact, a *PRINTER* command can be inserted anywhere in a line of text.

```
F1-Help  F2-File/Print  F3-Edit  F4-Format  F5-Dictionary  F6-Addresses

         This short paragraph is printed on the NEC Pinwriter P2200 at
         10 characters per inch, which is the normal font chosen for
         this printer in the Setup program.
         *PRINTER 27,103*
         This line is printed at 15 characters per inch.
         *PRINTER 27,80*
         Again, this line is printed at 10 characters per inch.

HOLD          Inserting                          0%     Line 1 of Pg 1
Esc-Main Menu 10 Pitch (LQ) P 12
```

Figure 10.12: Using special commands to control printer output

```
This short paragraph is printed on the NEC Pinwriter P2200 at
10 characters per inch, which is the normal font chosen for
this printer in the Setup program.

This line is printed at 15 characters per inch.

Again, this line is printed at 10 characters per inch.
```

Figure 10.13: The output generated from the screen in Figure 10.12, using a NEC Pinwriter 2200 dot-matrix printer

11

Drawing Lines and Using the Calculator

DRAWING LINES AND OTHER SHAPES

You can use different types of straight lines, boxes, and other shapes to enhance your documents. For instance, placing an important note or table in a box can help to set it off. Or you might want to use vertical or horizontal lines to separate different parts of a page. You can draw using a single or double line, a solid black line, or any other character of your choice. Figures 11.1 and 11.2 show how simple visual devices can dramatically emphasize a text.

HOW TO DRAW LINES

To begin line drawing, you must first select either the kind of line you want to draw or the character to be used as a drawing tool and then turn on the *draw mode*:

1. Position the cursor exactly where you want the drawing to begin.
2. Select *Draw lines* from the Edit menu (F3). When the Drawing menu appears (Figure 11.3):

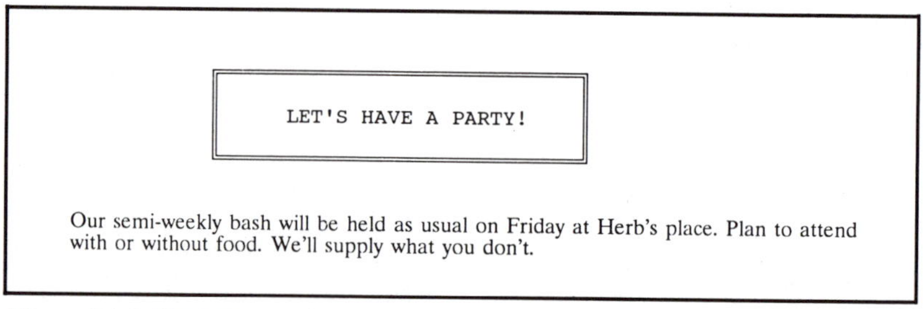
LET'S HAVE A PARTY!

Our semi-weekly bash will be held as usual on Friday at Herb's place. Plan to attend with or without food. We'll supply what you don't.

Figure 11.1: Boxes can enhance a page

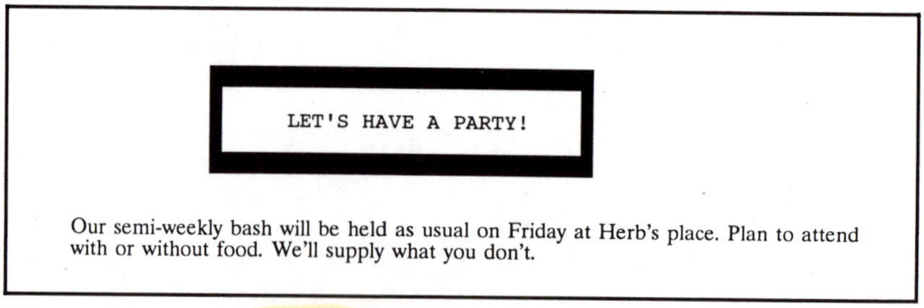
LET'S HAVE A PARTY!

Our semi-weekly bash will be held as usual on Friday at Herb's place. Plan to attend with or without food. We'll supply what you don't.

Figure 11.2: Use a reverse video box for a special effect

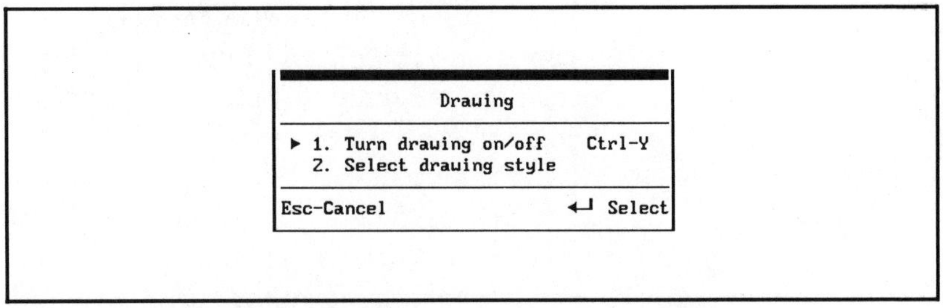

Figure 11.3: The Drawing menu

3. Choose *Select drawing style* and then make your choice from the Drawing Styles menu (Figure 11.4). You can select any of the following for drawing:

   - Single line
   - Double line
   - Inverse color line
   - Any other character of your choice

4. Return to the Edit screen by pressing ↵.

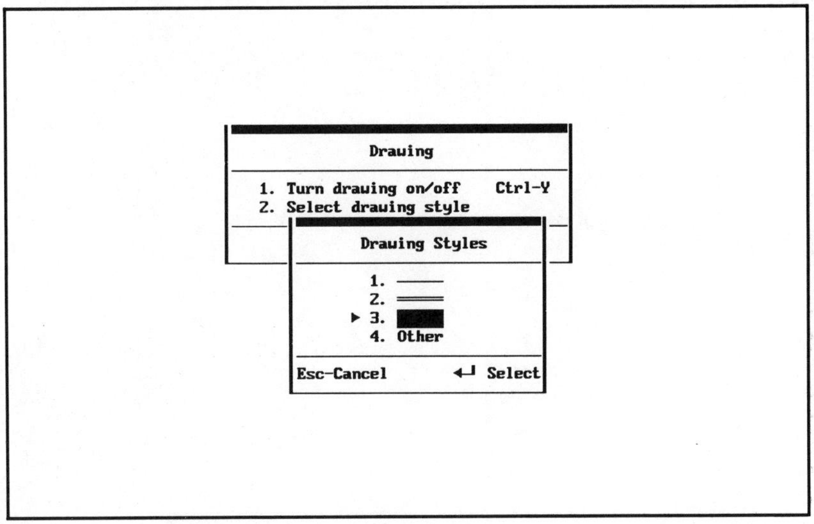

Figure 11.4: The Drawing Styles menu

You are now in the *draw mode*. When this mode is on, there are two changes to the normal Edit screen. First, the word *Drawing* appears near the bottom of the screen; second, the cursor appears as a blinking *line*, even if you were originally in the Insert mode.

To draw a line, press the appropriate cursor key. Figure 11.5 shows which keys to press for the different directions. For example, to draw a horizontal line from left to right, press **6**. You can draw the line rapidly by holding down the cursor key.

TIPS ON DRAWING LINES

Here are some handy techniques to use when drawing lines:

- **To change directions:** Press the appropriate cursor key whenever you wish. If you use only the four keys for horizontal and vertical motion, Professional Write takes care of making nice neat corners. Diagonal corners don't look very good—either on the screen or when printed.
- **To stop line drawing:** Press the speed key Ctrl-Y. This puts you back into the normal edit mode. You can use this key

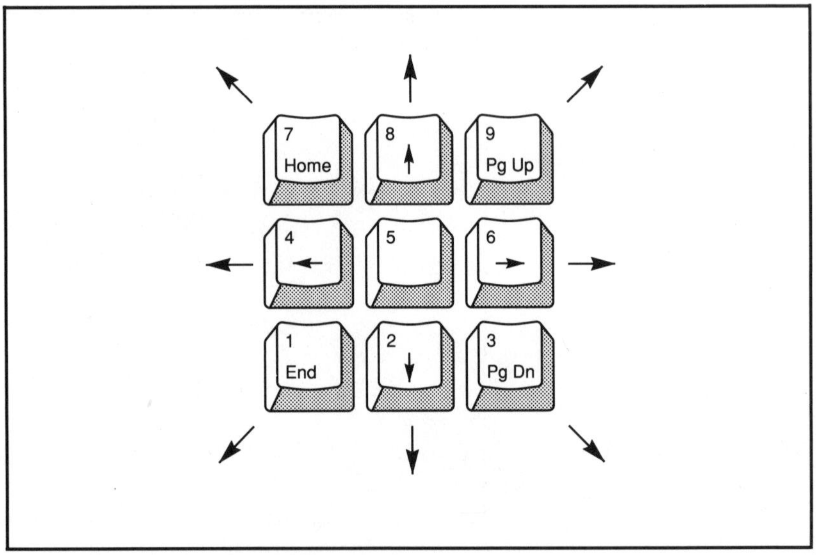

Figure 11.5: Use these keys for drawing lines

You can also turn off the draw mode by selecting *Draw lines* from the Edit menu (F3) and then selecting *Turn drawing on/off*.

when you are finished drawing or when you want to stop temporarily to move the cursor to another location.

- **To turn line drawing back on:** Press Ctrl-Y. In fact, you can enter the draw mode at any time with this key. The line or character that you selected last from the Drawing Styles menu will be used. Notice that the speed key Ctrl-Y is a toggle, turning the draw mode on and off.
- **To erase a line:** Hold down a Shift key and then move the cursor back over the line to be erased. To resume drawing, release the Shift key. This is a very handy way of correcting mistakes as soon as they occur. You can also use the ⟵ key and the spacebar to erase lines in the horizontal direction.

When you erase a line next to a corner, you'll see that the software can't anticipate what you want. You'll usually have to erase a bit more than you want and then redraw the line properly.

Overwriting Text

If you move the cursor over existing text while in the draw mode, that text is erased and replaced by the line. If you accidentally overwrite some text, turn off the draw mode (press Ctrl-Y), reenter the text, reposition the cursor, and then press Ctrl-Y again to resume drawing.

Keyboard Disabling

While you are drawing, most of the normal keys on the keyboard are disabled. However, you can still pull down any of the menus by pressing the appropriate function key. You can then use that menu in the ordinary way. In some cases, pulling down a menu turns off the draw mode. To resume line drawing, turn the draw mode back on by pressing the speed key Ctrl-Y.

After You Leave the Draw Mode

When you exit from the draw mode and return to the normal edit mode, any lines that you have drawn are treated like groups of normal characters. You can delete them, overwrite them, move them around, and so on. If you accidentally delete or overwrite part of a line, you can redraw it: position the cursor at the correct spot, press Ctrl-Y to enter the draw mode, and then move the cursor.

SELECTING OTHER DRAWING CHARACTERS

For more information about using special characters, see Chapter 2.

You can select any character you wish to use a drawing tool: In step 3 of the instructions listed above in "How to Draw Lines," select *Other* from the Drawing Styles menu. Then, enter the character you want to use. This is most useful when you want to use one of the special characters that you access by holding down the Alt key and then entering the ASCII code for that character on the numeric keypad. For example, to draw using the ASCII character 177, simply hold down the Alt key and then press 177 on the numeric keypad (you don't need to press NumLock). You can then draw the unusual box shown in Figure 11.6.

If you select a drawing character that your printer can't output, another character will be substituted. For instance, suppose you draw a box that's in a Times Roman font and then try to print the page on a laser printer. The output you'll see will be a poor imitation of a real box. The reason is that the Times Roman typeface doesn't have the characters for drawing either horizontal lines or corners.

WHICH FONTS YOU CAN USE

For two reasons, lines and boxes must be drawn using a monospaced font. First, most proportional fonts don't have single-line and double-line characters. The second reason has to do with the difficulty of aligning various types of lines with proportionally-spaced text.

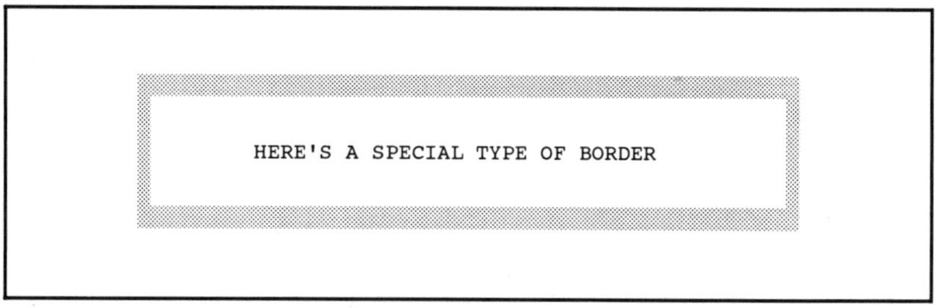

Figure 11.6: You can use special characters for unusual effects

Note that you can include lines and boxes within a document that contains proportional fonts. You just can't *combine* lines and proportionally-spaced characters. Here are some guidelines to follow when drawing:

The most commonly used monospaced typeface is Courier. There are also several others.

- When drawing any line, make sure you select a monospaced font *for the entire row*. This includes any text on the same row as the drawn line. If even a single character on that text row is in a proportional font, the printed results may not be what you want.
- If you include text within a box, select the same font for the text and the box.
- If you want to vertically align any text with adjacent horizontal lines, use the same font for that text and the lines.

Checking the Font of Your Lines

Here's an important point to remember: When you draw a line, it's assigned the normal font then in effect for that document, which may or may not be a monospaced font. If the normal font is a proportional font, you'll need to change the font of the lines you draw, as follows:

1. First draw the lines you want.
2. Using either a text or rectangular block, select the drawn lines, *as well as any text on the same rows*.
3. Select a monospaced font for that block.

For a discussion of how to select fonts, see Chapter 9.

You can always check the font assigned to a drawn line: Move the cursor over the line and find the font name on the bottom row of the screen. If the typeface is Times Roman, Helvetica, or some other proportional font, you'll need to change the font, using the above steps.

Using Preview to See Your Work

If you draw lines on the same page with proportionally-spaced text, the relative positions you see on the screen will most likely not be what will be printed. The reason is that the screen displays only monospaced characters. However, you can get a good idea of the relative positions of lines on the page by using the Preview feature: Press Ctrl-PrtSc and then press Alt-V if you want to see a magnified view.

Selecting a Monospaced Font

All dot-matrix printers have at least one or two monospaced fonts. For a laser printer, the available monospaced fonts will depend on what font cartridges and soft fonts are installed. In addition, for many laser printers, such as the Hewlett Packard LaserJet, the Courier and Line Printer fonts are built in. Other popular monospaced fonts include Letter Gothic and Prestige Elite.

Here's how you can determine which typefaces are monospaced:

1. Display a list of the supported fonts for that printer: Press Ctrl-PrtSc; when the Preview display appears, select *List available fonts* from the Fonts menu.
2. Scan the list. If a font is proportional, the word *Prop.* will appear in the column labelled *Pitch*. For a monospaced font, a number, usually 10 or 12, will appear in that column.

HANDLING DIFFICULTIES

In some circumstances, your lines may not be properly aligned when printed, even though they were drawn with a monospaced font, perhaps because the Font Format print style has been selected for the document and Professional Write is trying to align your lines with existing tab settings.

If you encounter this problem, you may be able to eliminate the difficulty as follows:

1. Delete all tab settings from that part of the text containing the lines or boxes you have drawn.
2. Turn off Font Format for that same part of the document. Figure 11.7 illustrates how: The commands *FORMAT NO* and *FORMAT YES* turn Font Format off and on.

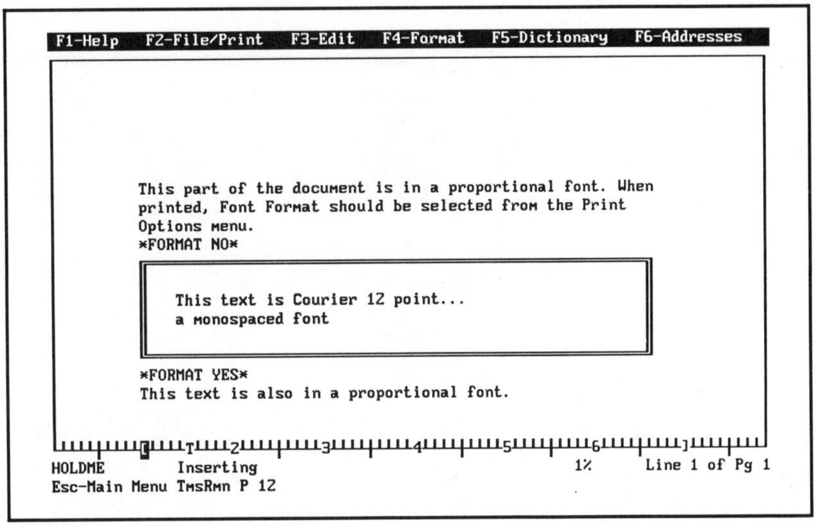

Figure 11.7: Turning off Font Format for part of a document

USING THE BUILT-IN CALCULATOR

Professional Write has a handy built-in calculator that allows you to perform simple arithmetic operations on groups of numbers. The calculator can be displayed at any time while you are working on a document. Numbers and numeric expressions can be entered directly into the calculator, or they can be transferred from the working copy. The results of a calculation are displayed in the calculator; they can also be transferred back into the working copy.

HOW TO MAKE A CALCULATION

To bring up the calculator display, select *Calculate* from the Edit menu (F3), or simply press the speed key Ctrl-M (M for Modest calculations only). When the calculator (Figure 11.8) appears, you can enter a numeric expression on the *Calculation* line. Press F9, and the result appears on the *Result* line.

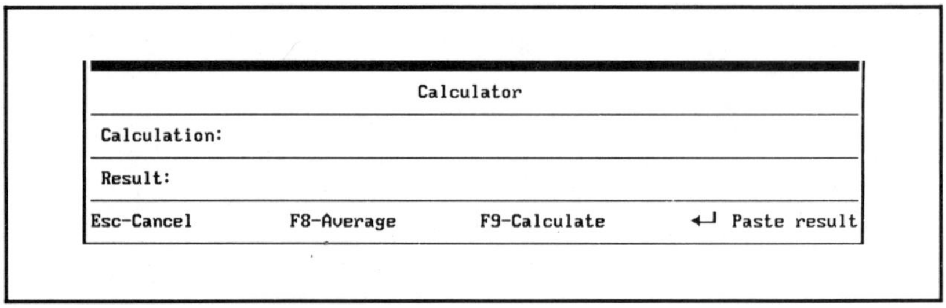

Figure 11.8: The calculator display

Example

Suppose you want to calculate the sum of five numbers. Here's how to do it:

The calculator begins in the Overwrite edit mode.

1. Press Ctrl-M to display the calculator.
2. Enter the following numeric expression: **10 + 20 + 30 + 40 + 50.** If you make a mistake, correct it by using the standard edit keys.
3. Display the result by pressing F9 (see Figure 11.9).
4. To return to the working copy, press Esc. Do not press ↵ unless you want to paste the result (see "Pasting the Result to the Working Copy," below).

Editing the Calculation

At any time while the calculator is displayed, you can edit the contents of the *Calculation* line:

You can toggle between the Overwrite and Insert edit modes by pressing the Ins key.

- Use the standard edit keys to modify the contents of the line.
- To delete the entire contents of the line, press Ctrl-E. You can then enter a new numeric expression.
- The contents of the *Result* line don't change as you edit the *Calculation* line. After you edit the *Calculation* line, you must press F9 again to recalculate the result.

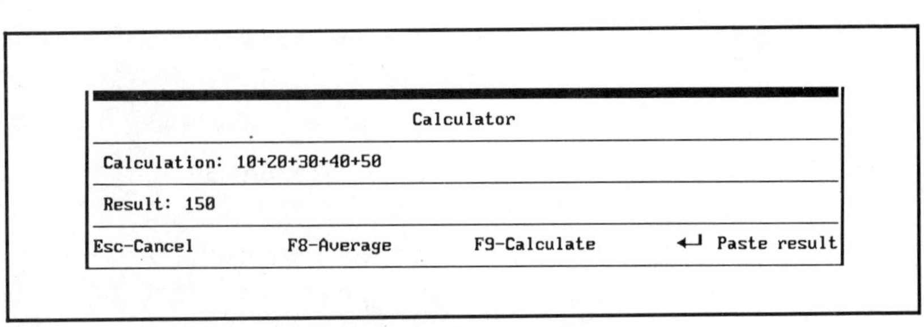

Figure 11.9: Calculating a simple sum

Editing the Result

You can also edit the contents of the *Result* line. For example, you might want to enter a dollar sign or commas. To edit the result:

1. Press Tab or ↓ to move the cursor to the *Result* line.
2. You can enter the Insert edit mode by pressing the Ins key.
3. Use the standard edit keys to make any changes you want.

If you subsequently press F9, your changes will be erased and the original form of the result will reappear.

Calculating an Average

You can use the calculator to compute the average of a group of numbers by entering the numbers on the *Calculation* line, separating the numbers with blank spaces, and then pressing F8. The average value of the numbers will appear on the *Result* line.

PASTING THE RESULT TO THE WORKING COPY

After you have made a calculation and the result appears on the *Result* line, you can then transfer the result back into the working copy:

1. Make sure that the result you want is displayed on the *Result* line. (If it isn't, press F9.)

2. Press ↵ to return to the working copy. (Look at the Status line.)
3. Paste the result: Move the cursor to the position where you want the result pasted, and then press ↵.

When the result is pasted into the working copy, text to the right is automatically pushed over to accommodate the number.

When you paste a number, you can have it line up with a decimal tab in the working copy:

1. After the calculator displays your result, press ↵ to return to the working copy.
2. Position the cursor at a *decimal* tab setting.
3. Press ↵ and the number will be pasted, with its decimal point aligned on the tab setting.

HOW TO USE NUMBERS

You can enter as large a number as you like in the calculator, but the calculator only maintains up to 16 significant digits in the computer's memory. If you enter more than 16 digits, the lower order digits are replaced by zeroes. For instance, if you enter the number 123,123,123,123,123,123,123, it's treated as the number 123,123,123,123,123,100,000.

A number can be entered either with or without a decimal point. However, note that both 1 and 1.0 are recognized by the calculator as the number 1, but 1. is considered by the calculator to be an illegal value. In other words, if you include a decimal point it must be followed by a digit.

You can enter either positive or negative numbers. A negative number can be written as –3, (3), or <3>. A number can contain commas and either a dollar sign or the pound sign (£). These various symbols will be carried along as part of the calculation but won't affect the numerical result.

CREATING NUMERIC EXPRESSIONS

A numeric expression consists of numbers and *arithmetic operators*. These operators are:

+	Addition
–	Subtraction
*	Multiplication
/ or ÷	Division *(Press Alt-246 to generate the ÷ symbol)*

Here's an example of an expression:

```
5 + 4 - 3 * 2/8.
```

The spaces between the numbers and operators are ignored when the calculation is performed.

The Order in Which Calculations Are Performed

When the calculator evaluates an expression, it performs operations in the following order:

1. Multiplications and divisions first, working from left to right.
2. Additions and subtractions next, again from left to right.

For example, if you enter the expression **3 + 2*4**, the result will be 11, because the multiplication is done first, followed by the addition.

If you want the addition to be performed first in the above expression, place parentheses around the numbers to be added. That is, if you enter the expression **(3 + 2)*4**, the result will be 20 because the addition (3 + 2) is performed first.

Why? Because of the following rules:

3. If an expression contains a calculation inside of a pair of parentheses, whatever is inside the parentheses is evaluated *before* the rest of the expression.
4. Within each set of parentheses, rules 1 and 2 above apply.

You can even include parentheses within parentheses. For example:

((3 + 4)*2 +4)*5

Here's the order of events when the calculator evaluates this expression:

1. Add 3 + 4.
2. Multiply the result by 2.
3. Add 4.
4. Multiply the new result by 5.

Long Expressions

You can enter as long an expression as you like on the *Calculation* line. When the screen fills up, the expression begins to scroll to the left. To edit the expression:

- Use the ← and → keys to scroll left and right.
- To jump to the beginning or end of the expression, use the Home and End keys.

HOW THE RESULT APPEARS

If a dollar sign, pound sign, comma, or decimal point is included in one or more numbers in an expression, the result will also contain the dollar sign, etc. Commas are automatically positioned properly in the result.

The number of decimal places appearing in the result will depend on the type of calculation and on how the numbers were entered:

- The number of decimal places in the result will be the same as the maximum number of decimal places appearing in any number in the calculation.
- If the expression contains a division, and if all of the numbers in the expression are integers, then the result will contain up to eight decimal places.

Here are some examples:

NUMERIC EXPRESSION	*RESULT*
3 * 5	15
3. 0 * 5	15.0
3. 0000 * 5	15.0000
(3*5) + 1.0	16.0
4/3	1.33333333
4/3.0	1.3
4/3 + 1.00	2.33

TRANSFERRING NUMBERS FROM THE WORKING COPY

You can perform calculations on a group of adjacent numbers in the working copy by transferring those numbers to the calculator. Or you can transfer an arithmetic expression from the working copy to the calculator, where it can be evaluated.

To transfer either a group of numbers or an expression, first select it as a text or rectangular block and then bring up the calculator display. The numbers are automatically transferred to the *Calculation* line, and you can then compute a result.

When you transfer a group of numbers to the calculator, Professional Write assumes that you want to sum these numbers, and a plus sign is attached to each number. If you want some other type of calculation to be performed on the numbers, you can edit the *calculation* line in any way that you wish. After you have finished editing the numbers, press F9 to display the result.

Example

The working copy shown in Figure 11.10 contains three columns of sales numbers. Suppose you want to calculate the total sales for all

When the numbers are transferred, plus signs are automatically attached to each number, and the sum is displayed.

months and for all three columns and then paste the result onto the Edit screen. Here's how to have the calculator do all this:

1. Select the three columns of figures as a block.
2. Press F10 and then select *Calculate* from the Block Operations menu. The calculator will appear with the result already in place (Figure 11.11).
3. Press ↵ to return to the Edit screen.

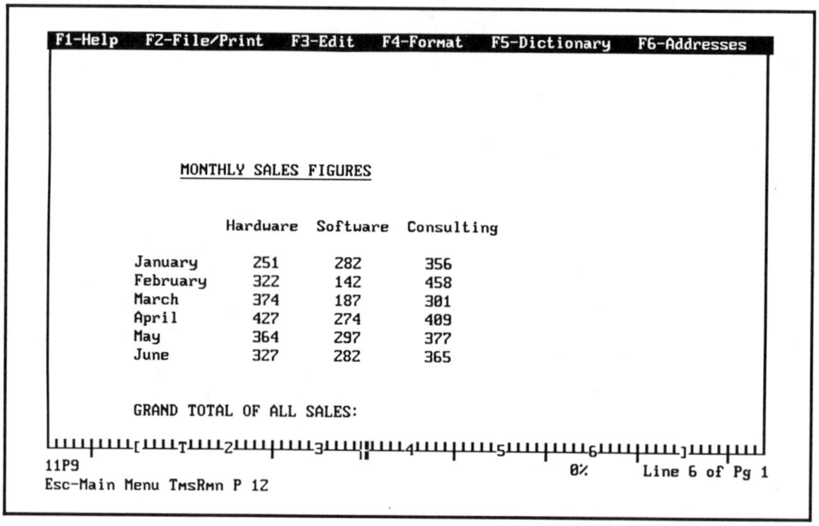

Figure 11.10: We can use the calculator to compute the sum of these numbers

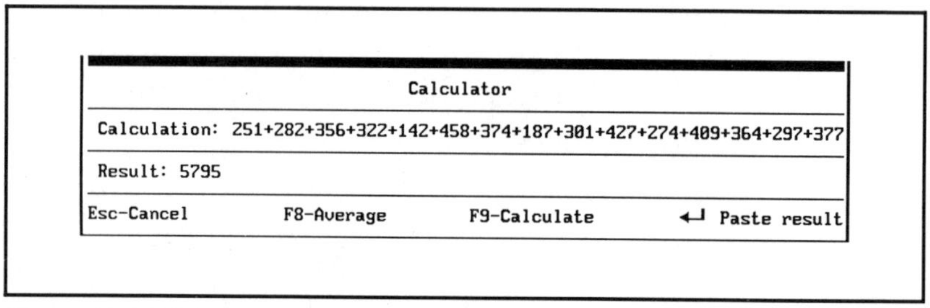

Figure 11.11: These numbers were transferred from the working copy shown in Figure 11.10

4. Move the cursor to the right of the line reading "GRAND TOTAL...".
5. Press ↵, and the result is pasted.

Points to Ponder

- You can use the speed key Ctrl-M, instead of step 2 above, to transfer a block to the calculator.
- If there are too many numbers to fit on the *Calculation* line, you can scroll back and forth by using the →, ←, Home, and End keys.

12 Previewing a Document

FOR SEVERAL REASONS, A DOCUMENT DISPLAYED ON the Edit screen may appear quite different from the way it will appear when printed. For example, the document may be printed in a proportional font, whereas the Edit screen displays only monospaced characters. Special commands embedded in the text can create differences between the displayed and printed page. For instance, the *NEW PAGE* command introduces a page break that doesn't show on the screen.

Professional Write's built-in Preview feature helps you to see on the screen how a printed document will appear. Preview utilizes the *graphics* mode of your screen. In order to be able to use Preview, your computer must have one of the following:

- Either a CGA, EGA, or VGA color monitor;
- A monochrome monitor with a Hercules-compatible control board (called a *display adapter*).

Because Preview uses the graphics mode of your computer, a great deal of computation is required to display a full screen of text. Consequently, you'll find that Preview takes quite a bit of time to display each screen, particularly with a PC or PC/XT (or compatible). On the other hand, PC/AT compatibles and computers based on the Intel-386 processor operate at much higher speeds, and the time delays when running Preview are quite brief with these machines.

Preview does much more than just display your document. For example, you can perform certain types of text modification while your document is being displayed. The advantage is that you can immediately see the results of any changes, much as they will appear when printed.

Here's a synopsis of Preview's main features:

- A full-page view can be displayed on screen, showing the general layout characteristics of one or two complete pages.
- A close-up view of part of a page can be displayed, showing details such as different font sizes and type styles.
- A list can be displayed of all fonts assigned to text in the working copy.

- A list can be displayed of all fonts currently supported by your printer.
- The font of selected text can be changed, with the effects immediately displayed on the screen.
- In a single step you can replace every occurrence of a particular font in the working copy with another font.

Some of these features may seem out of place in a module whose primary function is to display a preview of a document, but if you stop to think about it, there's a lot of sense in grouping these features in Preview. They allow you to make design changes to a document and then immediately see the results of these changes.

HOW TO PREVIEW A DOCUMENT

When you preview a document, it will appear on the screen *as it will be printed on the currently-selected printer* and with the print styles currently in effect. You can enter the Preview mode either from the Edit screen or from the Print Options dialog box.

PREVIEWING DIRECTLY FROM THE EDIT SCREEN

Normally, the quickest way to call up Preview is directly from the Edit screen. To preview a document directly from there:

1. Make sure that both the correct printer and the correct print styles have previously been set in the Print Options dialog box.
2. Scroll to the page to be displayed first when you enter Preview. If you want to begin with the first page, just leave the cursor at the beginning of the document.
3. Press Ctrl-PrtSc, and after a few seconds the Preview screen will appear.

PREVIEWING FROM THE PRINT OPTIONS DIALOG BOX

For a discussion of print styles, see "The Print Options Dialog Box" in Chapter 10.

If you want to change either the selected printer or one or more print styles before previewing a document, you must do so from the Print Options dialog box. You can then call up Preview directly from there:

1. Display the Print Options dialog box, either by pressing the speed key Ctrl-O or by selecting *Print working copy* from the File/Print menu (F2).
2. Select the printer you want from the *Print to* option.
3. Enter the page number you want to preview first in the option *Starting page*.
4. Enter the Print styles you want on the line labeled *Print styles*.
5. Press Ctrl-PrtSc. After a few seconds the Preview screen will appear.

See "Page Numbering" in Chapter 5.

A Note about Page Numbering

The number that you enter in the *Starting page* option (step 3 above) may or may not correspond either to the sequence number of the page that would be printed or to any page numbers that appear on the Edit screen. However, the number you enter *does* correspond to what Preview thinks is the printed page sequence number. This number will correctly correspond to the sequence number of the printed page only if

- There are no *JOIN* commands in your document;
- There are no *PRINTER* commands that reset the page position in the printer;
- The page size set in the Preview mode (see "Selecting the Correct Page Size," below) corresponds to the actual size of the pages being printed.

WHAT YOU SEE IN THE PREVIEW MODE

In the Preview mode, most of the features of a document will appear as they will be printed. For example, Figure 12.1 shows part of a document on the Edit screen, and Figure 12.2 shows the same part of the document in the closeup view in Preview.

Notice that because of the limited resolution of computer display screens, the clarity of the screen display in Figure 12.2 is only fair. Generally you'll find that the quality of the printout is far better than that shown on the screen. However, the screen display is good enough to show you roughly how things will appear when printed. If you want to get an absolutely perfect idea of how the printed document will appear, print the document.

ELEMENTS THAT DISPLAY CORRECTLY

Although the clarity of the Preview screen is limited, you can still easily distinguish many important page and text features. Be aware, however, that Preview displays some document features correctly and others incorrectly.

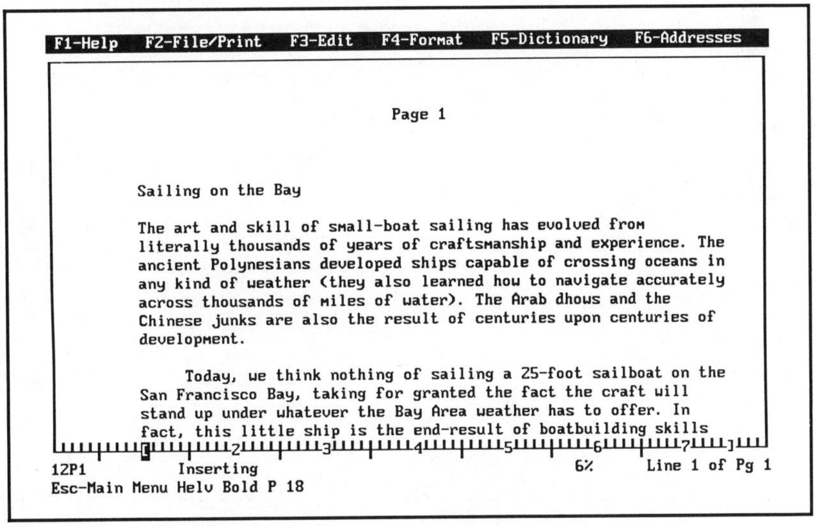

Figure 12.1: Part of a document on the Edit screen

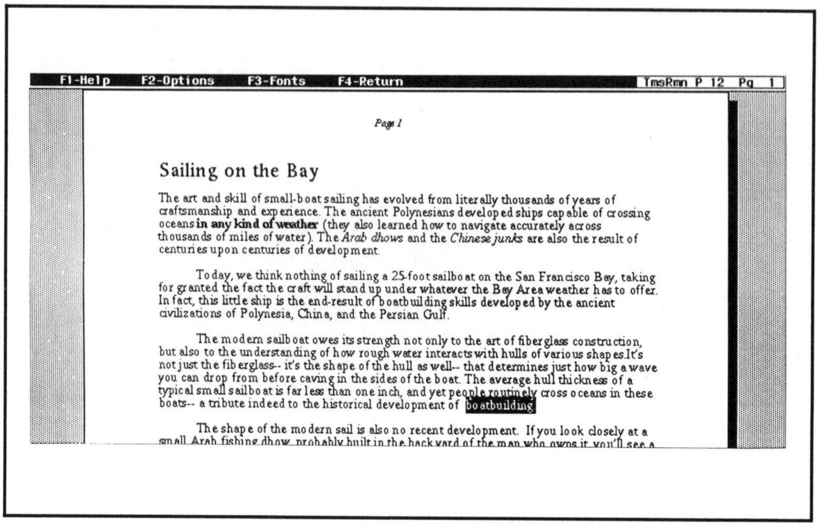

Figure 12.2: The same document of Figure 12.1, shown in the close-up view of Preview mode

Generally, the following elements are displayed accurately on the Preview screen:

- The relative sizes of fonts up to 30 points. Also, for dot-matrix printers, the relative sizes of normal, compressed, and expanded text.
- The various text styles, such as boldface, underline, and italics.
- Line breaks. Professional Write calculates the length of each line, based on individual character widths, and breaks the line accordingly. (Note that in Figures 12.1 and 12.2 the line breaks shown in Preview are entirely different from those shown on the Edit screen because the text is in Times Roman 12 point, a proportional font.)
- Blank space for each graph specified by a *GRAPH* command in the text. The *GRAPH* command itself isn't shown, nor is the actual graph.
- Page breaks created by *NEW PAGE* commands.

- Page breaks will correspond to the pages as printed if the following conditions are true: (1) There are no *JOIN* commands; (2) the page size set in Preview corresponds to the actual size of the printed page; and (3) there are no *PRINTER* commands that change the page position in the printer.
- Top, bottom, left, and right margins.
- Text and numeric columns that have been aligned on tab stops.
- Text lines that have been either centered or right justified.

ELEMENTS THAT DO NOT DISPLAY CORRECTLY

Although Preview shows you a good deal about how the printed pages will appear, there are several elements that are not displayed accurately. These include the following:

- Page breaks may not be shown accurately, usually because of a *JOIN* command in a document. Preview ignores the space occupied by the joined document when printed (although the *JOIN* command itself is displayed).
- Font sizes above 30 points don't display in correct proportion to other font sizes, making it impossible to tell how much space to leave above a line containing very large text. To determine this, you'll need to experiment by printing the document.
- The shapes of different fonts are not accurately displayed. In fact, all proportionally spaced typefaces look the same in Preview, and so do all monospaced typefaces. However, the Preview screen contains a little box that displays the font name of any selected text.
- The effects of *PRINTER* commands are ignored. For example, if you use a *PRINTER* command to output a block of text in compressed mode, that block won't display as compressed in Preview.

- Selected characters: Some of the characters that display in the Edit mode may not be available either in Preview or in the currently available fonts for your printer. If Preview can't print a character displayed on the Edit screen, a blank is substituted. On the other hand, Preview may be able to print a character that your printer can't. In that case, you may be in for a surprise when you print the document.

Other Limitations of Preview

You can't display a preview of a printed envelope. If you try (by selecting *Envelope* from the Print Options dialog box), Preview simply prints the document itself instead of the envelope. Also, output resulting from a merge can't be displayed in Preview, such as form letters and other types of output resulting from the merging of data with the text in the working copy.

THE FULL-PAGE VIEW

When you enter Preview for the first time during a word processing session, the *full-page view* is displayed. For example, Figure 12.3 is a full-page view of Figure 12.1. Although you can distinguish only the largest fonts in this view, you nevertheless get a clear sense of the page layout.

You can also display a *close-up view* of a page, where you can more clearly distinguish important details. (This view is discussed later on.) If you happen to be in the close-up view, you can switch to the full-page view by pressing the speed key Alt-V.

ELEMENTS OF THE FULL-PAGE VIEW

The Word Cursor

The word cursor is always somewhere on the Preview screen. Unlike the Edit screen cursor, it is always positioned over an entire word. You can move this cursor from one part of the page to another,

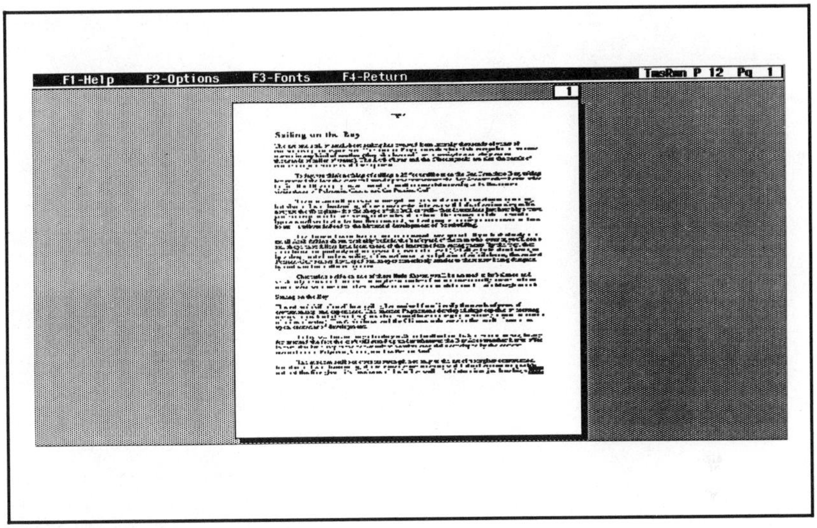

Figure 12.3: The full-page view

using keys that you'll learn about later. The word cursor has the following uses:

- To identify the font of a particular word.
- To establish a location that will be maintained when switching back and forth between Preview and the Edit display. This location is also maintained when you switch back and forth between the full-page and closeup views.
- To select a block of text for the purpose of changing its font.

The Menu Bar

Preview has its own menu bar, as shown in Figure 12.3. To select one of these menus, you simply press the corresponding function key:

F1-Help: This menu functions in the same way as the Help menu on the Edit screen: The help that's displayed on screen depends on what you are doing at the moment. For instance, you can highlight an item from another menu item and then press F1. You'll see helpful information about how to use that item.

F2-Options: This menu can be used for the following:

- Change the view, either to full-page or close-up
- Set the print styles for the entire document. These are the same styles that you can set from the Print Options dialog box, which is available from the Edit screen.
- Change the paper size that Preview uses in establishing where to display page breaks

F3:Fonts: From this menu, you can:

- Change the font of selected text in the document
- List all of the fonts that are currently assigned to text in the working copy
- List all of the fonts that are currently supported by your printer. These include both the printer's built-in fonts and also any fonts contained in the cartridges and font family selected during Setup.

F4: Return: Use this menu to return to the Edit menu. You can return either to the place corresponding to the current position of the cursor or to the position of the word cursor in the Edit menu when Preview was entered.

The Font Indicator

The font indicator does not show the style of the current word, such as boldfacing or italics.

The upper-right corner of the screen shows the *Font Indicator*. This displays the name of the font at the current location of the word cursor. For example, in Figure 12.3 the word cursor is positioned on a word whose font is TmsRmn P 12, or Times Roman 12 point, in Portrait orientation. The font indicator is helpful in deciding which fonts to use for various page elements, such as titles, column headings, and so on.

If a word consists of letters in different fonts, the font indicator displays the font name of the last letter in the word.

Page Number

In the very upper-right corner of the screen is the page number. In the full-page display, the page number also appears in a box above the page display. The displayed page number is *the number calculated by Preview*. As mentioned earlier, this number may have no correspondence either to page numbers appearing on the Edit screen or to the actual sequence of the printed pages.

THE TWO-PAGE DISPLAY

When you display the first page of a document in the full-page view, it appears alone on the Preview screen, as shown in Figure 12.3. However, as you begin to display additional pages, Preview displays two pages at once. For instance, Figure 12.4 shows the first two pages of a document.

The *active page* is the page on which the word cursor is located (page 2 in Figure 12.4). You can perform the various Preview operations only on the active page. You can also tell which page is active by looking at the page numbers in the boxes at the top of the two pages: The number of the active page is clearly visible, while the other one is shaded. You can change which page is the active one by using the PgUp and PgDn keys.

Preview shifts pages on the screen as you scroll through a document. For example, suppose that pages 1 and 2 are displayed in the

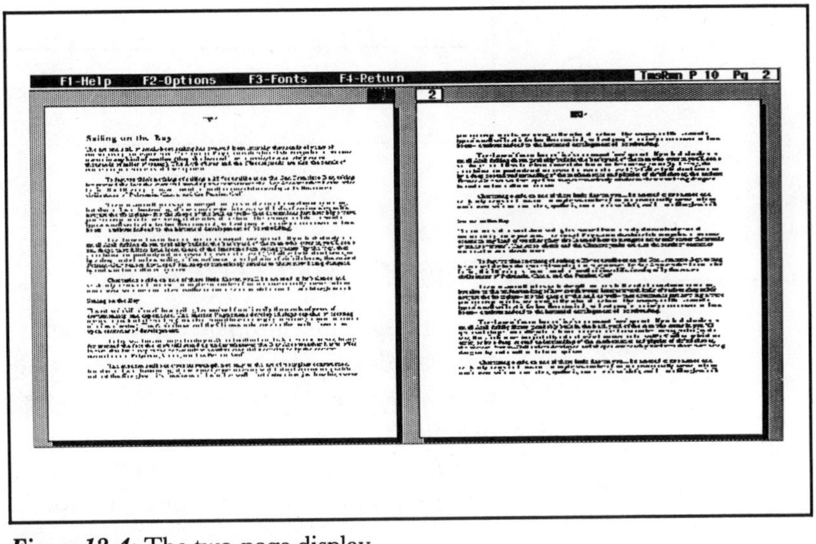

Figure 12.4: The two-page display

left and right halves of the screen. If you then instruct Preview to display page 3, page 1 is erased, page 2 shifts to the left half of the screen, and page 3 is displayed on the right.

MOVING AROUND THE DISPLAY

You can use various keys for moving the word cursor around the full-page view and for scrolling back and forth within a document. Table 12.1 lists these keystrokes.

Table 12.1: Cursor-Movement Keystrokes in the Full-Page Screen

To move the word cursor:	Press:
One word to the left, right, up or down	←, →, ↑ or ↓
To the beginning of the current line	Home
To the end of the current line	End
To the beginning of the current page	Ctrl-Home
To the end of the current page	Ctrl-End
To the beginning of the next page*	Ctrl-PgUp or PgUp
To the beginning of the previous page*	Ctrl-PgDn or PgDn

* These keys also shift the active page back and forth

THE CLOSE-UP VIEW

Although the full-page view is useful when you're working with the overall page layout, you must use the close-up view to see page details like individual letters and font styles. Figure 12.2 shows an example of a close-up view.

This is one of the few speed keys that uses the Alt key.

You can switch to the close-up view from the full-page view either by selecting *Change view* from the Options menu or by pressing the speed key Alt-V.

The various screen elements of the close-up view are virtually the same as those of the full-screen view. The main difference is that in a close-up view only part of a single page is visible on the screen.

You can move the word cursor around the page using the various keystrokes shown in Table 12.2.

Table 12.2: Cursor-Movement Keystrokes in the Close-Up View

To move the word cursor:	Press:
One word to the left, right, up or down	←, →, ↑ or ↓
To the beginning of the current line	Home
To the end of the current line	End
To the next part of the page, (up or down)	PgUp or PgDn
To the beginning of the current page	Ctrl-Home
To the end of the current page	Ctrl-End
To the beginning of the next page	Ctrl-PgUp
To the beginning of the previous page	Ctrl-PgDn

SELECTING THE CORRECT PAGE SIZE

Preview does not automatically set the page size to match the size set from the Edit screen. If you're using a page size other than 8½-x-11 inches, you must change the default page size used by Preview so that the line breaks (and in some cases the page breaks) displayed by Preview will match the actual printed pages.

Making this change can be a bother if you frequently use different page sizes with your printer; it means that you must set the page size *twice* within Professional Write.

To select a page size within Preview:

1. Select *Change paper size* from the Options menu.

2. Make your selection from the Paper Size menu that appears (Figure 12.5).

If you are using a paper size that doesn't appear in the Paper Size menu, then the line and page breaks shown in Preview probably won't match those actually printed.

Points to Ponder

The paper size you select in Preview has no effect on the margins and page length set from the Format menu in the Edit screen. Similarly, there is no effect on the actual printed page. The only effect of setting the paper size in Preview is to change the way the Preview display appears.

Even if you select the correct paper size, the page breaks shown in Preview may not match the actual printed pages. For more information, see "A Note about Page Numbering," above.

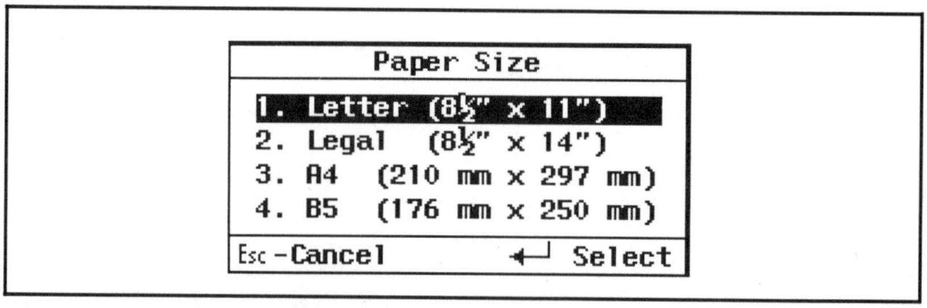

Figure 12.5: Select the proper paper size from this menu

LISTING THE CURRENT FONTS

Preview contains several powerful features for displaying and manipulating fonts within the current document. This section will describe how to display two different types of font lists. Subsequent sections will explain how to change fonts within the document.

You can display a list of the fonts that are currently supported by your printer (that is, those for which Professional Write is currently installed).

You can also display a list of all fonts currently assigned to text in the working copy. These features are useful in several ways. For instance, by comparing these two lists, you can determine if your document contains any fonts not currently supported by your printer.

FONTS IN THE CURRENT DOCUMENT

To display a list of fonts used in the working copy, select *List fonts in document* from the Fonts menu (F3). A font list appears, similar to the one in Figure 12.6. If necessary, you can scroll through this list with the PgUp and PgDn keys. (You can also display this list directly from the Edit screen by pressing Ctrl-0 to display the Print Options menu and then pressing the F8 key.)

If an asterisk appears before a font name in this list, it indicates that the current printer cannot support that font. However, this is not a reliable guide: Even if none of the fonts has a leading asterisk, one or more of them may not be currently supported by your printer. To determine if any fonts are unsupported, you must compare this font list with the list of all currently supported fonts.

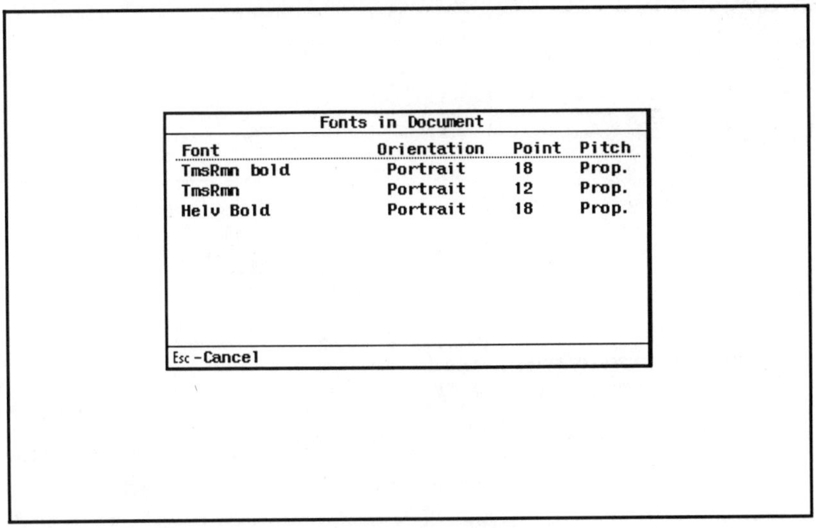

Figure 12.6: Fonts used in the current document

For more information about the currently supported fonts, see Chapter 8 and also Appendix A.

CURRENTLY SUPPORTED FONTS

The fonts currently supported by your printer are selected during Setup. These are the fonts that you can assign to text in the working copy. To display a list of these fonts, select *List available fonts* from the Fonts menu (F3). A list similar to the one shown in Figure 12.7 will be displayed. *This list applies to the printer most recently selected from the Print Options menu.*

Note that the list in Figure 12.7 is the same list that's displayed when you want to change the font of a block of text in the Edit screen.

Printer 1 Fonts

Font	Orientation	Point	Pitch
LJII-Courier	Portrait	12	10
LJII-Courier	Landscape	12	10
LJII-Line Printer	Portrait	8.5	16.66
LJII-Line Printer	Landscape	8.5	16.66
AC-TmsRmn	Portrait	6	Prop.
AC-TmsRmn	Portrait	8	Prop.
AC-TmsRmn	Portrait	10	Prop.
AC-TmsRmn	Portrait	12	Prop.
AC-TmsRmn	Portrait	14	Prop.

Esc-Cancel PgDn-More

Figure 12.7: These are the fonts currently available to your printer

CHANGING THE FONTS IN A DOCUMENT

Within Preview, you can change the font of a selected block of text, or you can replace every occurrence of a particular font with another one. These are powerful and useful features. For instance, if your document contains a font that's not currently supported, you can easily replace every occurrence of this font in the entire document with a font that is currently supported.

You can change the font of a block of text in a document and then immediately see how the new size appears in relation to the rest of the text on the page. This facility for changing fonts, coupled with the ability to display both full-page and close-up views, gives you the tools to perform reasonably sophisticated page design.

CHANGING SELECTED TEXT

Changing the font of a single word or some other small block of text must be done from the Edit menu.

You can change the font of a block of contiguous (that is, adjacent) text that's in the same font. However, you can't control the extent of this change. For instance, you can't change the font of a single word within a paragraph that's all in the same font. When you place the cursor on a word, then tell Preview to change its font, Preview automatically selects *all* text contiguous to that word that's in the same font.

To change the font of contiguous text in the same font:

1. Place the word cursor somewhere within the block of text whose font you want to change.
2. Select *Change a font* from the Fonts menu (F3). The entire block of text will be highlighted, and the Select Font or Size menu appears (see Figure 12.8). This menu displays all of the fonts that are currently supported by your printer.

The block may extend beyond the screen boundaries, so that you can't see where the block ends.

3. Select the new font from this menu and then press ↵.
4. When the query box shown in Figure 12.9 appears, leave the default value of **N** and press ↵.

After a short delay, the screen will be redisplayed with the new font. Remember: All proportional fonts look the same on the screen, so if the new font is the same size as the old one and if both the old and new fonts are proportional, there won't be any noticeable change on the screen.

Notice in Figure 12.8 that only a single paragraph has been highlighted. This indicates that the font of the adjacent paragraphs is different from that of the highlighted one.

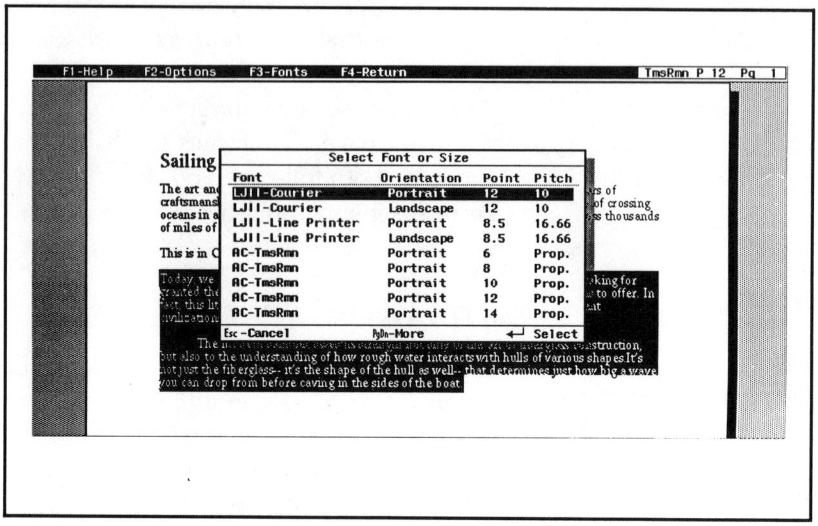

Figure 12.8: Select the new font for the highlighted block

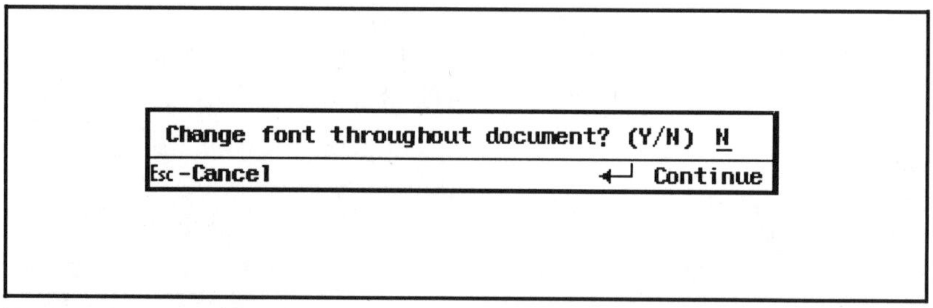

Figure 12.9: Do you want to replace every occurrence of a font?

CHANGING ALL OCCURRENCES OF A FONT

In a single operation, you can replace one font with another throughout the entire working copy. This is an extremely powerful feature that can be used in many ways. For instance, suppose that you have assigned the font Times Roman 14 point to every heading in a document. When you use Preview to display the document, you might decide that the headings need to stand out more. A few keystrokes will change them to a larger font, such as 18 point Bold, throughout the document.

This technique is also useful for replacing every instance of a font that is not currently supported in a document. This could occur, for example, if you change printers after creating a document, or if you change your selections of cartridges or soft font family.

Here are the steps for replacing every occurrence of a particular font in the working copy:

1. Place the cursor on any word that is assigned the font you want to change.
2. Select *Change a font* from the Fonts menu (F3). That word will be highlighted, as well as any adjacent text in the same font; and the Select Font or Size menu will appear (see Figure 12.8).
3. Select the new font from this menu and then press ↵.
4. When the query box shown in Figure 12.9 appears, enter **Y** and then press ↵.

Changing the Regular Font

The *Regular font* is the font assigned to text when you first create a new document, or to text written to a blank line.

If the word you selected in step 1 above is in the regular font of the document, the query box in Figure 12.9 will ask you if you want to replace all occurrences of the regular font. If you answer **Y**, then:

- All occurrences of the regular font will be changed to the new font.
- The regular font of the *document itself* will also be changed to the new font.

When you return to the Edit screen, any new text added to a blank line will then be in the new regular font you selected.

CHANGING THE PRINT STYLES

For more information on print styles, see "Print Style" in Chapter 10.

Normally, you assign print styles from the Print Options dialog box, which is accessed from the Edit display (F3). However, because the print styles can affect the way in which a document appears when printed, Professional Write has thoughtfully provided you with the ability to select new print styles from within Preview: You can change print styles and then immediately see their effect on the Preview display.

To change the print styles:

1. Select *Set print styles* from the Options menu. When the Print Styles menu appears (Figure 12.10):
2. Select the styles that you want by pressing the corresponding numbers. Each selected style is indicated by a triangle.
3. To remove a style that's already selected, press its number and the little triangle will disappear.
4. After you have selected the styles you want, press ↵.

You can also select or deselect a style by highlighting it and then pressing the spacebar.

The document will be redisplayed, showing the effects of the new styles. These styles become part of your document until you change them again either from Preview or from the Print Options menu.

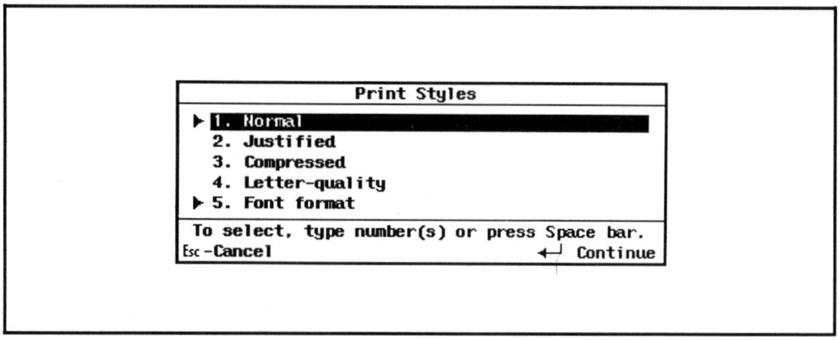

Figure 12.10: Select the new print styles from this menu

LEAVING PREVIEW

When you exit from Preview, you have a choice of where in the working copy you wish to return. To begin, press F4 to display the Return menu (Figure 12.11). Here are your choices:

- If you select *Return to current position*, the cursor in the Edit screen will be in the same position as the word cursor in the Preview display.
- If you select *Return to starting position*, the cursor in the Edit screen will be where it was when you entered Preview.

Notice that the Return menu indicates two speed keys you can use directly from the Preview display for returning to the Edit display: Press Esc to return to the current position, or press Alt-X to return to the starting position.

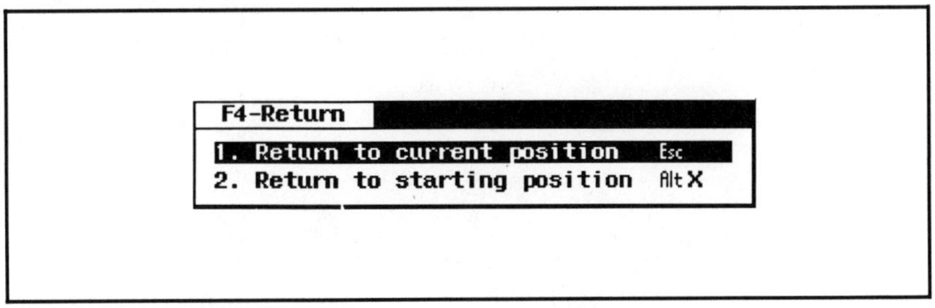

Figure 12.11: Select where to return in the working copy

13 Computerizing Your Address Lists

WITH THE ADDRESS BOOK FEATURE, YOU CAN KEEP computerized lists of names, addresses, phone numbers, and other information. An address book can be useful in many ways. For instance, if you're using Professional Write on a regular basis, an address book can be the fastest way to look up someone's telephone number or address. You can quickly paste selected data from an address book into the working copy. You can also create form letters and other standard forms, using selected information from an address book. And with an address book, you can easily maintain updated information about clients, friends, or other groups of individuals.

Working with an address book is straightforward, and you can easily add new data or modify or delete old information. You can browse through an address book, or print the entire contents. You can also limit your browsing or printing to specific groups of individuals. For instance, you might want to print out a list of clients who live in a particular city.

You can create and maintain several different address books, each containing data about particular groups of people. One book might be used for data on your current clients, while another might contain information on closed accounts.

Hard-disk computers can hold address-book data for 2,000 people, an upper limit that also applies to an address book stored on a 3½-inch floppy. For 5¼-inch floppies, however, the limit is approximately 1,000.

Work with an address book can begin from anywhere in the current working copy simply by selecting the Addresses menu (F6). There's no connection between the current contents of the working copy and what you do with an address book, unless you happen to want to copy some information from an address book into the working copy.

HOW AN ADDRESS BOOK IS STRUCTURED

An address book consists of a single file of information on a group of individuals, companies, or other entities. Data for each person or other entity is stored in a separate *record*. Each record consists of several *fields*, and each field contains a specific piece of information, such as a name or a telephone number. Each field has a name that identifies the type of information it holds.

For example, Figure 13.1 shows the contents of a single record in an address book. This record contains information about somebody named Sam Spade: The field called *First name* contains the value *Sam*, while the field *Last name* contains the value *Spade*.

HOW TO CREATE A NEW ADDRESS BOOK

To create or use an address book, you must begin from Professional Write's Edit screen. You can work with an address book regardless of the contents of the working copy.

WHERE TO STORE THE ADDRESS BOOK

You can store a file containing an address book on either a hard disk or a floppy. As usual, everything works much faster on a hard disk, so if you have a choice use the hard disk, but periodically save a backup copy on a floppy. You can create a special directory on your hard disk to save address books, or you can save them on any convenient directory.

CREATING THE NEW FILE

To create a new address book:

1. Begin by choosing *Select address book* from the Addresses menu (F6). The File Name dialog box shown in Figure 13.2 appears. When you first begin to use address books, the name of the sample address book that comes with the software, ADDRESS.SPC, is displayed in the dialog box.
2. Delete the current entry by pressing Ctrl-E.
3. Enter the name of the disk drive and/or directory where the file containing the new address book is to be written. **Don't**

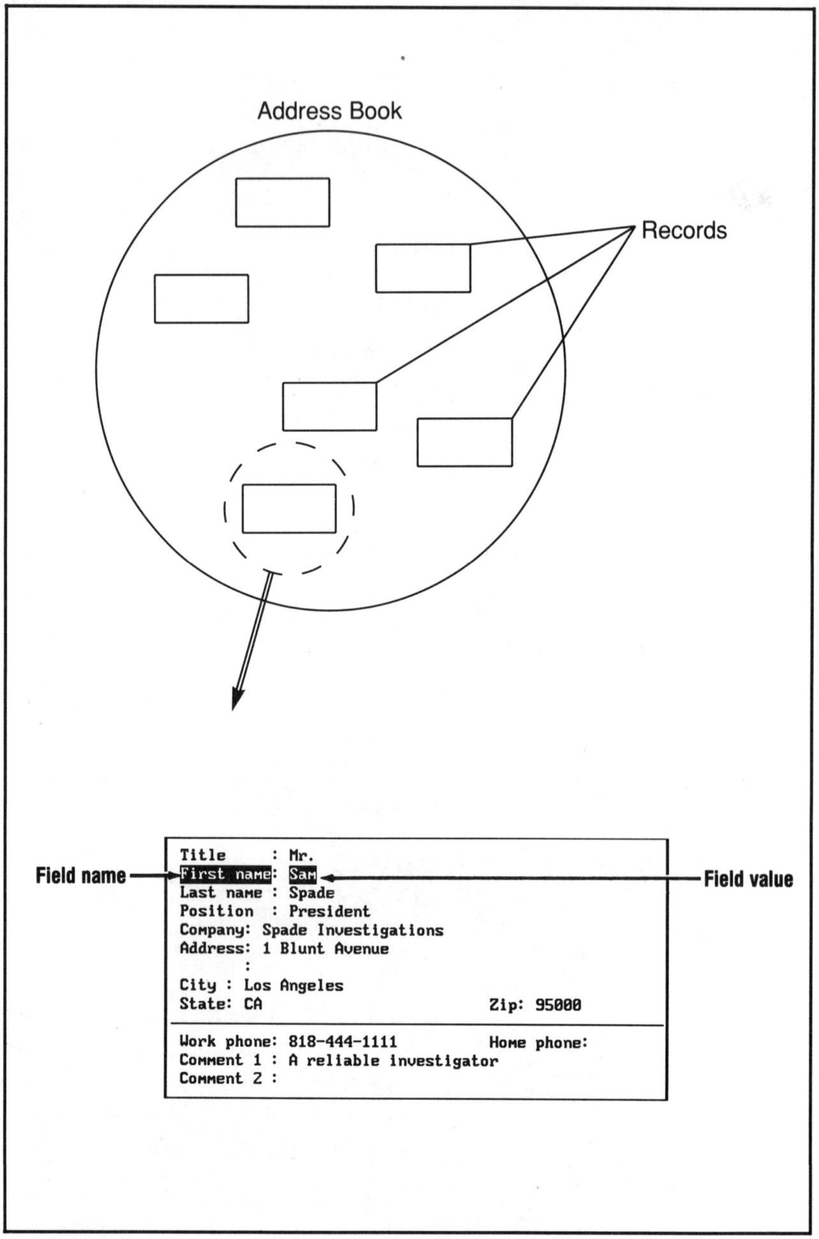

Figure 13.1: An address book consists of a file of records

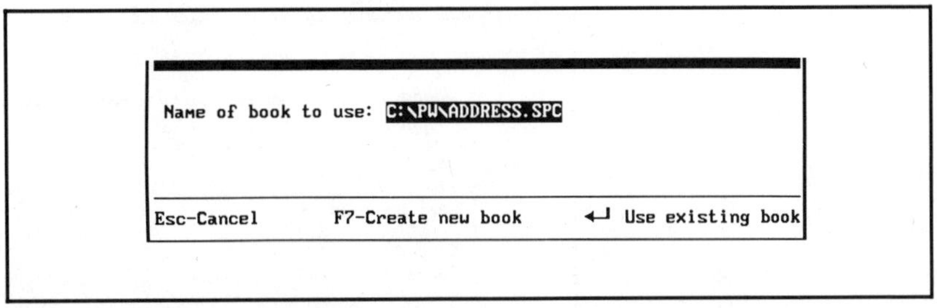

Figure 13.2: Enter the name of the new address book file here

press ↵. Be sure to include the complete path name of the directory.

Be careful not to overwrite an existing address book.

4. Enter the name of the file to hold your new address book and then press F7. If you enter the name of an existing file, a message appears on screen, warning that you may destroy valuable data.

5. If you wish, enter a description of the address book (up to 40 characters). This description will appear whenever this file name appears in the File Directory. Finish up by pressing the ↵ key.

You have now created an empty address book, and a blank *address form* appears on the screen (Figure 13.3). You can enter information about a person into this form (see "How to Add Records," below), or you can return to the Edit screen by pressing Esc.

Whenever you use the Addresses menu to work with an address book, Professional Write automatically uses the address book that was most recently accessed. Thus, once you have created a new address book following the above steps, Professional Write will automatically use it unless you specifically select another one (see "Maintaining Several Address Books," below).

HOW TO ADD RECORDS

A *record* is the information stored in an address book about a particular person. You can add new records whenever you wish. After a record has been added, it becomes a permanent part of the address book, unless you modify or delete the record at some later time.

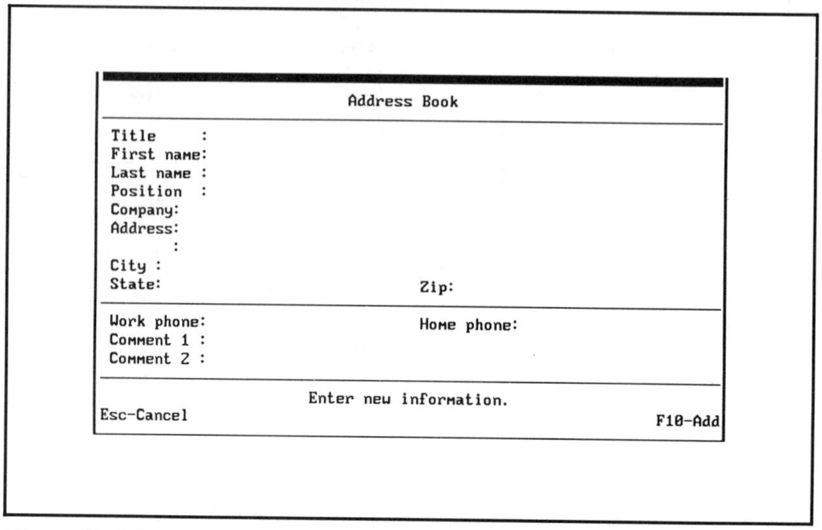

Figure 13.3: Enter data about a person into this blank form

THE ADDRESS FORM

To add one or more new records, select *Add an address* from the Addresses menu (F6). Professional Write automatically selects the address book you used (or created) most recently, and a blank address form appears on screen (Figure 13.3).

The address form consists of a set of field names. Each field name ends with a colon followed by blank space into which you can enter a value for that field.

To fill in this form, move the cursor from one field to the next, using the Tab and Shift-Tab keys. Enter data for as many fields as you wish, leaving the others blank. When you have finished entering data, press F10. The information is stored as a new record in the address book, and a new blank form appears.

Here are some points to keep in mind as you enter data:

- The data in the form doesn't become part of the address book until you press F10. Until then, you can move back and forth between fields to enter and edit field values.

- While editing, you can switch back and forth between the Insert and Overwrite modes by pressing the Ins key. Initially, the Overwrite mode is on when the address form is displayed.
- You can use any of the standard keys for editing field values.
- Be careful about capitalization; information will be saved exactly as it's entered.
- To erase a field value, press Ctrl-E.
- Data for the fields must fit within the space immediately after the field name. You can't extend a field value beyond the alloted space.
- To stop entering records and return to the Edit screen, press Esc. If you press Esc after beginning data entry for a record, a warning message appears, giving you a chance to save the data before exiting.
- As you add records to an address book, they are automatically arranged in alphabetical order by the values in the *Last name* field.

You can enter whatever information you like for any of the fields in an address form. Note that you can put any type of information you like into any field because Professional Write doesn't monitor the type of data you enter. For instance, you'll generally want to put address information into the field labeled *Address*—but not necessarily. You might have an application in which you don't need addresses, but you do want to save some other type of data—perhaps something like BALANCE DUE. You could save this information in the *Address* field, as long as you remember what you've done. Generally, try to be as consistent as possible with capitalization, punctuation, and particularly content.

The following five sections will discuss some of the fields on the address forms, with suggestions on how to use them effectively.

Title

Use this field for entries like *Dr.*, *Mr.*, *Ms.*, and *Professor*.

Last Name

Records are automatically sorted alphabetically by the values in this field, so be particularly careful about spelling. For the purposes of sorting, capitalization is ignored.

Position

This field is normally used for a person's position within an organization. Typical values would be *CEO*, *president*, and *sales manager*.

Address

This field has two lines for data in order to accommodate complex addresses such as *55 Park Street, Suite 12345*. You don't need to use both lines, and a blank line will be ignored when an address is output.

You can enter the address information on the two lines in any way that you want, but bear in mind that when the information is output, it will appear on the two lines exactly as you enter it. When entering the address information, use the Tab and Shift-Tab keys to move from one line to the other.

Comments

For more information about searching, see "Searching for Records," below.

Because you can search for selected groups of records using field values, the *Comment* fields can be particularly useful. For example, suppose one of your address books contains information about the employees in your company, which has many different departments. You could use one of the *Comment* fields to hold the department name for each employee. Then, you could scan the address book and display or print information about employees in a particular department.

As another example, suppose that your address book contains data about your clients, only some of whom are currently active. You could use one of the *Comment* fields to contain either of the values *ACTIVE* or *INACTIVE*. Then, when using the address book, you could selectively access either active clients, inactive ones, or all of them.

SEARCHING FOR RECORDS

Information is only as good as your ability to find and use it. Finding records in an address book is easy, provided you can supply the right amount and kind of information. For instance, if you want to display the data for Harry Johnson, the name *Harry Johnson* would be sufficient to identify the record you wanted. As you will later see, however, any search instruction that uniquely identifies a record will enable you to find it.

Here are some of the ways in which you can use an address book:

- Browse through each record in the book.
- Display a single record, based on information you supply to help locate the record.
- Browse through a selected group of records, again based on information you supply.

BROWSING THROUGH AN ADDRESS BOOK

You can scan an address book, displaying one record after another. The records will appear in alphabetical order based on the values in the *Last name* field. As each record is displayed, you have several options. You can

- Exit to the Edit screen.
- Go on to display another record.
- Edit the record, adding new data or updating information.
- Delete the record from the address book.
- Copy selected parts of the record to the working copy.

To browse through an address book, select *Find an address* from the Addresses menu (F6). When a blank address form appears, display the first record by pressing F10. Then

- To display the next record, press PgDn or F10.
- To display the previous record, press PgUp.
- To finish browsing and return to the Edit screen, press Esc twice.

FINDING A PARTICULAR RECORD

To find information about a particular person in the address book, you need to supply a set of *search instructions* to Professional Write so that it knows which record to find. You enter these search instructions on a *search form*, which is identical to a blank address form except that you are requested to "Enter search instructions." (See Figure 13.4.)

Suppose you want to display the information about a client named Pete Roberts. Here's how to do it:

Professional Write ignores capitalization in search instructions.

1. Select *Find an address* from the Addresses menu (F6).
2. When the blank search form appears, enter the instructions to select the record you want to find: Type in **Pete** and **Roberts** for the *First name* and *Last name* field, as shown in Figure 13.4.
3. Press F10, and Professional Write searches through the address book, finds the record, and displays it.

In this example, the values *Pete* and *Roberts* are the search instructions that Professional Write uses to find the matching record. However, you don't necessarily need to use both the *First name* and *Last*

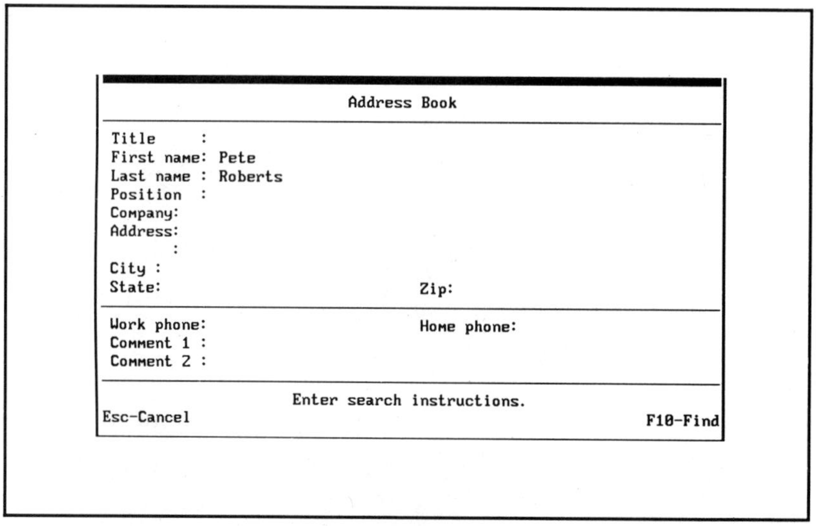

```
                      Address Book
Title      :
First name: Pete
Last name : Roberts
Position  :
Company:
Address:
       :
City :
State:                          Zip:

Work phone:                     Home phone:
Comment 1 :
Comment 2 :
                  Enter search instructions.
Esc-Cancel                                        F10-Find
```

Figure 13.4: The search instructions for finding information about Pete Roberts *name* fields to find a record. In fact, you can enter any search instructions that will uniquely identify the record, using as many fields as necessary. For instance, if there is only one record in your address book with a last name of Roberts, you could eliminate the first name and just enter **Roberts** in the *Last name* field. Professional Write would then find and display this record.

As another example, suppose you want to find the information about someone whose name you can't bring to mind, but who you know is your only client living in Anchorage. You could enter the value **Anchorage** into the *City* field, leaving the rest of the search form blank.

If there is more than one record with the value **Anchorage** in the *City* field, the first record found is displayed (see below for more details about finding collections of records).

FINDING SELECTED GROUPS OF RECORDS

You can use search instructions to find and display specific sets of records. For instance, you might want to display information about all clients who live in Boston. Or, you might want to display data on employees who work in a particular branch of your company.

As an example, suppose your address book contains information about your clients, and you would like to display only those records for clients living in California. Here are the steps:

1. As with any search, begin by selecting *Find an address* from the Addresses menu (F6).
2. When the blank search form appears, enter **CA** for the *State* field and then press F10.

Professional Write will display the first matching record in the address book, that is, the first record with a value of **CA** for the *State* field. To display the next matching record, press PgDn or F10. As each record is displayed, you can

- Make any necessary changes to the displayed information, or delete the record.
- Display the next matching record by pressing PgDn or F10.

- Display the previous matching record by pressing PgUp.
- Abort the data display and return to the blank search form by pressing Esc.

Points to Ponder

When you want to display one or more records, you need to enter search instructions only for one, two, or as many fields as necessary to specify the records you want.

Professional Write interprets a blank field to mean *any value*, as opposed to *no value*. This saves you the trouble of having to enter something for every field.

Although you don't need to be concerned with capitalization when entering search instructions, spelling is crucial. If you misspell part of a search instruction, Professional Write won't be able to find the record(s) you want. For example, suppose you enter **CA** as a search instruction for the *State* field. Records with values of *CA* for *State* will be displayed, but those with values of *California* will not (the computer just isn't that smart).

Professional write ignores leading spaces when matching search instructions with information in an address book. However, the number of spaces *within* a field value must match. For example, if you enter the search instruction **CEO** for the *Position* field, it won't match records with a value of *C E O*.

USING WILDCARDS

If you're not sure about the exact spelling of a field value, such as a person's name, you may still be able to find the information by using a *wildcard*, which consists of two consecutive periods (..).

A wildcard stands for *any character or group of characters*. For example, suppose you want to locate the record for a particular person. You can't remember the exact spelling of his last name, but you know that it's something like *Petrofsky* or *Petrovich*. You could solve this problem by entering the search instruction **Pet..** for the *Last name* field.

When Professional Write uses this search instruction, it will display every record whose *Last name* field contains a value starting with

Pet. If there are several such records, you can scan them until the correct one appears.

You can use as many wildcards as necessary within a set of search instructions. You can even use two wildcards within a single value. Table 13.1 gives a few examples.

Table 13.1: Wildcard Examples

VALUE ENTERED AS A SEARCH INSTRUCTION	VALUES THAT WILL MATCH
John..	John, Johnson
..John	John, Upjohn
..John..	John, Upjohn, Johnson
..	Any non-blank value

Note that if you enter a wildcard by itself for a field value, a record will match only if it contains a *non-blank value* for that field. You could use this, for instance, to display only those records for which the zip code was known: Enter a wildcard for the *Zip* field.

Table 13.1 also illustrates a slight inconsistency in the way in which Professional Write handles wildcards. If a wildcard is used as part of a value, such as *John..*, then the wildcard is interpreted as either *any set of characters* or *no characters*. This contrasts with the interpretation of a wildcard used by itself, which is *any non-blank group of characters*.

Other Examples of Using Wildcards

Wildcards can be used for many purposes. For instance, if you want to find all records for clients whose zip codes begin with *951*, you would enter the search instruction **951..** for the *Zip* field.

You can also use a wildcard as a shortcut when entering a long value as part of a search instruction. For instance, to find the record for Bernard Willinofsky, you can simply enter the value **Wil..** for the *Last name* field. If there is more than one matching record, you can quickly scan them to find the correct one.

EDITING AND DELETING RECORDS

You can easily modify the information stored in an address book. You may, for example, want to change the phone numbers for one or more records or alter other field values. You can also delete one or more selected records from an address book.

To edit or delete a record, it must first be displayed on the screen by using the techniques described above in "Finding Selected Groups of Records." When the record appears on the screen, you can then either make the necessary changes to it or remove it from the address book.

CHANGING EXISTING INFORMATION

To modify one or more records,

1. Enter the appropriate search instructions into a blank search form, describing the record(s) you want to edit. Finish by pressing F10. Then, as each record appears,
2. Move the cursor to each field to be edited using the Tab and Shift-Tab keys. Then make the necessary changes.
3. To enter these changes in the address book and go on to the next record, press either F10 or PgDn.
4. To stop editing records, press Esc. If you were in the middle of changing a record, Professional Write asks you to verify that you want to abandon the changes you were making: Press ↵ to ignore the changes and go on, or press Esc to return to that record. However, your search instructions are discarded and a blank search form appears. If you then want to continue editing, you'll have to reenter the search instructions.

You can also press PgUp, which enters the changes and then moves back to the previous record.

REMOVING RECORDS FROM AN ADDRESS BOOK

To delete one or more records, enter the appropriate search instructions into a blank search form, describing the record(s) you want to delete. Finish by pressing F10. As each record appears onscreen,

- You can delete the record by pressing F9. Verify that you really want to delete it by pressing ↵ (or if you change your mind, by pressing Esc.)
- If you decide not to delete the record currently displayed, press F10 or PgDn to go on to the next record.
- To abort the display of records, press Esc, and a blank search form will appear on screen.

Note that you can combine the editing and deleting process. For instance, you can scan through selected records (or through every record) in an address book; as each record appears, you can then decide whether to edit or delete it.

TRANSFERRING ADDRESS BOOK INFORMATION TO THE WORKING COPY

You can copy information from one or more records into the working copy. However, before you transfer any data, you must first specify the format of the data to be transferred from each record. This includes selecting the fields to be included as well as the order in which this information is to appear when copied to the working copy. You can also include boilerplate (that is, standard) text to be transferred along with the information from each record.

After you have established the standard format for data transfer, you can then copy information from whatever record or records you wish into the working copy. To do this, you display each record by entering the necessary search instructions onto a blank search form. When the record appears, press the appropriate key, and information is transferred to the working copy.

SELECTING THE INFORMATION TO BE COPIED

The format of the information to be copied from records to the working copy is controlled by the *copy format* for your address book. To display the current copy format, select *Specify copy format* from the Addresses menu (F6). (See Figure 13.5.) When this display first appears, it contains the default copy format supplied by Professional Write, which you can either leave unchanged or modify in any way you wish.

How the Copy Format Works

The copy format contains the names of the fields to be copied from each record, the order in which they are copied, and any other additional standard text to be included. Each line on the copy format contains the names of one or more fields, with each field name enclosed in asterisks. Each line represents one line of information to be transferred to the working copy from a record, with the following exceptions:

- If a field contains no data, then nothing is transferred. If none of the fields listed on a line contains any data, that line is not written to the working copy.

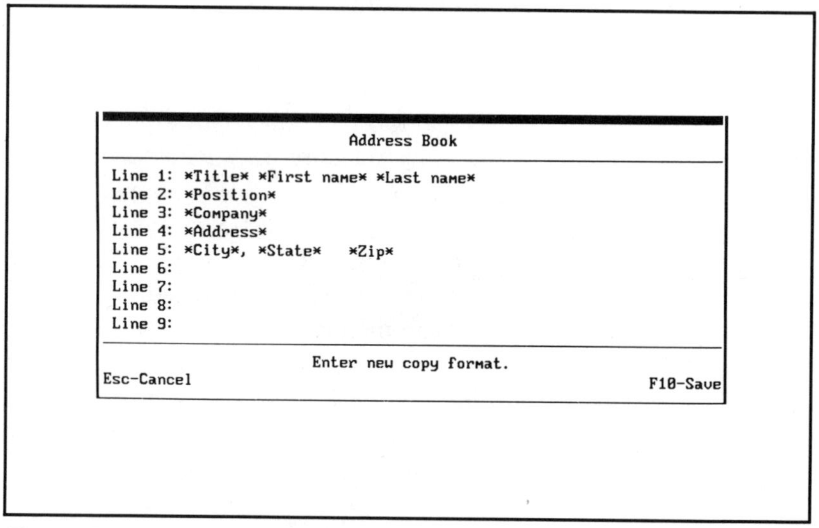

Figure 13.5: The default copy format

- If the *Address* field contains two lines of information, they will be transferred as they appear in the record.

Any text or punctuation outside the asterisks is transferred exactly as it appears on a line. For instance, in line 5 of Figure 13.5, a comma and space separate the *City* and *State* fields. These two characters will be copied to the working copy along with the values of the two fields. In fact, even if both fields are empty, the comma and space will be copied (creating a very strange looking line).

Figure 13.6 shows a sample record, and Figure 13.7 shows the result of copying data from this record to the working copy, using the copy format shown in Figure 13.5. Notice that because there is no data for the *Position* field, nothing is copied. Also, the *Address* field contains two non-blank lines, both of which are copied exactly as they appear in the record.

How to Modify the Copy Format

You can delete the entire contents of a line by pressing Ctrl-E.

You can modify the copy format to suit your own particular needs. To edit a particular line, first select *Specify Copy Format* from the Address menu (F6). Then move the cursor to that line and edit it,

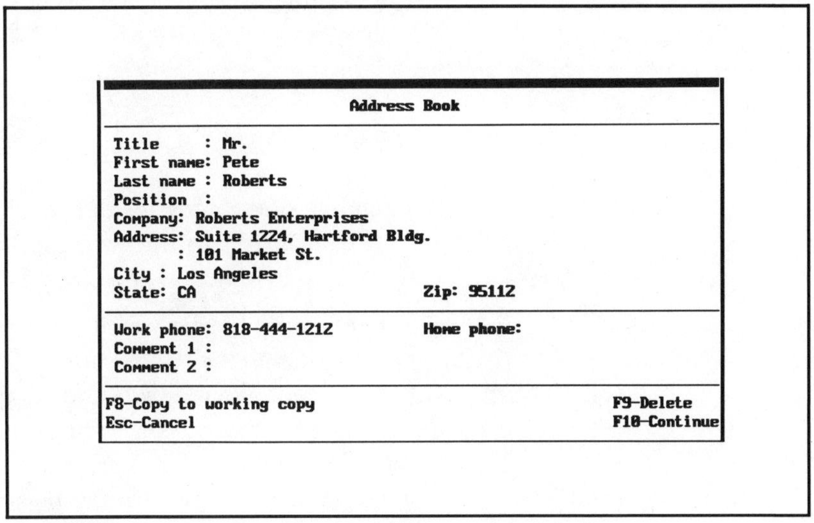

Figure 13.6: A sample record

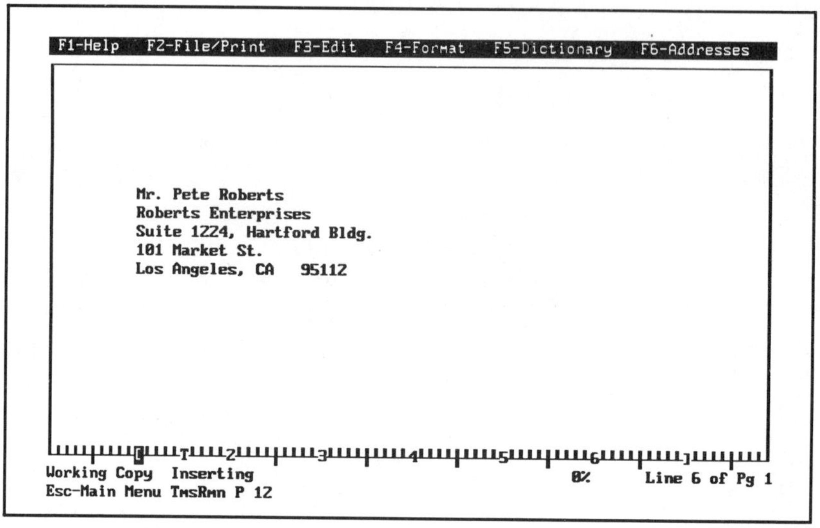

Figure 13.7: This data was transferred to the working copy from the record shown in Figure 13.6

deleting unwanted field names and entering the field names you want, as well as any other punctuation or text.

When you are finished editing, press F10 and the new copy format will be saved by Professional Write. On the other hand, if you want to abandon making changes, press Esc and the original copy format will be restored.

Points to Ponder

- Each line of the copy format represents one line of information transferred to the working copy, with the exceptions noted above in "How the Copy Format Works."
- When editing the copy format, enter each field name exactly as it appears in the address forms (except that you don't need to worry about capitalization). If you misspell a field name, you won't get what you want when data is transferred from records to the working copy. For field names containing two words, make sure to include the separating space when you enter the field name.
- Enclose each field name with asterisks.

- Enter as many field names as you like on each line.
- If you want standard text or punctuation to be copied with each record, enter it wherever you want it to appear. Make sure it's *outside* any asterisk pairs enclosing field names.
- The copy format is stored as part of the address book, and each address book can have only one copy format at a time. If you are using several address books, each will have its own copy format. If you want to change which data is to be copied from records, you'll have to modify the copy format for that address book.

COPYING INFORMATION FROM RECORDS

After you have set up the copy format the way you want, you can then copy data from one or more records into the working copy. To transfer information from a record,

1. On the Edit screen, place the cursor exactly where you want data from the records to be copied.
2. Select *Find an address* from the Addresses menu (F6).
3. Enter the appropriate search instructions into a blank search form, describing the record you want. Finish by pressing the F10 key.
4. When the record is displayed, press F8 and the information will be written to the working copy.

As information from a record is copied, text to the right of the cursor is automatically pushed over and down to make room.

EXAMPLE: CREATING AN INSIDE ADDRESS

When you want to create a business letter, you can use the default Copy Format, shown in Figure 13.5, for quickly entering the inside address of the letter. Here's how:

1. Starting with a blank working copy, enter the current date and then add one or two blank lines.

2. Display the record for the person to whom you are writing the letter by entering the appropriate search instructions (such as the person's name).
3. Press F8, and the inside address will be copied to the working copy. You can then continue writing your letter.

Note that this works *only* if the Copy Format has been previously set as shown in Figure 13.5. If you routinely use a different Copy Format, it's not worth the trouble to change it just for a single letter: Enter the inside address manually.

MAINTAINING SEVERAL ADDRESS BOOKS

You can create and maintain as many address books as you wish, using the techniques described in this chapter. To create each new address book, follow the steps described in "How to Create a New Address Book" in this chapter.

To use information from an existing address book,

1. Choose *Select address book* from the Addresses menu (F6).
2. When the File Name dialog box appears (see Figure 13.2), delete the current entry by pressing Ctrl-E.
3. Enter the name of the disk drive and/or directory containing the address book you want to use.

4a. If you know the exact name of the address book you want, enter that name immediately after the name of the disk drive and/or directory. Then press ↵.

4b. If you want to look through the current directory, do not enter a file name: Instead, press ↵ and the File Directory will appear. Select the address book from the File Directory and then press ↵.

For information about using the File Directory, see Chapter 7.

When you select an address book, Professional Write makes a notation in its permanent files. From then on, whenever you use the

Addresses menu to add records or search for records, this address book will be automatically accessed. To change to another address book, repeat the steps listed above.

PRINTING INFORMATION FROM AN ADDRESS BOOK

You can print information from an address book. The entire contents can be printed, or only selected fields from specific groups of records.

The easiest way to print information from several records is by creating a special form letter. Details on how to do this are covered in Chapter 14. However, you can output the contents of a single record as follows:

1. Start with a blank working copy.
2. Using suitable search instructions, display the record you want.
3. Transfer data from the record to the working copy by pressing F8. Exactly which information is transferred will be dictated by the current contents of the Copy Format for this address book (see "How the Copy Format Works," above).
4. In the working copy, add any additional information to be printed along with the address book data.
5. Print the contents of the working copy.

14 Form Letters and Other Standard Forms

MANY TYPES OF STANDARD FORMS CAN BE CREATED by merging information from a data file with standard text in the working copy. The most common type of form is the form letter, where merged information usually consists of names and addresses placed into specific locations within the letters. Generally, information from a data file can be merged into any location within the text in the working copy, giving you the ability to create many different types of forms. (See Figure 14.1.)

Here are some examples of forms that you can create:

- Form letters;
- Standard data forms. For instance, each form might contain demographic information about various clients, such as name, address, and telephone number;
- Lists of information from a Professional Write address book.

You can merge information from any of the following data sources with standard text in the working copy:

- A Professional Write address book
- A dBASE III or dBASE III PLUS database file

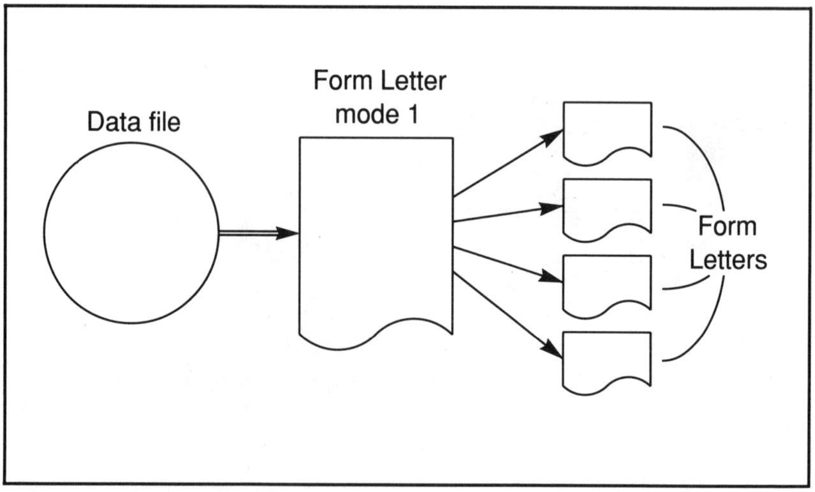

Figure 14.1: Forms are generated from standard text in the working copy and a data source

- A Professional File data file
- A delimited ASCII file

CREATING FORM LETTERS FROM ADDRESS BOOK DATA

You can merge information from a Professional Write address book with standard text to produce a set of customized form letters. You can print one letter for each record in an address book, or you can select which records to merge for printing. You can control the precise placement of each merged data item in the printed letters.

Suppose that you want to send personalized letters, similar to the one shown in Figure 14.2, to a group of customers. Assume that you have a Professional Write address book called CLIENTS, which contains information about these customers—one record per customer.

CREATING THE FORM LETTER MODEL

To begin, you create the standard text, which is called the *form letter model*, shown in Figure 14.3. Notice that this differs from the letter shown in Figure 14.2, in that specific information has been replaced

June 25, 1989

Mr. Albert Krasnowitch
49 Hampton Way Court
Phoenix, AZ 12345

Dear Mr. Krasnowitch:

We would like to thank you for your recent business. Please keep in touch with us, Albert. We would be happy to mail merchandise prepaid, even to Phoenix!

Sincerely,

Joe Pringlesbury
SALES MANAGER

Figure 14.2: A personalized form letter

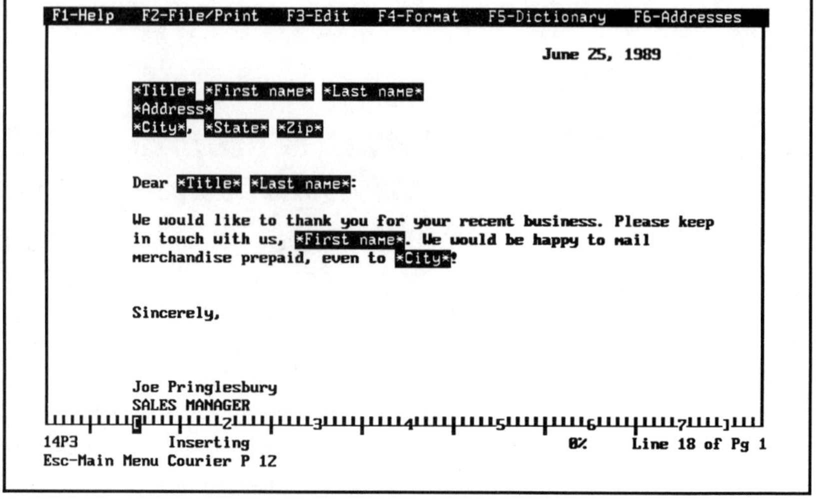

Figure 14.3: This form letter model contains field names

by items enclosed in asterisks. Each of these enclosed items is a *field name*, corresponding to one of the fields in your address book. When the letters are printed, actual field values from the CLIENTS address book will replace the field names in the form letter model.

Using Field Names

Here are a few things to keep in mind when creating a form letter model:

- Each field name must be enclosed in asterisks.
- Place each field name exactly where you want the field value to appear in the final letters. Normally, the field value will begin at the position of the asterisk preceding the field name. For more information on placing field values, see "Controlling the Position of Merged Data," below.
- You don't need to worry about capitalization, but the spelling of a field name must be exactly as it appears in the address book.
- When the value of a field is printed, all leading and trailing blanks are ignored.

See Chapter 13 for details about field name spellings.

- You can include any text or punctuation between field names. These will be printed with each form letter. For example, in Figure 14.3 notice that a space is included between *Title* and *First name*, and also between *First name* and *Last name*. As you can see from Figure 14.2, these spaces are printed.
- A field name can be used as many times as desired in a form letter model. For example, in Figure 14.3 the field *City* has been used twice.

Forcing Automatic Rewrap

If you insert a field value into the middle of a line of text, you may find that the surrounding text doesn't always get reformatted properly because of the length of the field value. For example, in Figure 14.3, the field name *First name* appears in the second line of the body of the text. If the value of this field happened to be very long, that text line might not rewrap properly (text might be lost from the end of the line).

There must be a space between the field name and the position indicator.

You can avoid this possibility by inserting the *position indicator* **T** along with the field name, as follows: *First name (T)*. This will ensure that no matter how long a field name is, any surrounding text will be properly reformatted.

PRINTING THE LETTERS

For information about filling in the Print Options dialog box, see Chapter 10.

After you have created the form letter model, you are ready to print the form letters. To begin, you must enter a couple of selections in the Print Options dialog box, including which address book to use. Then you must select which records from the address book are to be merged for printing.

Selecting the Address Book and Other Print Options

To start the printing process, you need to fill in various options in the Print Options dialog box. Most of the options shown in Figure 14.4 will be applicable, except that a different pair of printers will probably be displayed under the *Print to* option.

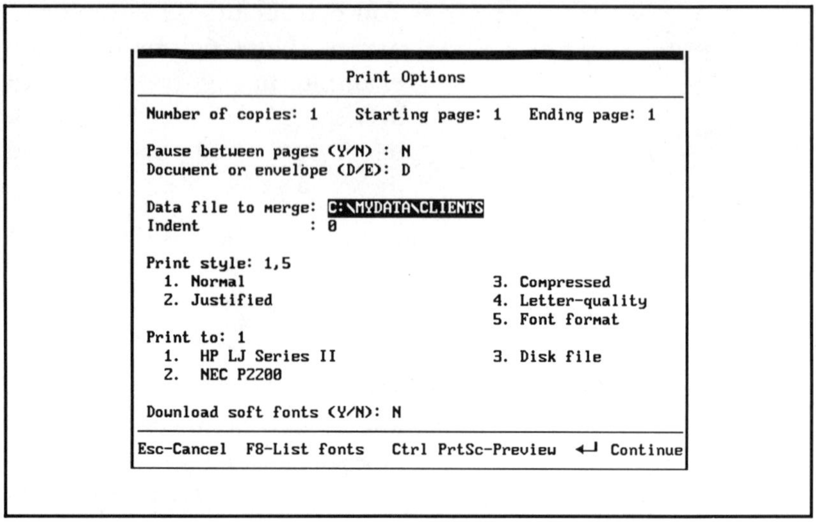

Figure 14.4: Enter the name of the address book in this dialog box

Here's how to get started with the printing:

1. Make sure that your form letter model is in the working copy.
2. Select *Print working copy* from the File/Print menu (F2) (or press the speed key Ctrl-O). When the Print Options dialog box appears (Figure 14.4):
3. Select the appropriate print styles and the printer to be used.
4. In the line labeled *Data file to merge:*, enter the name of the address book file to be used. If the file is not in the default data directory defined by the Setup program, you must include the name of the disk drive, as well as the full pathname.
5. After filling in the Print Options dialog box, press ↵ and a blank search form will appear (Figure 14.5).
6. If you want to generate a form letter for every record in the address book selected in step 4 above, simply press F10 and printing will begin.

For information about using search instructions, see Chapter 13.

7. If you want to select a particular group of records to merge, enter the appropriate search instructions on the search form.

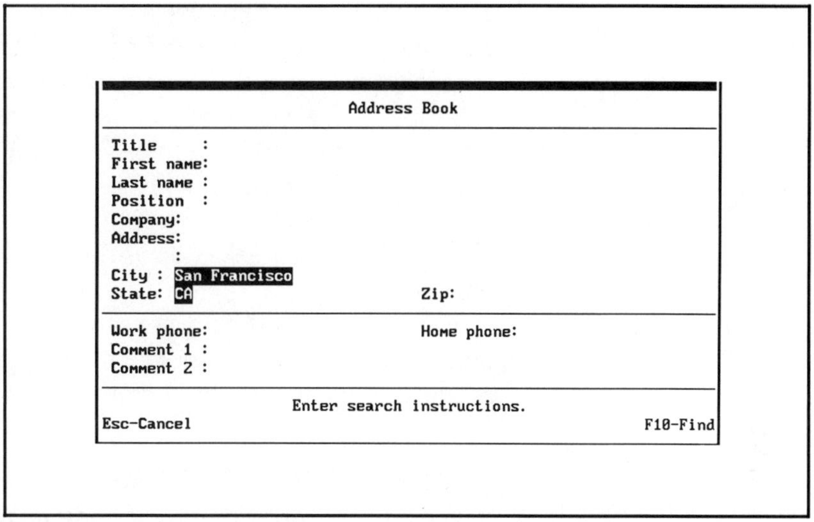

Figure 14.5: Enter the search instructions in this search form

For example, if your address book contains records for various clients, the search instruction in Figure 14.5 will select only those records for clients from San Francisco, California.

8. After you have entered your search instructions, press F10, and printing will begin. A separate letter will be generated for each record merged from the address book.

Saving the Form Letter Model

If you plan to use the same form letter model again, save it to a file. When you do, the name of the address book that you entered in the Print Options dialog box will also be saved in that file. The next time you retrieve the form letter model, this information is also retrieved, and you won't have to reenter it in the Print Options dialog box.

CONTROLLING THE POSITION OF MERGED DATA

Normally, when a form letter is printed, each field value will be printed in the position dictated by the position of the asterisk preceding the field name in the form letter model. For example, in Figure 14.3, the entry **First name** begins one space after the entry **Title**. When each form letter is printed, the value of the field *First name* will be printed one space after the value of *Title*, regardless of the length of *Title*.

Suppose, however, that you want to position a field value at a precise *physical* position on a line. For instance, you might want each name to begin exactly 2.5 inches to the right of the left edge of the paper. If you were entering data into preprinted forms, you would likewise want each field value to be printed at a specific location on the page.

You can control the precise physical positioning of field information in a number of ways. The method depends on the type of font assigned to the text in the document.

Using a 10-Pitch Monospaced Font

With a monospaced font printing at 10 characters per inch, you can use the Ruler line to set the exact position of field information: On the form letter model, position the left asterisk of the field name at the location on the line where the field data is to be printed. You can use the Ruler line as a guide because each vertical line represents one-tenth of an inch, corresponding in this case to the width of each character.

For instance, in Figure 14.6, the entry *Last name* begins at character position 25. When each form is printed, the value in the *Last name* field will begin 2.5 inches in from the left edge of the page.

Other Fonts

For proportional fonts (as well as monospaced fonts not in 10-pitch) you can set the physical position of each field on a line as follows:

1. Before creating the form model, create a tab setting at the exact position where you want data for the field to appear when printed, again using each Ruler line mark as one-tenth of an inch.
2. When you create the form model, position the beginning of the field name (that is, the left asterisk) at this tab setting.

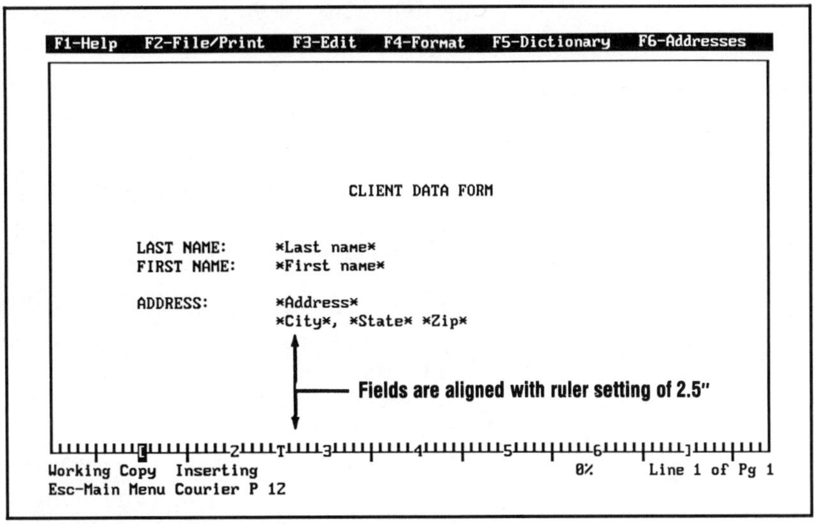

Figure 14.6: Fields on each line will begin printing 2.5 inches from the left margin

3. In the Print Options dialog box, select *Font Format* as one of the print styles.

To position several fields at different horizontal locations, create a tab setting at each location and then make sure that each field name is lined up with that tab setting.

For example, in Figure 14.6 there is a tab setting at position 25 on the Ruler. This setting applies to the entire page, so that when each form is printed, the fields will line up 2.5 inches in from the left edge of the paper.

If you want to reposition one or more fields after you have constructed a form, you must then reset the tabs of the lines containing the field names. For more details, see "Changing the Tab Settings of Existing Text" in Chapter 5.

Right-Aligning Field Values

Occasionally, you may want to right-align a field value in a form letter. That is, you want the end of the value to occur at a particular horizontal position on a line. This can be useful, for example, if you want to line up columns of numbers on a page. Here are the steps to follow:

1. Select a monospaced font (see "Points to Ponder," below).
2. Enter the field name so that the right-hand asterisk is positioned at the spot where the data values are to end.
3. Include the position indicator **(R)** as part of the field name.

Here's an example: *CURRENT BALANCE (R)*. Make sure to include a blank space between the field name and the position indicator.

Points to Ponder

When aligning the rightmost asterisk of a field name, use the Ruler line as a guide: The left end of the Ruler line corresponds to the left edge of the printed page, and each ruler mark is equivalent to one-tenth of an inch.

You must use a monospaced font for the text when right-adjusting any fields, or you won't be able to position the field values properly. Using a 10-pitch font is the easiest because you can use the Ruler line as a guide when lining up the field name in the form letter model. If you use another size font, you'll need to use some trial-and-error to determine the correct positioning of the field names to be right justified.

PRINTING ADDRESS BOOK INFORMATION

Using the techniques described in the preceding section, you can print selected bits of information from an address book. For example, suppose that you want to print the name, address, and phone numbers from selected records in an address book. You could use the form model shown in Figure 14.7, or you could improve this form model by including some identifying information for the field values, as shown in Figure 14.8.

Normally, the information from each record would be printed on a separate page. However, because this information occupies only a few lines, a lot of paper would be wasted. You can save paper by

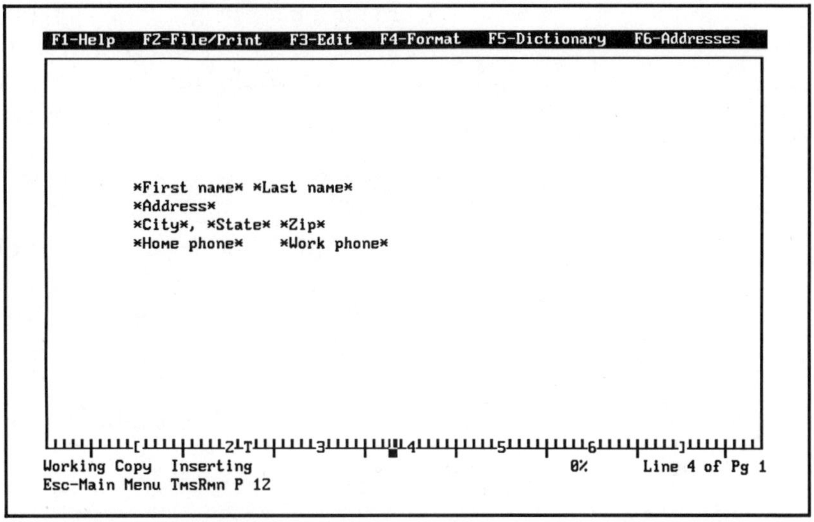

Figure 14.7: A simple form model for printing address book information

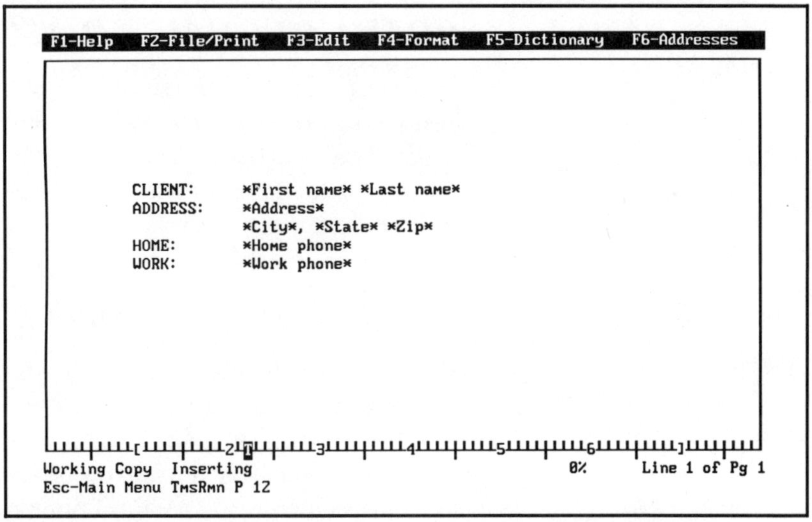

Figure 14.8: Identifying information in a form model can enhance a printed list

printing data from several records on each page, as follows:

1. Select *Set top/bottom margins & length* from the Format menu (F4).
2. Enter zero for *Top margin* and *Bottom margin*.

3. Enter a page length that's long enough to include the information from each record. In addition, the page length must allow a whole number of "pages" (that is, individual records) to fit onto a single printed page.

The reason for the last suggestion in step 3 is to guarantee that data from a single record won't be split across a page boundary. For example, nearly all dot-matrix printers output 66 lines per page, so you would select one of the following values for page length: 6, 11, 22, or 33. On the other hand, most laser printers print 60 lines per page, so you would select a page length of 6, 10, 12, 15, 20, or 30.

Notice that "page length" as used by Professional Write refers to the number of lines taken up by each record—not to the physical length of each page.

CREATING FORM LETTERS FROM A DELIMITED ASCII FILE

You can merge a standard form letter with information from a delimited ASCII file to produce a set of customized form letters. This type of file is useful because many different types of software products can output data in this format, including database programs, spreadsheets, and word processors.

THE FORM OF A DELIMITED ASCII FILE

This type of file contains field values only—not field names.

Figure 14.9 illustrates the way in which data is structured in this type of file. Each line contains the contents of a single *record* and ends with a hard return (you can't see a hard return because it's a nonprinting character). Each record consists of a set of field values. Each field value is enclosed by a pair of double quotation marks called *field delimiters;* and fields are separated by commas called *field separators*. Every record in a delimited ASCII file has exactly the same fields.

When this type of data file is used, every record in the file is merged to generate a separate letter. That is, you can't selectively merge records as you can with a Professional Write address book.

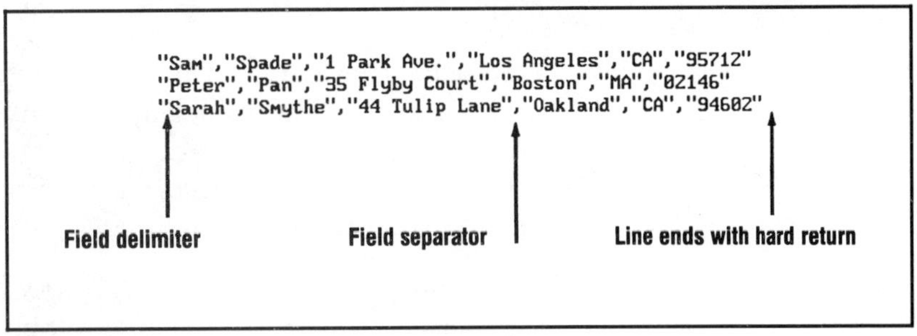

Figure 14.9: Structure of a delimited ASCII file

CREATING THE FORM LETTER MODEL

Figure 14.10 shows a form letter model that could be used with the data file illustrated in Figure 14.9. In this case, each field value is represented by a number enclosed in asterisks. *The number represents the relative position of a field in the ASCII file.* For example, the first field of each record in Figure 14.9 is a first name, and therefore you place ***1*** at each position in the form letter model where the first name is to appear. Similarly, the fourth field in each record contains the name of a city, so you would enter ***4*** in the appropriate positions of the form letter model.

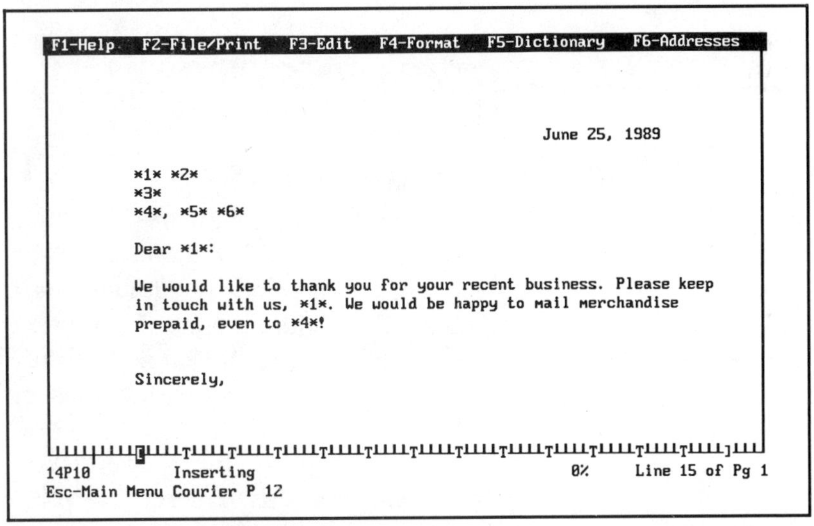

Figure 14.10: This form letter could be used with the delimited ASCII file shown in Figure 14.9

PRINTING THE LETTERS

After you have created the form letter model, you are ready to print the form letters. To begin, you must enter a couple of values in the Print Options dialog box, including which address book to use. Then the data from each record in the ASCII file will be merged with the form letter model to produce a separate letter:

1. Make sure that your form letter model is in the working copy: Either retrieve the file, or create a new one.
2. Select *Print working copy* from the File/Print menu (F2) (or press the speed key Ctrl-O). When the Print Options dialog box appears (Figure 14.4):
3. Select the appropriate print styles and the printer to be used.
4. In the line labeled *Data file to merge:* enter the file name of the delimited ASCII file to be used. If this file is not in the default data directory defined by the Setup program, you must include the name of the disk drive, as well as the full pathname.
5. After filling in the Print Options dialog box, press ↵ and the letters will be printed.

CREATING FORM LETTERS FROM OTHER TYPES OF DATA FILES

You can create form letters using information from either Professional File or dBASE data files. The basic techniques and ideas are the same as those described above for merging data from a Professional Write address book. However, with either of these types of files, you have a good deal more flexibility in controlling the entire merging process than you do when merging a Professional Write address book.

You can print one letter for each record in a data file, or you can select which records to merge for printing. In addition, you can control the order in which letters are printed. For instance, you could have the letters printed in zip code order.

Because some field names can be quite long, you have the option of using synonyms for these names when you create the form letter model. Also, when merging data from either of these types of files, you have a good deal of control over how these values look in the printed letters. For example, when printing dates, you can select from a variety of different formats, such as *04/03/91* or *April 1, 1991*.

Here are the basic steps to follow when creating a set of form letters:

- Create the form letter model in the working copy, using either the actual field names in the data file or using synonyms of your choice for the field names.
- Display the Print Options dialog box, then fill in the name of the data file to use and specify any other print options that are needed.
- Select the records to be merged by entering the appropriate search instructions.
- Specify the order in which the records are to be printed by entering the appropriate sort instructions.
- Specify any synonym names you used instead of actual field names.
- Enter instructions for formatting the values in the various fields.

CREATING THE FORM LETTER MODEL

As an example, assume that you want to generate a series of form letters to a group of clients and that the client data is to be merged from a dBASE file whose records contain the fields shown in Table 14.1.

To begin, you create the *form letter model*, similar to that shown in Figure 14.3. You might want to review the material on form letter models in the section "Creating Form Letters from Address Book Data," above.

As you build the form letter model, place each field name exactly where you want the actual field data to be merged. As usual, each field name must be enclosed by asterisks.

Table 14.1: Fields in the CLIENTS File

FIRST	*(client's first name)*
LAST	*(client's first name)*
STREET	
CITY	
STATE	
ZIP	
PHONE	
BAL_DUE	*(amount owed to you)*
DUE_DATE	

If you want to control the exact placement of a field on the printed output, use preset tab positions. For details, see "Controlling the Position of Merged Data" earlier in this chapter.

You can substitute any synonyms of your choice for the actual field names used in the data file. This substitution is not particularly valuable for dBASE files, where field names are limited to ten characters or fewer (although you can always use a longer and more descriptive synonym for a short field name). However, Professional File field names can be longer than you could believe, so being able to substitute a short synonym can be very useful.

If you do use one or more synonyms, make a note of them: Later on, you'll need to supply these names to Professional Write so that it can make the correspondence between actual field names and your synonyms.

PRINTING THE LETTERS

After you have created the form letter model, you are ready to print the form letters. To begin, you select which data file to use and also fill in any other necessary items in the Print Options dialog box.

For information about filling in the Print Options dialog box, see Chapter 10.

Include any file extension that's part of the name. For example, dBASE files have the .DBF extension.

Selecting the Data File and Other Print Options

1. Make sure that your form letter model is in the working copy.
2. Select *Print working copy* from the File/Print menu (F2) (or press the speed key Ctrl-O). When the Print Options dialog box appears (Figure 14.4):
3. In the line labeled *Data file to merge:*, enter the name of the data file to be used. If the file is not in the default data directory defined by the Setup program, you must include the name of the disk drive and also the full pathname.
4. Enter any other necessary print options.
5. After filling in the Print Options dialog box, press ↵ and a blank search form will appear, similar to that shown in Figure 14.11. Note that these search instructions are quite different from those used with a Professional Write address book.

Selecting the Records to Be Merged

The search form contains a list of the fields in the data file. Note that these are the actual field names, not the synonyms you may have used in the form letter model.

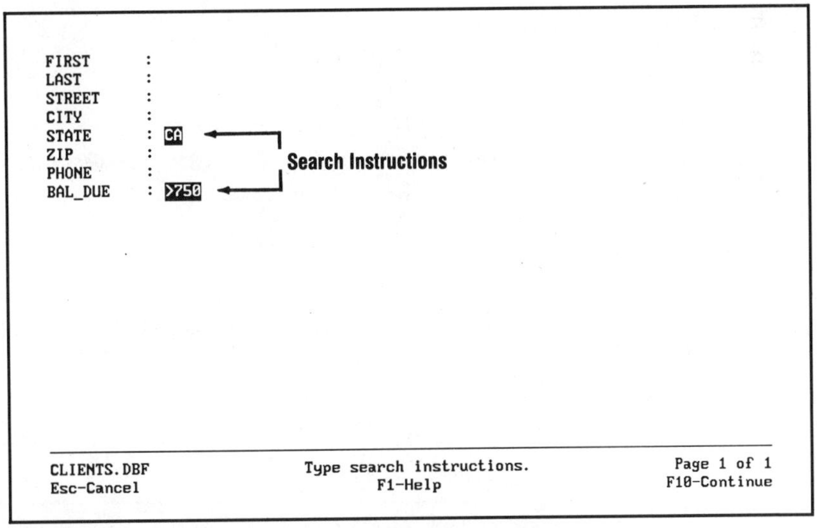

Figure 14.11: Enter search instructions on this form

If you want to merge every record in the data file, just press F10 when the search form appears. However, if you want to select a particular group of records to merge, enter the appropriate *search instructions* on the search form. For example, if you want to merge only those records for clients living in California who owe you more than $750, you would enter the search instructions shown in Figure 14.11

For a complete discussion of the search instructions that can be used with Professional File and dBASE data files, please refer to "Using Search Instructions with Professional File and dBASE Files" later in this chapter.

You can enter search instructions in as many fields as you wish. To move between fields, use the Tab and Shift-Tab keys. When you have finished entering your search instructions, press F10, and another similar form—the Sort and Identifier form—will appear (Figure 14.12).

Specifying the Sort Order and Synonym Information

For a complete discussion of how to use sort instructions, refer to "Using Sort Instructions," below.

If you want to control the order in which letters are printed, you can enter one or more *sort instructions* on the Sort and Identifier form shown in Figure 14.12. If you don't enter any sort instructions, the records will be merged and printed in the order in which they are written on the data file.

For example, in Figure 14.12, the number **1** next to the ZIP field indicates that the letters are to be printed in zip code order. In addition, the number **2** following the LAST field indicates that if two or

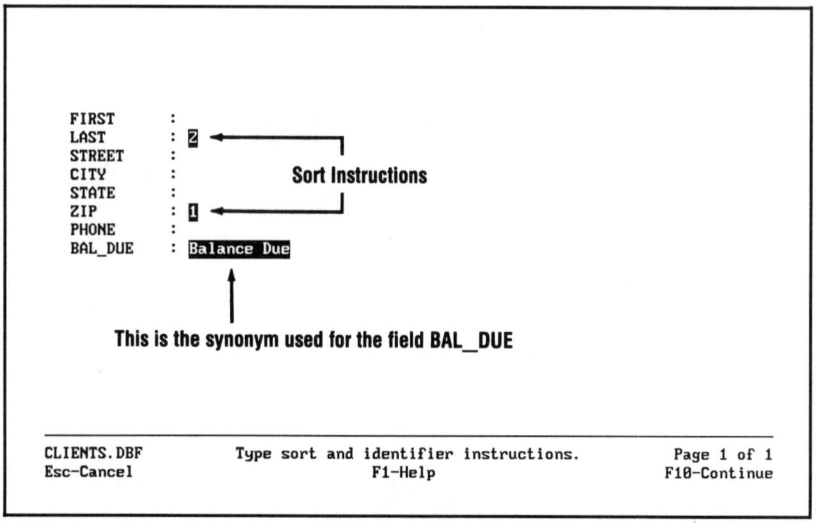

Figure 14.12: Enter sort instructions and synonym information on this form

more letters have the same zip code, then they will be printed in order according to the values in this field, last names.

If you used any synonyms for field names when you built the form letter model, you must enter these synonyms here. For example, if you used the synonym *Balance Due* for the field *BAL_DUE*, then you would enter **Balance due** next to the field name, as shown in Figure 14.12.

If you enter both a sort instruction and a synonym name for the same field, follow these rules:

- The synonym name should not include the asterisks that appear in the form letter model.
- Enter the sort instruction first, then a semicolon, then the synonym name.
- The only blanks that you enter should be those contained in the synonym (for example, *Balance Due*).

When you are done entering any sort instructions and synonyms, press F10 and a blank Format Instructions form will appear (see Figure 14.13).

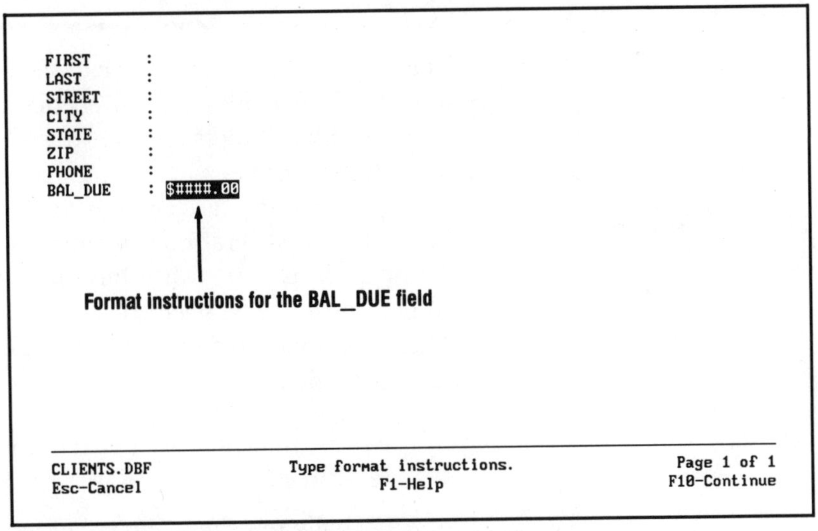

Figure 14.13: Enter format instructions on this form

Controlling the Format of Field Data

You have a great deal of control over the exact appearance of the field values that appear in the printed letters. To exercise this control, you enter various types of *format instructions* on the form shown in Figure 14.13.

For example, in the BAL_DUE field in Figure 14.13, the following characters appear: $####.00. This is a format instruction that forces every printed value for this field to begin with a dollar sign and to end with two decimal places.

For a complete discussion of how to use format instructions, refer to "Using Format Instructions" in this chapter.

You can enter format instructions for as many fields as you wish, or you can leave this form blank. If you don't enter a format instruction for a particular field, then Professional Write will select a default format for that particular data type.

When you have finished entering format instructions, press F10 and the letters will be printed.

SEARCH INSTRUCTIONS FOR PROFESSIONAL FILE AND DBASE FILES

The search instructions that can be used with either Professional File or dBASE data files are entirely different from the search instructions used with a Professional Write address book, and they are also much more extensive.

Search instructions are entered on a search form, such as the one shown in Figure 14.11. You can enter search instructions for as many different fields as you wish. Only those records that satisfy *all of the search instructions* will be selected.

There are many different types of search instructions. You can specify that a field value:

- Exactly matches a specified numeric or character value (such as "Zip code = 96402")
- Partially matches a character value ("first name begins with *Smy*")

- Does not match a particular value ("city is not *Berkeley*")
- Falls within a range of values (age is between 25 and 70)
- Exactly matches one of a specified group of values ("city is either *Oakland* or *Berkeley*")

Search instructions can be used with three different types of fields: Character, Numeric, and Date. Generally, when you use a search instruction for a field, the instruction must match the data type assigned to that field. However, in a few cases Professional Write can recognize a data type even when it's in a field that has been assigned a different type. For instance, a numeric value in a character-type field will be recognized correctly.

INSTRUCTIONS FOR CHARACTER FIELDS

A character field contains strings of characters (as opposed to dates or numbers). You can specify exact matches, partial matches, negative matches, range matches, and combination matches. When making comparisons between two strings of characters, capitalization is not considered.

Exact Matches

Specify the exact value that you want:

SAMPLE SEARCH INSTRUCTION	MATCHING VALUES
John Smith	John Smith, john smith

Partial Matches

Use the following wildcards to select values based on partial matches:

? (stands for any single character)

.. (stands for any group of characters)

SAMPLE SEARCH INSTRUCTION	*MATCHING VALUES*
John..	John, Johnson
..John	John, Upjohn
..John..	John, Johnson, Upjohn
..	any non-blank value

Range Matches

For more information on how characters are ordered, see "The Rules for Character Sorting" later in this chapter.

Specify a range of values. Use the symbol -> (the hyphen then the right angle-bracket):

SAMPLE SEARCH INSTRUCTION	*MATCHING VALUES*
a – >g	Any value starting with any of the letters a through g (regardless of capitalization)

Combination Matches

This is an *either/or* search condition, created by listing two or more individual values separated by semicolons:

SAMPLE SEARCH INSTRUCTION	*MATCHING VALUES*
CA; AZ	CA or AZ
CA..; AZ..	Any value starting either with CA or AZ
CA; AZ..	Either the value CA, or any value starting with AZ.

Negative Matches

Specify what you *don't* want, using the slash character:

SAMPLE SEARCH INSTRUCTION	*MATCHING VALUES*
/John	Any value except John
/..John..	Any value that doesn't contain John

/John..	Any value not beginning with John
/a – >g	Any value not starting with any of the letters a through g.
/CA..; AZ..	Any value not starting either with CA or AZ

Points to Ponder

- When a slash (/) is used, it must be at the beginning of the search instruction.
- A slash applies to the *entire* search instruction (see the last example above).

INSTRUCTIONS FOR NUMERIC FIELDS

A numeric field is one that contains only valid numbers. Professional Write will treat a number correctly, even if it is written in a character-type field, provided that each number begins with a relational operator (these are discussed below).

Exact Matches

SAMPLE SEARCH INSTRUCTION	*MATCHING VALUES*
=25	25, 25.00

Relative Matches

This search condition compares two values, using one of the following *relational operators*:

OPERATOR	*MEANING*
=	is equal to
<	is less than
>	is greater than

⩽	is less than or equal to
⩾	is greater than or equal to

SAMPLE SEARCH INSTRUCTION	*MATCHING VALUES*
=25*	25, 25.00
<25	0, −5, 24, 24.99
>25	25.1, 30
⩽25	0, −5, 24, 24.99, 25
⩾25	25, 25.1, 30

*You must include the equal sign to specify an exact match.

Range Matches

This search condition specifies a range of values, using the symbol -> (hyphen, then the right-angle bracket):

SAMPLE SEARCH INSTRUCTION	*MATCHING VALUES*
=5->25*	Any value between 5.00 and 25.00

*You can omit the equal sign before the second number.

Combination Matches

Use a semicolon to separate values:

SAMPLE SEARCH INSTRUCTION	*MATCHING VALUES*
=5; =25	Either 5 or 25
<5; >25	Any value not in the range between 5.00 and 25.00
=5; 25->50	Either 5, or any value between 25 and 50.

Negative Matches

Specify what you *don't* want, using the slash character:

SAMPLE SEARCH INSTRUCTION	*MATCHING VALUES*
/ =10	Any value not equal to 10.00
/<25	Any value greater than or equal to 25
/ =5; =25	Any value except 5.00 or 25.00
/ =1->100	Any value outside the range between 1 and 100

INSTRUCTIONS FOR DATE FIELDS

Enter the year first in a search instruction, then the month.

A date field is one that has been defined to contain only valid dates. Many different formats are used for holding date values, and Professional Write will recognize nearly all of them. You can use any of the relational operators discussed above in a search instruction. However, when you write a search instruction, you must enter the date in one of the following forms: 1990/12/25 or 90/12/25.

Note that you can use this type of search instruction only with fields that have been specifically designated to contain date-type information. For instance, you can't use these search instructions on a character-type field that happens to contain date values.

SAMPLE SEARCH INSTRUCTION	*MATCHING VALUES*
=1989/12/25	December 25, 1989
>1985/01/05	Any date after Jan. 5, 1985
<85/01/05	Any date before Jan. 5, 1985

EXAMPLES USING SEARCH INSTRUCTIONS

A few examples will help you see how to use the various types of search instructions described above. The fields of the CLIENTS file shown in Table 14.1 will be used.

Example: Find all clients who live in Berkeley, California.

Search Instructions:

CITY: Berkeley

STATE: CA

Example: Find all clients who live either in Berkeley or Oakland (both in California).

Search Instructions:

CITY: Berkeley; Oakland

STATE: CA

Example: Find all clients whose last names begin with the letters A through G.

Search Instructions:

LAST: A -> G

Example: Find all clients who don't live in Berkeley or Oakland (both in California).

Search Instructions:

CITY: /Berkeley; Oakland

STATE: /CA

Note that if you leave off the condition on STATE, any client living in Oakland, Tennessee, would be incorrectly excluded.

Example: Find all clients who live in San Francisco and who don't owe you any money.

Search Instructions:

CITY: San Francisco

BAL_DUE: =0.0

You can't use sort instructions with a Professional Write address book.

SORT INSTRUCTIONS FOR PROFESSIONAL FILE AND DBASE FILES

When merging data from either a Professional File or a dBASE data file, you may want to control the order in which form letters are printed. To do this, enter the appropriate sort instructions on a Sort and Identifier form similar to that shown in Figure 14.12. You can sort on the values of any type of field.

When you issue sort instructions, you can select the following:

- The *primary sort field*. Sorting is done on the basis of the values of this field.
- The *secondary sort field*. For equal values in the primary sort field, sorting will be done on the basis of the values of this field.
- Whether the sort is done in ascending or descending order.

THE BASIC SORT INSTRUCTIONS

Use these instructions for controlling sorting:

1: Enter this value next to the primary sort field

2: Enter this value next to the secondary sort field

D: Enter this character next to a field to be sorted in descending order

N: Use this character to specify a numeric sort

Points to Ponder

Here are a few things to keep in mind when using sort instructions:

- If you want to sort on one field only, enter the number 1 next to that field name.
- By default, sorting is normally done in ascending order.
- If you want to do a numeric sort you must always use the **N** sort instruction.

- If you include more than one sort instruction in a field, the number 1 or 2 must come first, then the remaining instructions.
- If more than one sort instruction is used for a field, place them together (for example, *1D* or *2N*).

AN EXAMPLE OF SORTING

Using the fields shown in Table 14.1, Figure 14.14 shows how to use a set of sort instructions. The sorting will be done first on the field BAL_DUE. Because a numeric sort is to be done, the sort instruction N is included. Also, because the sort instruction D is included, the sort will be done in descending order. Finally, if two or more records have the same value for this field, then they will be sorted by the values of the field LAST.

THE RULES FOR CHARACTER SORTING

When a pair of character values is compared during the sorting process, the "smaller" value is moved up or down, depending on whether the sort is ascending or descending. When Professional Write compares two character values, it strips off any leading blanks, then makes a character-by-character comparison. As soon as a

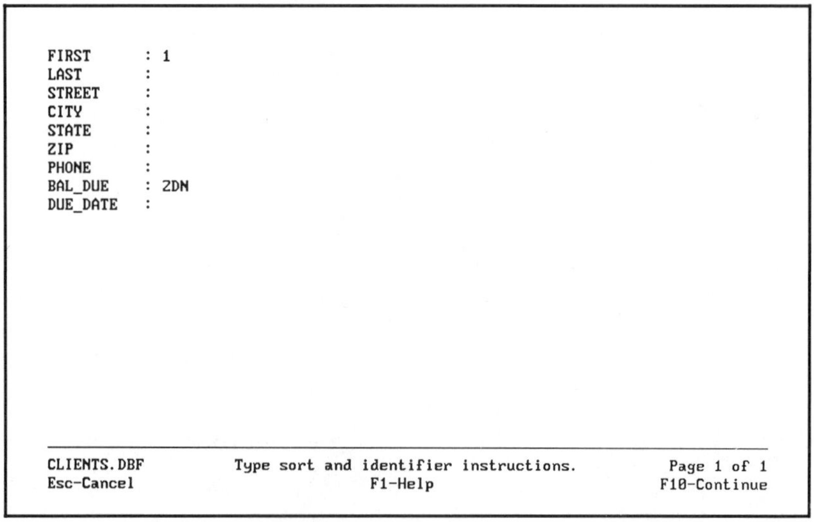

Figure 14.14: A set of sort instructions

mismatch is found between two corresponding characters, the "lower" of those two characters determines which of the two strings will appear first in the sorted list.

In comparing pairs of characters, the following *sort order* is used:

1. Blank space (the lowest of all characters)
2. Special characters, such as ?, $, and #.
3. Digits (0–9)
4. Letters (A–Z) *(uppercase and lowercase are equivalent)*

According to this sort order, any special character is lower than any digit or letter; and any digit is lower than any letter. In fact, the special characters have their own sort order, but we'll skip that complication here.

Table 14.2 illlustrates these rules with several examples. Notice that a blank space within a character value is significant. Digits are

Table 14.2: Sorting Examples

This entry is less than	This entry
$	1
1	2
1	11
21	1
1 3	12
A	B
A	AA
A B	AA
AAAAA	AB
A B	A$B

All special characters come before either digits or letters. No distinction is made between uppercase and lowercase.

treated as ordinary characters when used in a character sort, and this can lead to problems. For example, the value "12" comes before the value "2" when they are treated as characters. If you plan to sort on a series of numeric values, you must use the **N** sort instruction for that field.

One final note about sorting should be mentioned. If you plan to do any sorting, you must specify a *work drive* in the Setup program. This drive is used for temporary storage during the sorting process. See Appendix A for details about using the Setup program.

FORMAT INSTRUCTIONS FOR PROFESSIONAL FILE AND DBASE FILES

When merging data from either a Professional File or a dBASE data file, you may want to control the format of the merged data that appears in the form letters. To do this, you enter the appropriate *format instructions* on the Format Instructions display (Figure 14.13). If you don't enter a format instruction for a field, then its values will be printed in their original form in the data file.

You can use format instructions for the following data types:

- Character
- Numeric
- Date
- Time

Most format instructions consist of a set of single characters that describes how to treat corresponding characters in the data file. For example, suppose you write the instruction "AAaaaaaaaa" for a particular field. This instruction has the following meaning: For each printed value of this field, capitalize the first two letters, then print the remaining eight letters in lowercase.

FORMAT INSTRUCTIONS FOR CHARACTER FIELDS

These instructions apply to fields containing character values. You can control the capitalization of each character value, as well as allow for digits within the field. If you have trouble understanding the following information, refer to the examples that follow; they'll help you to get a grip on how these instructions work.

FORMAT INSTRUCTION	*MEANING*
a	Print a lowercase letter
A	Print an uppercase letter
N or n	Print a digit (0–9)
x	Print either a number or a lowercase letter
X	Print either a number or an uppercase letter
E or e	Print either a number or a letter in its original capitalization
A Special character	Insert this character, shifting data over to make room for it. You can use nearly all of the special characters on the keyboard, such as #, ?, and !.
¦	Determines whether the printed values are left- or right-justified (see below for details). Also permits variable-length data.

Points to Ponder

- If there isn't an exact one-to-one correspondence between the characters in a search instruction and the character in the field value, then the ¦ character must be either the first or last character of the instruction.

- If a format instruction begins with ¦, then trailing blanks are stripped from the printed value.
- If a format instruction ends with ¦, then the number of places indicated by the format instruction is printed (including leading blanks), and the value is right-justified.
- If a value contains one or more digits, and you don't put N or E in the corresponding positions in the format instruction, then other parts of the format instruction may not work correctly (such as the insertion of special characters).
- When a special character is inserted, any text to the right is shifted to make room, unless the special character falls on a blank, in which case the blank is replaced by the character.

Examples

FORMAT INSTRUCTION	*FIELD VALUE*	*PRINTED VALUE*
Aaaa	john	John
¦Aaaaaaaaaaaaa	john	John
¦aaaaaaaaaaaaa	John	john
Aaaaaaaaaaaaaa¦	John	^^^^^^^^^^John**
Aaaaaaaaaaaaaa*	john	john
XXX-XXX-XXXX	415 555 1212	415-555-1212
XXX-XXX-XXXX	415-555-1212	415-555-1212
XXX-XXX-XXXX	4155551212	415-555-1212
(XXX)XXX-XXXX	(415)555-1212	

*This instruction doesn't work, because the total number of characters in the format instruction doesn't match the number of characters in the field value. Consequently, the ¦ character must be included as part of the format instruction.

** ^ = space

FORMAT INSTRUCTIONS FOR NUMERIC FIELDS

These instructions apply to fields containing numeric values. You can exercise a great deal of control over the appearance of printed numbers. Some instructions consist of a single character that controls the appearance of corresponding digits when printed. Other instructions determine the printing of special characters like commas, minus signs, and so on. Several examples at the end of this section will help you understand these instructions.

FORMAT INSTRUCTION	*MEANING*
#	Print a digit; Don't print a leading blank, but do print a trailing zero.
9	Print a digit; Print a leading blank or a trailing zero.
0	Print a digit; Print a trailing zero, or print a zero for a leading blank.
*	Print a digit; Print an asterisk for an unused leading position.
.	Print a decimal point, moving over any digits to the right.
,	Print a comma.
-	Print a minus sign for a negative number, or no sign for a positive number.
+	Print a plus or minus sign, depending on whether the value is positive or negative.
<> or ()	Print <> or () around the number if it's negative.
$ or £	Print this character.
"Text"	Print any characters exactly as they appear in the instruction. This includes any letters or special characters on your keyboard. Any text must be enclosed in double quotes.

Points to Ponder

- You can't put an asterisk after a decimal point in an instruction.
- If you include text as part of an instruction, make sure that it's enclosed by double quotes.
- Text can't be inserted in the middle of an instruction. Place it either at the beginning or the end.

Examples

FORMAT INSTRUCTION	*FIELD VALUE*	*PRINTED VALUE*
999.99	515.00	515.00
999.99	515	515.00
999.99	25	^25.00*
###.00	25	25.00
000.00	25	025.00
$###.##	25	$25.00
$****.99	25	$**25.00
999.99" dollars."	25	^25.00 dollars.
(###.##)	-25	(25.00)
(###.##)	25	25.00

* ^ = space

FORMAT INSTRUCTIONS FOR DATE FIELDS

You can control the appearance of values from fields defined to hold date-type information. You can use any of the format instructions described below with any dBASE or Professional File field that's been defined specifically to hold date values. This is true regardless of the format of the values in the field.

As before, if the instructions below seem a bit confusing, the examples that follow should help clarify things.

FORMAT INSTRUCTION	*MEANING*
0y	Print the year as a two-digit number (such as *87*, *88*, *89*).
yy	Print the year as either a one- or two-digit number.
yyyy	Print the year as a four-digit number (such as *1990*).
0m	Print the month as a two-digit number.
mm	Print the month as a one- or two-digit number (such as *1* or *11*).
January	Print each month as its full name (such as *February*, *March*).
Jan.	Print each month as a three-letter abbreviation.
0d	Print the day as a two-digit number.
dd	Print the day as a one- or two-digit number.
Separators	You can use almost any special character to separate the three parts of a date (month, day, and year). The most common separators are the blank space, slash (/), and colon (:). (See examples below.)

Points to Ponder

- If the format instruction *yyyy* is used for the year, and if a value for the year is supplied as a two-digit number (such as in *04/11/87*), the century is assumed to be 1900s.
- If a month instruction such as *Jan.* is used, the capitalization and punctuation used in this instruction is duplicated in all month values printed. For example, if your format instruction is *Jan* then dates will be output as *Feb*, *Mar*, etc.

- If Professional Write can't recognize the form of a date value in a field, it prints the contents of the field exactly as it appears in the data file.
- Generally, format instructions won't be able to interpret a date value in a field unless that field has been specifically designated to hold date-type values.

Examples

FORMAT INSTRUCTION	*FIELD VALUE*	*PRINTED VALUE*
January dd, yyyy	04/29/90	April 29, 1990
mm/dd/yy	04/29/90	4/29/90
0m/0d/yy	04/29/90	04/29/90
mm:dd:yy	04/29/90	4:29:90
Jan. dd, yyyy	01/05/90	Jan. 5, 1990

FORMAT INSTRUCTIONS FOR TIME FIELDS

You can control the appearance of values from fields that contain time information. Generally, these format instructions will work provided that the data in a field can be recognized as a valid time value.

FORMAT INSTRUCTION	*MEANING*
0h	Print the hour as a two-digit number.
hh	Print the hour as either a one- or two-digit number.
0m	Print the number of minutes as a two-digit number.
mm	Print the number of minutes as either a one- or two-digit number.

0s	Print the number of seconds as a two-digit number.
ss	Print the number of seconds as either a one- or two-digit number.
c0	Print the number of centiseconds (hundredths of a second) as a two-digit number.
cc	Print the number of centiseconds as a one- or two-digit number.
Separators	You can use almost any special character to separate the parts of a time value. The most common separators are the slash (/) and the colon (:).
"Text"	Print any characters exactly as they appear in the instruction. This includes any letters or special characters on your keyboard. Any text must be enclosed in double quotes.
a.m or p.m.	Print this text, punctuated and capitalized exactly as it appears in the instruction.

Points to Ponder

- If you use the instruction *cc*, then the output may be confusing. For instance, see the fourth example below.
- If you use either *AM* or *PM* as part of an instruction, it must come after the parts that describe the time itself.
- Time values are not rounded. For instance, in the sixth example below the printed time is *5:15*, although the actual time is closer to 5:16.

Examples

FORMAT INSTRUCTION	*FIELD VALUE*	*PRINTED VALUE*
hh:mm:ss	5:1:25	5:1:25
0h:0m:ss	5:1:25	05:01:25

hh:mm:ss.c0	5:15:25.05	5:15:25.05
hh:mm:ss.cc	5:15:25.05	5:15:25.5
"Current time: " hh:mm	5:15:25	Current time: 5:15
hh:mm	5:15:55	5:15
0h/0m/0s AM	5:01:55	05/01/55 AM

15 WORKING WITH MACROS

IF YOU HAVE TO PERFORM THE SAME TASKS WITH Professional Write on a routine basis, you may be able to simplify your work by automating it, using a *macro*. A macro is a set of keystrokes that you can "play back" by hitting a single key combination. For instance, suppose that you routinely enter the name of your organization at the top of each letter you write. You can set up a macro to do this for you: Press the appropriate macro key combination and the letterhead will automatically be entered.

To create a macro, you tell Professional Write to begin recording keystrokes, and then you enter the keystrokes to perform whatever operation you want. When you have finished, you tell Professional Write to stop recording. Then you assign an Alt-key combination (Alt plus another key) as the name of the macro you have just recorded. From then on, whenever you press that Alt-key combination, your recorded keystrokes will be played back exactly as you entered them.

You can have a macro pause during playback to allow you to enter text from the keyboard. For example, if you routinely use an address book, you can create a macro to select the address book and then pause temporarily to allow you to enter the name of the person whose address or phone number you want to find.

You can create a macro to record just about anything you can do within Professional Write, with one exception: You can't access the Preview mode while recording a macro.

You can begin a macro from anyplace within Professional Write except Preview. For instance, you can begin recording a macro from the Edit screen, a dialog box, or even the Main menu.

You can use macros effectively in countless ways. A few examples are given at the end of this chapter, and Chapter 16 is filled with additional examples of different ways to use macros. As you work with Professional Write, you'll probably find many uses for macros. Up to 35 different macros can be stored, and at any time you can delete or replace a macro that you have previously defined.

You have 35 different macro names to use: Alt-A through Alt-Z and Alt-1 to Alt-9. However, you can't use Alt-0 because that's the speed key for creating macros. For each macro you create, try to select a letter or number that is somehow related to the action performed by that macro. For instance, if you create a macro to retrieve a file, you might name it Alt-R (R for *retrieve*). Obviously, you can do this only to a limited extent (what would X stand for?). If you forget the name you assigned to a macro, you can list all of the current macros on the screen.

HOW TO CREATE AND USE A MACRO

To create a macro, begin by deciding exactly what you want to do. Then, position Professional Write at the precise location where you want the macro to begin. For example, if you want to start the macro from the Main menu, display that menu. Next, tell Professional Write to begin recording the macro. From then on, every keystroke you enter will be recorded as part of the macro. When you are finished, tell Professional Write to stop recording and then assign the Alt-key combination you want as the name of the macro.

EXAMPLE: CREATING A STANDARD LETTERHEAD

This first example shows how to create a macro to automatically enter a standard letterhead (shown in Figure 15.1) at the top of a blank working copy. The key combination Alt-T (T for *tuners*) will be assigned to the macro.

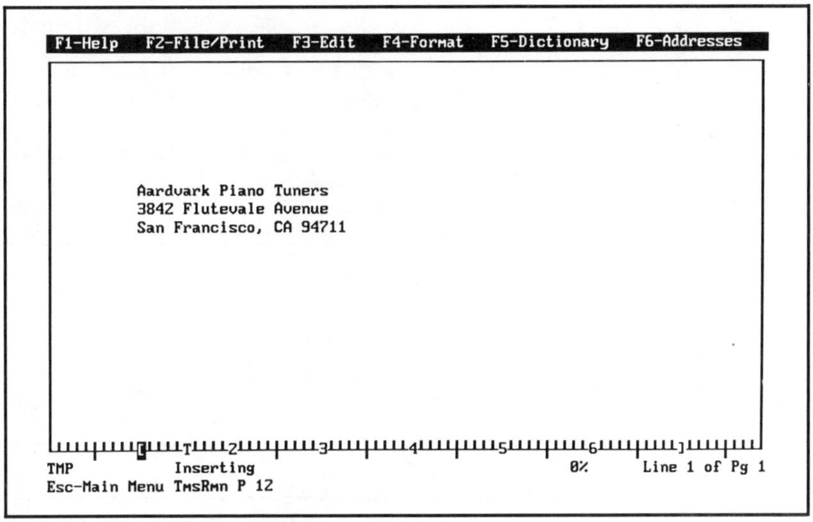

Figure 15.1: You can create a macro to generate this letterhead

When you are recording a macro, the word **Recording** appears at the bottom of the screen.

1. Position the cursor where you want the macro to begin (in this example, it's the top of the document).
2. Begin creating the macro: Select *Use macros* from the File/-Print menu (F2), or press the speed key Alt-0 (zero).
3. When the Macros menu appears (Figure 15.2), select *Record a macro*. You'll see a message telling you that you're about to begin recording a macro. Just press ↵ to go on.
4. Begin entering the keystrokes you want to become part of the macro. In this example, enter the three lines shown in Figure 15.1, and then press ↵ twice to skip down two lines.
5. After you have finished entering all of your keystrokes, stop recording: Press Alt-0, and a menu of choices is displayed (Figure 15.3). At this point, you have the following options:
   - Pause to allow user input (this option is discussed later)
   - End the recording process and save the keystrokes
   - Resume recording keystrokes (press Esc)
   - Cancel the entire operation
6. In this case, you'll save the macro: Select *End and save recorded keystrokes*. The Save Recorded Keystrokes menu appears (Figure 15.4).
7. Select the key combination (that is, the macro name) you want to assign to this macro. In this case, scroll through the list and highlight *Alt-T*.
8. Enter a short description of the macro (up to 20 characters), then press ↵.

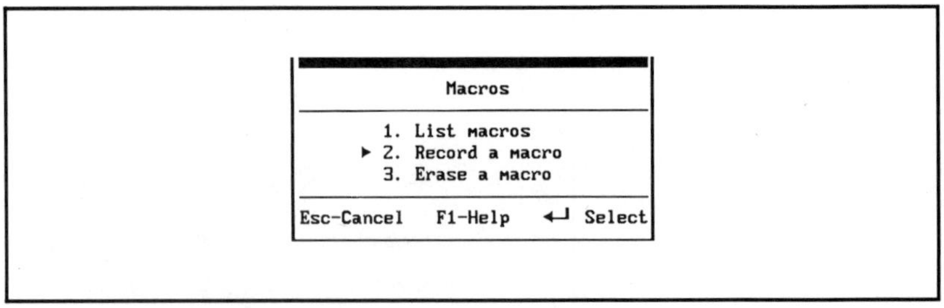

Figure 15.2: The Macros menu

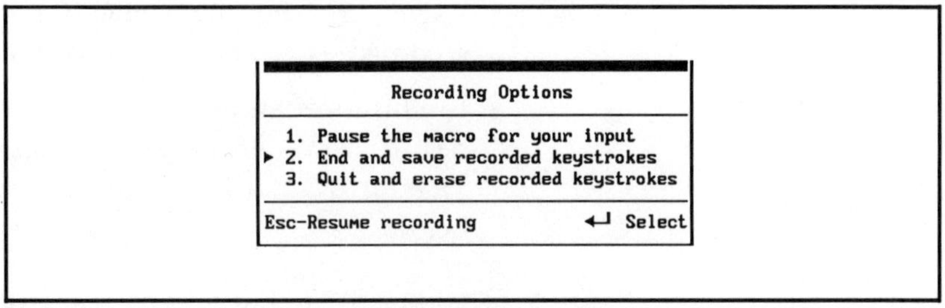

Figure 15.3: Your options while recording a macro

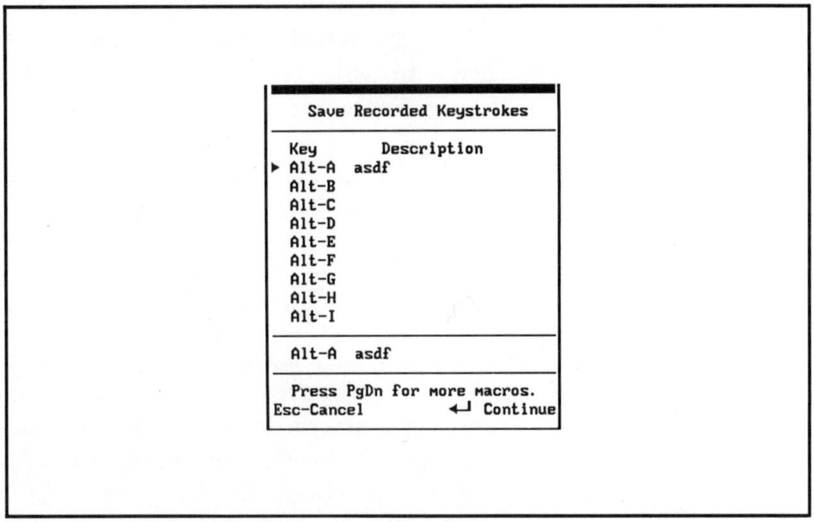

Figure 15.4: Select the macro name from this menu

Your macro is now stored in the file PW.MAC, in the same directory as the other Professional Write files, where it will remain until you delete or replace it (or until a system crash destroys the file).

Points to Ponder

- When recording a macro, you can include any set of keystrokes you like, with one exception—you can't play back another macro.
- If you select a menu item as part of a macro, enter the number of that item—don't use the cursor-control keys to highlight the item you want.

- As you are recording a macro, *every single keystroke* you enter is recorded—even errors that you make and then correct.
- If you make an error while recording a macro, it's best to begin over again because Professional Write has a limited amount of total available space for recording macros (see below).

Professional Write has a limited amount of *total* space for storing macros. For a hard-disk computer, this amounts to approximately 1,400 keystrokes for all of the macros (for floppy-disk computers, the total is about 600). You can allocate this total available space in any way you wish. For example, you could use it all up in one giant macro containing a huge amount of text. It is more likely, however, that each of your macros will use only a few keystrokes, perhaps including a couple of text lines, so that you'll probably have enough space for as many macros as you can dream up.

HOW TO PLAY BACK A MACRO

To play back a macro that has been previously recorded, all you have to do is press its name, that is, the Alt-key combination for that particular macro. Professional Write will play back every keystroke you pressed when the macro was recorded.

Playing Back under the Right Circumstances

Whenever you play back a macro, make sure that Professional Write is in the proper condition to play back the macro. For instance, if you create a macro to select *Create/Edit* from the Main menu and then print a particular file, make sure that the Main menu is displayed before playing back that macro.

If your macro is designed to create output on the printer, the printer must be ready to receive input from the computer. Otherwise, Professional Write pauses with a "Printer not ready" message, which is not what the macro expects. This then throws off the sequence of keystrokes being played back, and the macro won't do what it is supposed to.

DISPLAYING A LIST OF YOUR MACROS

If you can't remember the name of a particular macro, you can display a list of all existing macros. When you find the correct one, you can play it back directly from the displayed list:

1. Select *Use macros* from the File/Print menu (F2), or press Alt-0.
2. Select *List macros* from the Macros menu. When the list of macros appears:
3. Scroll through the list of macro definitions (Figure 15.5), using the PgDn and PgUp keys, until you find the correct macro.
4. To play back the macro you want, highlight it and then press ↵.

MACROS THAT WAIT FOR INPUT

You can create a macro that will pause while it's playing back, letting you enter whatever you wish. For instance, you could create a macro that prints data from an address book; at the appropriate time,

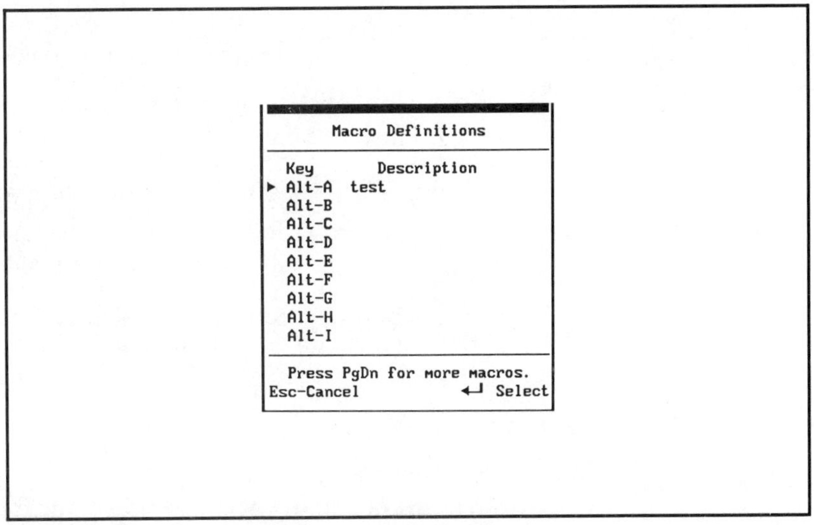

Figure 15.5: This menu lists all currently defined macros

the macro pauses to allow you to enter specific search instructions so that only select portions of the address book are output. The steps for creating this type of macro are nearly the same as for ordinary macros.

CREATING A MACRO

To illustrate how this type of macro works, let's create one that outputs the following sentences:

> My name is *My Name*. Please send me a letter.

The italicized part of this sentence is *variable information* that you input while the macro is playing back. A pause in macro execution allows you to do this.

Assuming that the Edit screen is displayed, here are the steps for creating the macro:

1. Begin creating the macro: Press Alt-0 to display the Macros menu, select *Record a macro*, and then press ↵ to begin recording the macro.
2. Enter the following text: **My name is** {*include an ending space*}
3. Create a pause in the macro: Press Alt-0, then select *Pause the macro for your input*. Press ↵ to continue.
4. Enter your name. *This part is not recorded* (see "A Point of Confusion," below).
5. Press F9 to resume recording.
6. Enter the following text: **. Please send me a letter.** (Note the period (.) preceding the word "Please.")
7. End macro recording: Press Alt-0, select *End and save recorded keystrokes*, and then select an Alt-key combination for the macro name.

A Point of Confusion

At the beginning of step 4 above, the following message appears at the bottom of the screen: **Recording paused. Type your data and then**

press F9. This is a little confusing because you are creating a macro, not entering real data. In step 4, you can enter whatever you want, but *it's not recorded.*

The reason for this part of the macro is that in some circumstances you must enter data in order for the correct sequence of events to occur while the macro is being recorded. For example, suppose you are creating a macro to retrieve a document into the working copy, and the macro pauses at the Filename dialog box so that you can enter the name of the document to be retrieved. While you are creating the macro, you must enter a document name at this point, or Professional Write won't be able to proceed correctly. (Later in this chapter you'll see an example of a macro that retrieves a file for you.)

PLAYING BACK THE MACRO

Let's see what happens when you play back this macro:

1. Before beginning, make sure that the Edit screen is displayed. (Can you understand why?)
2. Start playing back the macro: Press the Alt-key combination assigned to the macro. The following immediately appears on the screen, starting at the current cursor location: **My name is**
3. Now enter whatever you want. This is the *variable data.* (Notice the message at the bottom of the screen.)
4. After you finish entering the variable data, press F9. The macro continues playing back, and you'll see the following appear: **. Please send me a letter.**

Points to Ponder

If you forget to press F9 after entering the variable data, but instead continue whatever you are doing, the macro remains in a paused state, waiting to play back the rest of its recorded keystrokes. Sooner or later, you'll have to press F9 to let the macro play itself out. Then you may have to clean up the mess resulting from the effects of the unwanted keystrokes.

MACROS WITH SEVERAL PAUSES

You can introduce as many pauses as you need in a single macro, using the steps outlined in the above example. To create each pause:

1. Press Alt-0.
2. Select *Pause the macro for your input*, and then press ↵.
3. Enter whatever variable data you want.
4. Press F9 to resume recording.

When the macro is played back, it will wait for your input at each pause you created.

HANDLING SPECIAL CIRCUMSTANCES

When you create a macro, you expect to use it later on in circumstances similar to those in which the macro was created. This doesn't always happen, and various types of strange results can occur.

To interrupt playback of a macro, press Alt-0.

The most obvious error occurs when you press the wrong macro name. Usually, you'll immediately get the idea that something is wrong because you'll probably see something completely unexpected appear on the screen—a clue that either the macro isn't working properly, or you played back the wrong macro.

If Professional Write gets stuck while the macro is playing back, try pressing Esc until something familiar appears on the screen. Then, check the bottom of the screen: If *Playback* appears, the macro is still trying to go on. In that case, press Alt-0 to cancel the macro playback.

If Professional Write encounters an unusual circumstance while a macro is being played back, it may cancel the playback, or it may simply continue the playback hoping for the best.

For example, suppose you create a macro that retrieves a file into the working copy, then performs some standard operation on that file. As part of the playback, the macro pauses to allow you to enter the file name. If you enter a file name that can't be found, Professional Write not only issues a message to that effect, but it then continues to play back the macro. The result is a fairly messy looking screen, but usually no substantial damage is done.

DELETING AND EDITING MACROS

You can delete a macro simply by selecting it from the appropriate menus:

1. Select *Use macros* from the File/Print menu (F2), or press Alt-0.
2. Select *Erase a macro* from the Macros menu.
3. Select the macro you want from the Erase a Macro menu (Figure 15.6): highlight the macro name and then press ↵.
4. Professional Write gives you a chance to change your mind: Press ↵ to erase the macro, or press Esc to forget the whole thing.

Unfortunately, there is no simple way to edit an existing macro. You must reenter the entire macro, being careful to make the changes you want. This can be a considerable inconvenience if you want to make a tiny change to a long macro, but there is no alternative.

EXAMPLE: RETRIEVING A DOCUMENT

This example demonstrates how to use a macro to automatically enter most of the keystrokes for retrieving a Professional Write document. This macro is designed to be used from the Main menu. When you start the macro, it will enter the Edit screen and then go through the steps for retrieving a document, pausing to allow you to enter the name of the document you want.

Here are the steps for creating this macro:

1. Display the Main menu.
2. Begin macro recording.
3. Press **1** to Select *Create/Edit* from the menu.
4. Begin retrieving a file: Press Ctrl-G.
5. Pause the macro: Press Alt-0, **1**, ↵.
6. Enter the name of a file containing one of your documents.

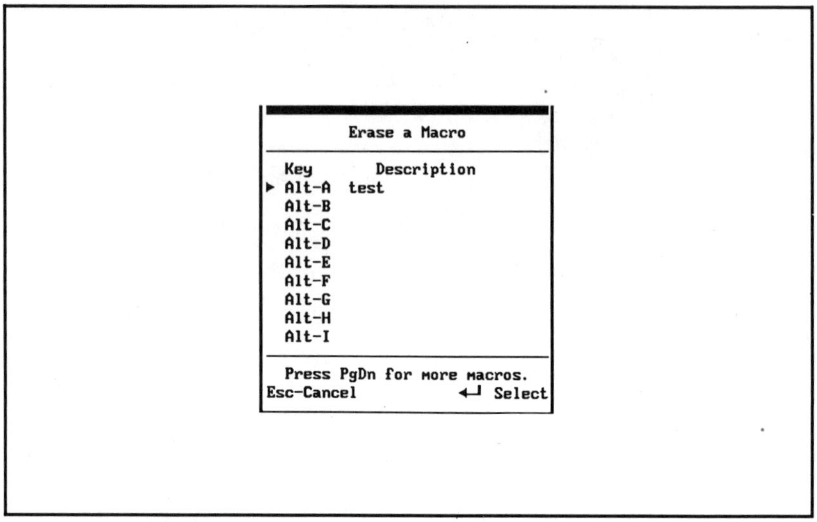

Figure 15.6: Select the macro to be erased from this menu

7. Press F9 to resume macro recording.
8. Press ↵. The document you named should be retrieved.
9. Stop macro recording and assign a name to the macro.

PLAYING BACK THE MACRO

To play back this macro, display the Main menu, and then simply press the Alt-key combination you assigned in step 9 above. The entire series of keystrokes you recorded will be played back exactly as you recorded them. When the macro pauses, enter whatever variable data is necessary and then press F9 to resume the macro playback.

Points to Ponder

- This macro should be run from an empty working copy. Otherwise, if you try to retrieve a document, Professional Write might display a message to the effect that you are about to overwrite information that hasn't been saved.
- If you accidentally press ↵ instead of F9 after entering the document name, the document will be retrieved, but

the message *Playback paused. Type your data and then press F9* will continue to appear on the bottom of the screen. When you eventually do press F9, an extra blank line will appear at the current cursor position because of the final ↵ supplied by the macro.

- If the document you retrieve isn't a normal Professional Write document, you'll have to select the document type and then press ↵.

16 Using Macros for Advanced Applications

THERE IS VIRTUALLY NO LIMIT TO THE OPERATIONS that can be incorporated into a macro. As you gain experience with Professional Write, you may begin to notice that you perform a particular set of operations over and over—perhaps with only minor changes from one time to the next. This kind of routine task is an ideal candidate for a macro. Several different macros for different types of applications are described in this chapter. You may want to modify some of them, adapting them to suit your particular needs.

As you read this chapter, pay particular attention to the sections labeled "Points to Ponder." They help to explain why in some circumstances a macro may not work correctly. If you understand what these circumstances are (a printer isn't ready, you pressed the wrong key, and so on), you can probably figure out why a macro has failed to work—and, even more important, how to avoid these failures.

CHANGING THE STANDARD PRINTER

If you are working with two printers, you may periodically want to use the Setup program to switch the printer currently assigned to Printer 1. (Remember that there's not much point in ever using Printer 2 because you can't use different fonts with it.) To automate this process, you can create two macros, one for selecting each of your printers as Printer 1.

This section will describe how to create a macro to select the HP LaserJet II as Printer 1. This macro will:

- Select the HP LaserJet II as Printer 1
- Select *B_TMS Proportional 1* as Cartridge 1
- Select *AC-TmsRmn & Helv Base Set* as the soft font family
- Select *AC TmsRmn Portrait 12* as the regular font

CREATING THE MACRO

Some of the steps described below may seem very roundabout, but they are necessary to guarantee that the correct selections are made, regardless of the previously assigned printer (for additional explanations, see "Starting from a Known Position," below).

To create the macro, carefully follow these steps:

1. Begin macro recording (from *anywhere* inside Professional Write).
2. Press Esc five times.* (The Main menu should appear.)
3. Start the Setup program: Press **2**.
4. Select the HP LaserJet II as Printer 1:
   - Press **1**;
   - Press Pg Up three times and then PgDn once*;
   - Highlight *HpLJ Series II* and then press ↵.
5. Select Cartridge 1:
   - Press **1**;
   - Press PgDn once and then PgUp twice*:
   - Highlight *B-TMS Proportional 1* and then press ↵.
6. Select the soft font family:
   - Press **3**;
   - Press PgDn once and then PgUp once*;
   - Highlight *Ac-TmsRmn & Helv Base Set* and then press ↵.
7. Select the regular font:
   - Press **4**;
   - Press PgDn once and then PgUp four times *;
   - Highlight *AC-TmsRmn Portrait 12* and then press ↵.
8. Return to the Edit screen: Press Esc twice and then press **1**.
9. Turn off macro recording and assign a name to the macro.

   *These steps must be carried out exactly as directed, regardless of what the screen displays!

Starting from a Known Position

Several of the above steps (those marked with asterisks) seem to do a lot of extra button pushing for no apparent reason. Here's the idea behind all this button pushing: As a macro is recording, it notes every keystroke you enter, including each ↑ and ↓ keystroke you use to select a menu item. This can lead to problems because the number of required ↓ or ↑ keystrokes depends on your starting point on the screen.

To understand the problem better, look at the details for selecting the new printer in step 4 above: When you press **1** to select Printer 1, *the previous selection appears highlighted*. For instance, if the IBM Color Printer was previously assigned as Printer 1, it would be highlighted (Figure 16.1.)

If you were to press the ↑ or ↓ keys to highlight the new printer, those exact keystrokes would be recorded. Then, when you later played back the macro, it would work correctly *only if you started from the same previous location*; namely the IBM color printer.

This means that the macro would work properly whenever the IBM printer was assigned; but it would not work correctly if you ran it when any other printer was assigned.

To solve this problem, you must make sure that *each time you make a menu selection, you start from the same location, regardless of the previous selection*. Here's the trick to accomplish this: Begin by pressing either PgDn or PgUp to guarantee that you scroll *off of* the screen you want to eventually display. Then scroll back to that screen and select the item you want.

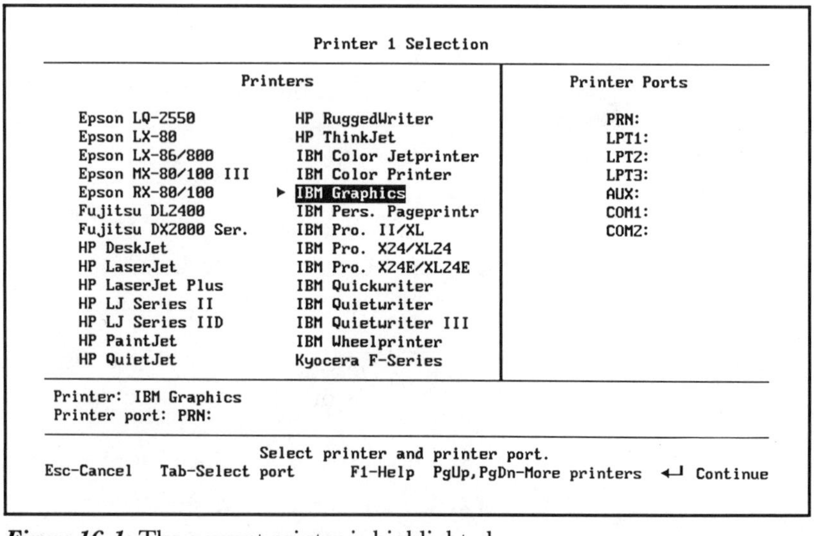

Figure 16.1: The current printer is highlighted

The crucial point is that when you then move back to the display containing the printer you want, *the highlighting is now at the top of the menu*. You can now use the ↓ key to highlight the new printer and then select it.

Points to Ponder

- The reason for step 2 above is to allow you to run the macro from anywhere within Professional Write. For instance, if you are deep within a set of menu choices, you can always back out to the Edit screen by pressing Esc enough times. Pressing it once more returns you to the Main menu. The extra Esc keystrokes do no harm, because they are ignored when the Main menu is displayed.
- You can easily modify the above steps for whatever printers, cartridges, etc., you want to use.
- This macro will work as long as Professional Write's list of printers doesn't change. If you someday get an update for the software, you may need to recreate the macro.

PLAYING BACK THE MACRO

You can play back this macro from just about anywhere inside Professional Write: Press the name of the macro (that is, the Alt-key combination) to begin playback.

When the macro is finished, it returns to the Edit screen, but *probably not to where you were in Professional Write when you began playing back the macro.*

CHANGING THE REGULAR FONT

Suppose that you often use a variety of choices for the regular font. For example, you might use a Times Roman typeface for some documents, but for others you might want to use something a little fancier.

You can create a macro to select a particular font as new regular font, following the steps outlined in the previous example as a guide. For instance, here's how to select Helvetica 12 point as the regular font (assuming that it's accessible from the current selections of cartridges and soft font family):

1. Begin macro recording (from anywhere inside Professional Write).
2. Press Esc five times. The Main menu should appear.
3. Enter Setup and select the current printer (you have to do this in order to select the new regular font): Press **2**, **1**, and then ↵.
4. Select the regular font:
   - Press **4**;
   - Press PgUp four times to scroll to the top of the font selections.
   - Press PgDn as many times as necessary to display Helvetica 12 point Portrait.
   - Highlight the font and then press ↵.
5. Return to the Edit screen: Press Esc twice and then press **1**.
6. Turn off macro recording and assign a name to the macro.

Points to Ponder

You can create many different macros to change from one setup to another, using the above two macros as guides. For instance, you might want to create one macro to change to a different cartridge and perhaps another macro to select a particular soft font family. Or, you might have one or two sets of standard printer control codes that you use for different documents. You could create a macro for each of these changes and save yourself quite a bit of work.

SWITCHING BETWEEN FONT SIZES

You can improve the appearance of a document by using different size fonts for titles and headings. You can make this font switching a breeze by creating a different macro to select each font. For example, you could create a macro for assigning a large font to your headings, perhaps naming it Alt-H (H for *heading*). To create the heading, you simply type it in, select it as a block, and then press Alt-H.

Here's a sample macro to select Times Roman 18 Point Bold as the font for a heading. This macro assumes that this particular font is accessible to your printer, either as a built-in font or through a cartridge or a soft font family.

Remember: To change the font of some text, you must first select that text as a block. The macro can't do this for you, so it must begin macro recording *after* you make the selection.

Here are the steps for creating the macro:

This macro won't work for rectangular blocks.

1. Select any text block. You can choose any text because the block is only a model to be used by Professional Write while creating the macro.
2. Turn on macro recording.
3. Display the Text Block Operations menu: Press F10.
4. Select a new font: Press 4. When the font menu appears:
5. Press PgDn enough times to scroll to the bottom of the Font menu. Then press PgUp until *TmsRmn Bold Portrait 18* appears on the screen.
6. Use the ↓ key to highlight this font and then press ↵ to select it. The text block you selected should now be displayed in boldface on the screen.
7. Turn off macro recording and assign a name to the macro.

If this font is on the bottom of the font list, you'll need to use a different strategy: Press PgUp several times first, then scroll back down.

PLAYING BACK THE MACRO

To play back the macro, you must first select the text block whose font is to be changed. Then press the macro name to begin playback of the macro. After a short pause, that block should be boldfaced, and the name of the new font should appear at the bottom of the screen.

Points to Ponder

If you change the selection of fonts that are currently available, this macro may then not work properly. The reason is that the keystrokes in steps 5 and 6 may no longer result in the correct font being highlighted, because the items displayed on the menu may be different. If this happens, you'll need to recreate the macro, following the above steps.

This macro will not work with rectangular blocks because in step 4 above the key **4** is pressed to select the correct menu item for choosing a new font. Unfortunately, in the Rectangular Block Operations menu this same item is numbered 5 rather than 4. However, you could create a similar macro for changing the font of a rectangular block: Duplicate the above steps, but replace the number 4 with 5 in step 4.

PRINTING SELECTED ADDRESS BOOK INFORMATION

Suppose that you periodically print selected records from a particular address book. For instance, one week you might want to print records from customers in Arizona, the next week customers from California, and so on.

You can create a macro that will automate this process by performing the following steps:

- Retrieve the form model into the working copy.
- Begin the process of printing the data.
- Pause to input the search instructions specifying which records are to be printed.
- Carry out the printing.

For a discussion of printing address book data, see "Printing Address Book Information" in Chapter 14.

In this example, assume that you have previously created and stored the form model (shown in Figure 16.2) in the file *CLINFO*. This form model is used for merging the address book information. In addition, assume that the name of the address book file was selected and stored in this file as well (see "Saving the Form Letter Model" in Chapter 14).

Here are the steps for creating the macro:

1. Begin macro recording from a blank working copy.
2. Retrieve the file CLINFO into the working copy.
3. Begin the printing: Press Ctrl-O. When the Print Options dialog box appears,

4. If necessary, enter the full name of the address book file on the line *Data file to merge*, and then press ↵. The Search Instructions display should appear (Figure 16.3).
5. Create a pause in macro recording: Press Alt-0, **1**, and then ↵.
6. Enter whatever search instructions you want (but don't press F10 yet.)
7. Resume macro recording: Press F9.
8. Press F10, and the information selected by your search instructions will be printed.

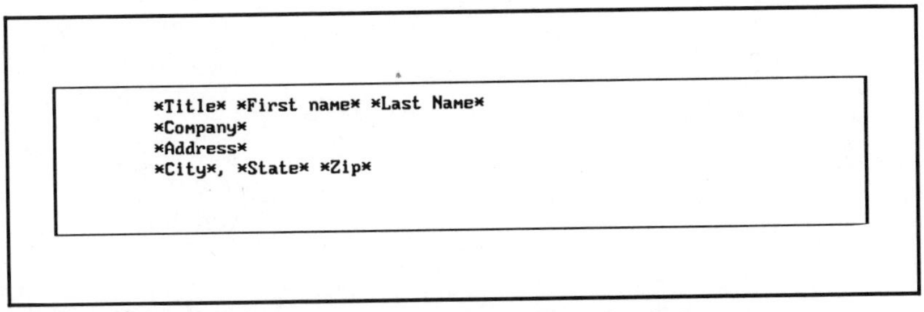

Figure 16.2: The form model for creating address book data

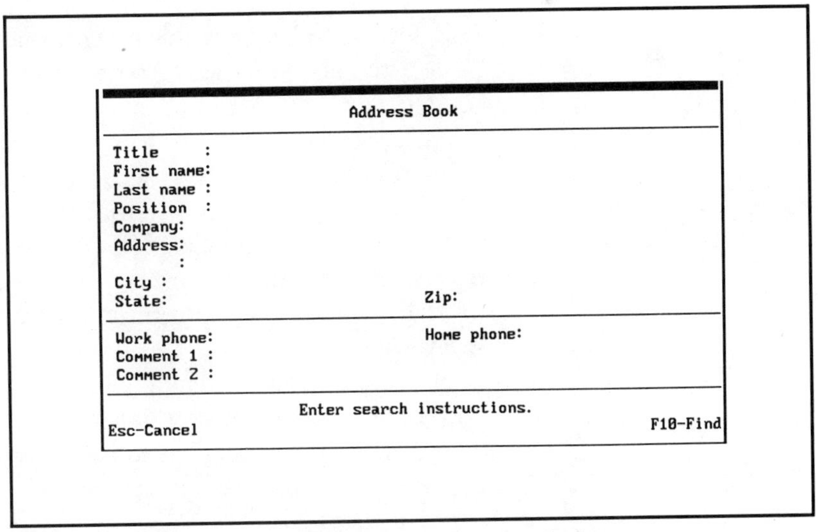

Figure 16.3: Enter any search instructions on this display

9. Follow any instructions on the screen to print the records.
10. Stop macro recording and assign a name to the macro.

Points to Ponder

Before recording this macro, you must make sure that:

- The form model has been stored in the file CLINFO (or whatever file name you wish to use).
- When the form model was stored to a disk file, the name of the correct address book was stored with it (by entering it in the Print Options dialog box).
- The printer is on and ready to receive data from the computer. Otherwise, Professional Write will pause with a warning message that the printer isn't ready. You'll then have to enter extra keystrokes, which will mess up your macro recording. Sooner or later, you'll then need to press F9 to cancel the macro recording, fix up the printer, and start over again.

PLAYING BACK THE MACRO

Before you play back this macro, make sure that all of the conditions listed above under "Points to Ponder" are correct. If any of these conditions isn't in effect, then Professional Write will require extra keystrokes, which will throw off the timing of the keystrokes being played back by the macro.

When you play back the macro, it will pause with the Search Instructions screen displayed (Figure 16.3). You can then enter whatever search instructions you want or leave the screen blank. Then press F9, the macro will continue, and the records that you specify will be printed out.

Note that if you accidentally press F10 instead of F9 at this point, you'll have to finish up by pressing the appropriate keys manually. Then, after the printing has finished, you can press F9 to let the rest of the macro play itself out harmlessly.

PRINTING ENVELOPES

You can use a slight variation of the macro described in the preceding section to print envelopes from selected information supplied by an address book. Before going on, please carefully review the previous section, "Printing Selected Address Book Information."

As in the previous example, assume that you have created and stored the form model shown in Figure 16.2 in the file *CLINFO*. This form model is used for merging the address book information. Also assume that the name of the address book file was selected and stored in this file as well (see "Saving the Form Letter Model" in Chapter 14.)

This macro will pause, allowing you to enter appropriate search instructions for selecting the records for the envelopes that are to be printed. Remember: As you create this macro, you need to go through the entire sequence for printing envelopes—up to and including actually printing them.

Here are the steps for creating the macro:

1. Make sure that your printer is set up for printing envelopes.
2. Begin macro recording from a blank working copy.
3. Retrieve the file CLINFO into the working copy.
4. Display the Print Options menu: press Ctrl-O. Then:
5. Create a pause before each page is printed: Press Tab three times and then enter **Y**.
6. Set up for printing envelopes: Press Tab once and then enter **E**.
7. If necessary, enter the full name of the address book file on the line *Data file to merge*, and then press ↵. When the Search Instructions form appears:
8. Create a pause in macro recording so that you can enter search instructions: Press Alt-0, **1**, and then ↵.
9. Enter whatever search instructions you want (but don't press F10 yet.)
10. Resume macro recording: Press F9.
11. Press F10, and the printing will begin.

12. As soon as the first message appears on the screen, stop macro recording and assign a name to the macro.
13. You can then either continue printing or you can abort printing by pressing Esc. In either case, the macro has been saved and is ready for use.

PLAYING BACK THE MACRO

Before playing back the macro, make sure that the printer is ready to receive data from the computer, and also that it's set up to print envelopes. When you play back the macro, Professional Write will pause before each envelope is printed, giving you a chance to insert the envelope in the printer. For more details, see the previous section labeled "Playing Back the Macro".

CREATING A CUSTOMIZED LETTERHEAD

If you have a laser printer, or a very high quality dot-matrix printer, you can print a customized letterhead at the top of each letter. You can even create different letterheads for different situations.

By using a suitable macro, you can create an entire letterhead with a single keystroke. As an example, this section will describe how to create a macro for generating the letterhead shown in Figure 16.4. In this figure, the top line is printed in Times Roman 30 Point Bold. The remaining lines are in Times Roman 14 Point Italic.

This particular macro will work only on a laser printer, but you can modify it to work on any type of printer.

User-Friendly Consulting Service

3853 Canon Avenue
Oakland, CA 94602
(415) 530-6653

Figure 16.4: You can create a customized letterhead with a macro

1. Starting with a blank working copy, begin macro recording.
2. Enter the entire letterhead (in this example, the text shown in Figure 16.4).
3. Change the font of the first line:
   - Select the line as a text block and then press F10.
   - Select *Change font or size* from the Block Operations menu.
   - Press PgUp several times*, until the top of the Font menu appears, then press PgDn until *TmsRmn Portrait Bold 30* appears.
   - Press ↓ until this font is highlighted, then press ↵ to select it.
4. Select the remaining lines as a text block.
5. Change the font of this block to Times Roman Portrait 14 Point, using steps similar to those described in step 3.
6. Again select the same lines as in step 4 as a text block and then press F10.
7. Select *Change style* from the Block Operations menu. When the Style menu appears:
8. Select *Italic*: Press 3 and then press ↵.
9. Turn off macro recording and select a name for the macro.

   *See "Starting from a Known Position," above, for an explanation of the keystrokes in this step.

Points to Ponder

You can create or play back this macro only if the fonts you select are currently available to Professional Write and your printer. That is, each font must exist either in a cartridge or soft font family that's currently selected.

If you change the selection of fonts that are currently available, this macro may then not work properly. The reason is that in step 6, the keystrokes needed to select the new font may change because the items displayed on the menu may be different. If this happens, you'll need to recreate the macro, following the above steps.

Each printer has memory limitations, so that if you try to download too many fonts to a printer, it will cease to function properly. If you want to use more fonts than your printer's memory will allow, you'll need either to get more memory for your printer, or reduce the number of fonts you are using. See Chapter 8 for more information about printers.

A
Installing Professional Write

THIS CHAPTER DESCRIBES THE HARDWARE YOU NEED to run Professional Write. It also describes how to create a set of backup diskettes for daily use so that the originals can be saved for special occasions. Also described in this chapter is the process for customizing Professional Write for your particular hardware setup, including specifying your printer, as well as other parameters that affect how you interact with Professional Write.

HARDWARE REQUIREMENTS

Installation of the Professional Write is straightforward, and only standard hardware is required. Before installing the program, read this section to make sure that you have the appropriate hardware. Professional Write is designed to run on a computer that is compatible with the IBM PC, IBM PC/XT, IBM PC/AT, or PS/2 (models 25, 30, 60, 70, and 80.) The computer can be either a hard- disk or floppy-disk machine. In addition, the computer must be equipped as follows:

Memory: The computer must have at least 512K of memory, preferably 640K.

If you plan to use Professional Write extensively, it's a good idea to use a computer with a hard disk. If your computer does not have one, you might consider purchasing a hard disk for it; the modest investment will be well worth it.

Disks: Professional Write will run with a hard disk and one or two floppy-disk drives ($5\frac{1}{4}$- inch or $3\frac{1}{2}$-inch); or with two floppy-disk drives of either type.

Monitor: Professional Write will work with most types of monochrome monitors and color monitors. If your computer uses a monochrome monitor and you want to use Professional Write's Preview feature, the computer should also have a Hercules-compatible display adapter (the board that controls the monitor).

Printer: Professional Write directly supports a great many printers, including all of the popular laser and dot-matrix varieties. In addition, the software will work with just about any other printer, even if it is old and the manual for it has disappeared.

MAKING BACKUPS

Before you install Professional Write, you should make backups of the original floppy disks that contain the Professional Write programs. A *backup* is a duplicate of an original disk. After you've made backups of all the original Professional Write disks, store the originals in a safe place and use the duplicates for working with the software. Then, if the duplicate disks are damaged in any way, you can make a new set of duplicates from the originals.

Protect your disks against accidental erasure. If you're using $5\frac{1}{4}$-inch disks, attach a *write-protect tab* to each of the original Professional Write disks. This tab should cover the little rectangular notch along one side of a disk. If you're using $3\frac{1}{2}$-inch disks, set the write-protect tab to the *protect* position.

As you read through the following sections, which describe how to make a set of duplicate disks for either hard-disk or floppy-disk computers, take careful note of the following terminology, which you'll see displayed on your computer's screen:

- **SOURCE diskette:** The original Professional Write disk
- **TARGET diskette:** The blank disk that is to become the backup for the original. This disk must be formatted.

HARD-DISK COMPUTERS

Remember: The symbol ↵ means to press the Enter key.

This section describes how to make backups of your original Professional Write diskettes with a hard-disk computer. Before going on, make sure that your computer is running, and that the C prompt (something like *C:\>*) is showing on the screen.

Here are the steps for copying one of your original Professional Write source diskettes to a blank disk:

1. Type in the following command: **DISKCOPY A: A:** (put a space between the first colon and the second *A*) and then press ↵. If the screen displays the message *Bad command or*

file name, you'll have to get assistance from someone familiar with your computer in order to find the program named DISKCOPY.

2. Insert the source diskette into drive A.
3. Press any key to continue.
4. Continue following the instructions that appear on the screen for inserting and removing disks. You may do a bit of disk switching, so be careful not to get the disks confused.
5. When the copy process is finished, the message *Copy another diskette (Y/N)?* will appear on the screen. Type in **N**.
6. Remove the backup disk and label it to match the label on the original, adding the word *BACKUP* to the label.

Store the original disks in a safe place and use only the backup disks.

Repeat the above procedure for each of your original Professional Write source diskettes. You can then install Professional Write on your hard disk, using the backup disks that you have just made.

FLOPPY-DISK COMPUTERS

This section describes how to make backups of your original Professional Write diskettes with a floppy-disk computer. Before going on, make sure that your computer is running, and that the A prompt (something like *A*>) is showing on the screen. Here are the steps for copying one of your original Professional Write diskettes to a blank disk:

Remember: The symbol ↵ means to press the Enter key.

1. Type in the following command: **DISKCOPY A: B:** (put a space between the first colon and the letter B) and then press ↵. If the screen displays the message *Bad command or file name,* you'll have to get assistance from someone familiar with your computer in order to find the program DISKCOPY.
2. Remove the DOS disk from drive A and insert the source diskette.
3. Insert a blank formatted disk into drive B.
4. Press any key to continue.

5. When the copy process is finished, the message *Copy another diskette (Y/N)?* will appear on the screen. Type in **N**.
6. Remove both disks from the computer.
7. Label the backup disk to match the label on the original disk, adding the word *BACKUP* to the label.

Store the original disks in a safe place and use only the backup disks.

Repeat the above procedure for each of your original Professional Write source diskettes. You can then start up Professional Write, using the backup disks that you've just made.

INSTALLING PROFESSIONAL WRITE ON A HARD-DISK COMPUTER

This section describes how to install Professional Write on a hard disk (no special installation is required for floppy-disk computers). Once you have installed Professional Write on a hard disk, it is there more or less permanently and can be easily run.

Here are the steps for installing the software:

1. Turn on the computer. Make sure that you see the DOS prompt, which will look something like *C:*\>.
2. Create a new subdirectory called \PW for storing the Professional Write programs. Enter the following commands:

```
MD \PW ↵
CD \PW ↵
```

After you have entered the above two DOS commands, you should again see a DOS prompt. You are now "in" the new subdirectory called PW—that is, any file manipulations that take place will normally be in and out of this subdirectory.

Now you're ready to copy the Professional Write programs into the subdirectory.

3. Insert the backup floppy labeled *Start Up Disk; Disk 1* into drive A. (For 3½-inch floppies, the disk is labeled *Start Up and Program Disk.*)

4. Copy the programs from this floppy disk onto the hard disk with the following command:

```
COPY A:*.*
```

5. Repeat steps 3 and 4 for each of your backup floppy disks. (You should have a total of either six 5¼-inch or three 3½-inch disks.)

Your Professional Write programs are now "permanently" stored on the hard disk in the directory \PW, from which they can be easily started at any time. Store the floppy disks in a safe place. You'll need them only if something accidentally damages the programs on the hard disk.

CUSTOMIZING PROFESSIONAL WRITE FOR YOUR COMPUTER

The first time you run Professional Write, you'll need to use the Setup program to customize the software for your particular hardware. Setup is menu driven and very easy to use; you make your selections from a series of menus displayed on the screen. This section will describe the various selections you can make, which are:

- The printer attached to your computer.
- A secondary printer that may be occasionally used with Professional Write.
- Any codes that must be sent to your printer before and after a document is printed.
- The name of the default directory you plan to use for storing your documents.
- The name of the work drive to be used by Professional Write when it performs various housekeeping chores.
- The color format to be used for Professional Write's displays.
- The speed at which Professional Write updates the information on your screen.

- The default edit mode set by Professional Write each time you begin using the program.

The selections you make with Setup aren't written in stone. At any later time you can enter Setup from within Professional Write and change any of the current selections. For example, if you someday attach a new printer to your computer, you can then enter Setup and make the new printer selection.

As you work with Professional Write, you'll find that some changes you want to make must be done from Setup. For instance, if you want to select a different regular font (the font in which most of the text will be printed) for a particular document, you would enter Setup and then choose the new font. This type of operation usually takes less than a minute.

You can use Professional Write's context-sensitive Help system at any time while you are using Setup: Press the Help key (F1) and helpful information about what you are doing at the moment will be displayed. For more information about the Help system, see "Getting On-Line Help" in Chapter 1.

STARTING UP PROFESSIONAL WRITE

Before you can customize Professional Write, you must first start it up:

Hard-disk computers: type in the following two DOS commands, *remembering to press ↵ after each command*:

```
CD \PW
PW
```

Floppy-disk computers:

1. Insert the disk labeled "Start Up" into drive A.
2. Type **PW** and then press the ↵ key.
3. If you are using 5¼-inch disks, follow the instructions on the screen to swap disks.

If your display is unreadable, skip to the section "Setting Display Colors" in this chapter.

When Professional Write begins to run, the Main menu will appear on the screen (Figure A.1).

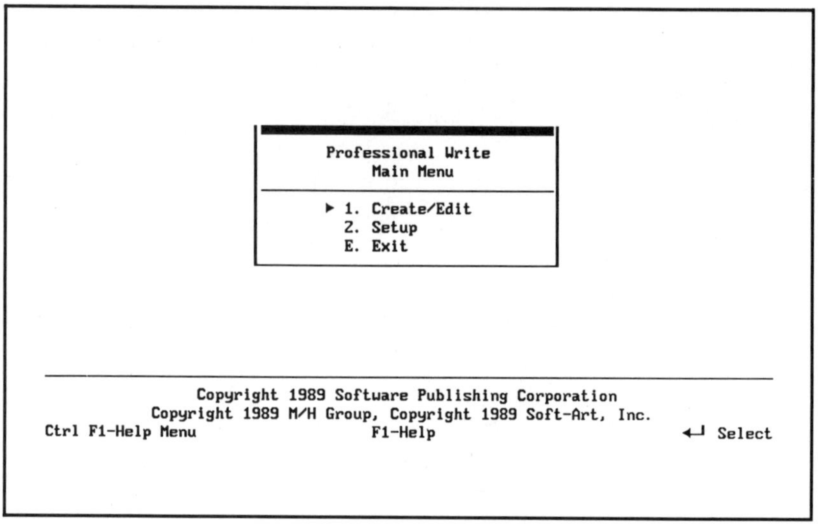

Figure A.1: The Main menu

RUNNING THE SETUP PROGRAM

To run the Setup program, select *Setup* by pressing the number **2** on the keyboard (use the number key at the top of the keyboard). When Setup runs, the Setup menu appears (Figure A.2). This is the menu you use to begin selecting the various options you want.

To leave the Setup program and return to the Main menu, press Esc when the Setup menu is displayed.

HOW TO SELECT A PRINTER

For more information about printers and fonts, refer to Chapter 8.

You can set up two printers to use with Professional Write—Printer 1 and Printer 2. For various technical reasons explained in the main text, there is little reason ever to use Printer 2, so this section will describe only how to select Printer 1. If you want to select a second printer, follow the instructions below, substituting *Printer 2* for *Printer 1*.

When you select a printer, you may also need to make other choices as well, depending on the printer type and other considerations.

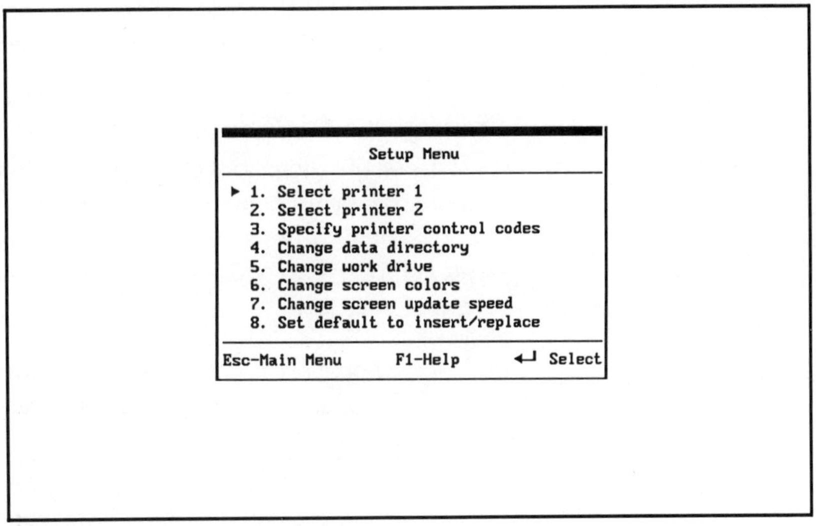

Figure A.2: Begin selecting each option from this menu

These include:

- **Font cartridge selection.** Some laser printers have plug-in slots for one or two font cartridges. If you are using a cartridge with your printer, you'll want to select it as part of the printer selection process.
- **Soft fonts.** With some laser printers, you can download soft fonts from your computer's hard disk. If you plan to do this, you'll want to tell the Setup program which group of soft fonts you will be using.
- **The regular font.** Most printers can output in several different fonts. If yours is one of these, you must select which font is to be used as the *regular font*, that is, the standard font for your documents. For a dot-matrix printer, the selection is limited to fonts built into the printer's hardware. For a laser printer, the font selection is determined by all of the following: (1) the built-in fonts, (2) the font cartridges plugged into the printer, and (3) the fonts included in the soft font family that you select as part of the printer selection process.

- **Soft font directory.** If you are using soft font files, you must specify the directory in which these files are stored.

Selecting the Printer

This section describes the steps for selecting a printer. If you have a dot-matrix printer, not all of these steps will apply. In addition, if your printer can output in only one font, then most of these steps won't apply. The text below indicates which steps apply to which types of printers.

1. Choose *Select printer 1* from the Setup menu, by pressing **1** on the keyboard. The Printer menu appears on screen (Figure A.3).
2. Scroll through the list, using the PgDn and PgUp keys, until the name of your printer appears. If you can't find the printer's name, select a printer that you think is similar to it, such as a later model by the same maker or one that's compatible with yours. Otherwise, select *Unlisted Printer.*
3. Highlight the printer's name, using the four cursor keys. **Don't press ↵ yet.**

The port is initially set by Professional Write as *PRN* because the majority of printers are attached to this port. If you're not sure which port is attached to your printer, you'll need to consult higher authority.

Before leaving this menu, you may need to specify the port (the connection on your computer) to which your printer is attached. The port currently assigned is shown on the third line up from the bottom of the screen (see Figure A.3). If this isn't correct, change it as follows:

1. Press Tab and the printer port that's currently selected is highlighted on the right side of the screen.
2. Select the correct port name: Highlight the name of the port to which your printer is connected and then press ↵.

If you selected Unlisted Printer, press ↵ and then skip to "Selecting an Unlisted Printer," below.

If your printer doesn't print in more than one font, skip to the section labeled "Customizing for a Serial Port," below.

```
                         Printer 1 Selection
                   Printers                          Printer Ports

 ▸ Unlisted Printer         Diablo 635                    PRN:
   ALPS ALQ 200/300         Epson EX-800/1000             LPT1:
   ALPS P2400C              Epson FX-80/100 III           LPT2:
   Apple LaserWriter        Epson FX-85/185               LPT3:
   Apple LaserWriter +      Epson FX-86e/286e             AUX:
   Apple LW II NT           Epson FX-850/1050             COM1:
   AST TurboLaser /PS       Epson GQ-3500                 COM2:
   Brother HR Series        Epson JX-80
   Brother Twinriter dp     Epson LQ-500
   Brother Twinriter wp     Epson LQ-800/1000
   C. Itoh Prowriter Jr     Epson LQ-850/1050
   Canon BJ 130             Epson LQ-950
   DEC LN03                 Epson LQ-1500
   Diablo 630 ECS           Epson LQ-2500

 Printer: Unlisted Printer
 Printer port: LPT1:

                    Select printer and printer port.
Esc-Cancel   Tab-Select port    F1-Help   PgDn-More printers    ↵ Continue
```

Figure A.3: Select your printer from this menu

Selecting the Soft Font Family

This section applies only to Hewlett-Packard laser printers and compatibles. If you are not using one of these, skip to the section labeled "Selecting the Regular Font," below.

For more information about soft fonts, see Chapter 8.

After you have selected your printer from the Printer menu, a Setup menu similar to that shown in Figure A.4 will appear.

Professional Write can access only certain fonts: those built into your printer, those in the font family you select, and those in the font cartridge(s) you select. Therefore, before selecting a font family, decide on which fonts you plan to use most frequently.

Professional Write can access only one soft family at a time, even if you have fonts from several families on your hard disk. If you want to use a new set of fonts, you must select the corresponding font family, using this part of Setup. This is the only way that Professional Write can gain access to the fonts in that family.

To select the soft font family you plan to use:

1. Choose *Select soft font family* by pressing **3** in the Setup menu. The Soft Font menu shown in Figure A.5 appears.

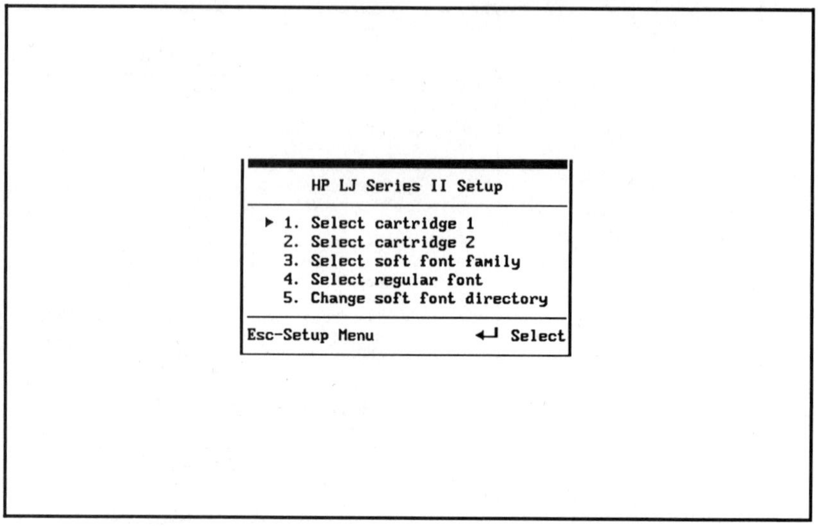

Figure A.4: A Setup menu for a printer that supports cartridges and soft fonts

2. Select the soft font family: scroll through the list, using the PgDn and PgUp keys. When the family name that you want appears, highlight it by using the ↑ and ↓ keys and then press ↵. The Setup menu for your printer will reappear.

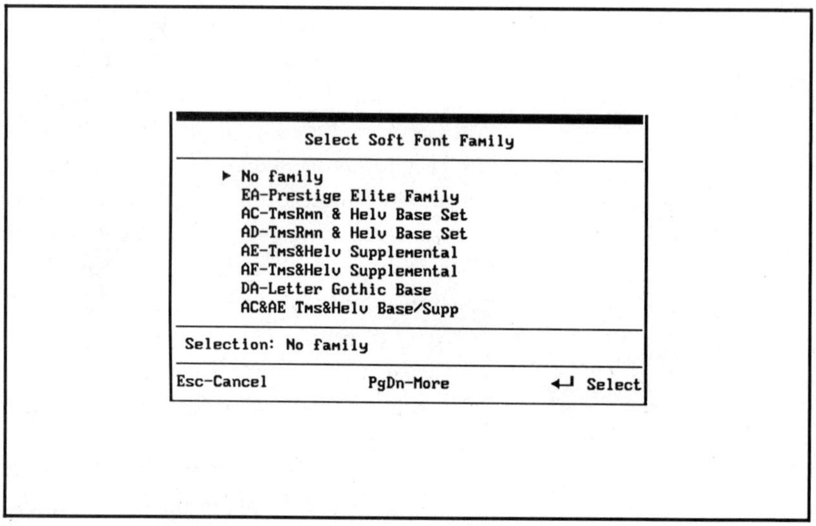

Figure A.5: Select the soft font family from this menu

Points to Ponder

- Before selecting a soft font family, make sure that all of the fonts in this family are installed on your hard disk.
- If, for some reason, you decide to stop using soft fonts, enter this part of the Setup program and then select *No family* from the Soft Font menu.

Selecting the Soft Font Directory

You need to tell Professional Write where to find your soft font files. To do this:

1. Select *Change soft font directory* from the Setup menu. When the dialog box appears (Figure A.6):
2. Enter the name of the disk drive and/or directory where your soft font files are stored, and the setup menu for your printer will reappear. You can now specify any cartridges you plan to use with your printer.

Copy your soft font files to this directory before you try to use any of these fonts with Professional Write.

Selecting the Printer Cartridges

If your printer doesn't have slots for installing font cartridges, skip to the section labeled "Selecting the Regular Font," below.

If you plan to use one or two cartridges with your printer, you need to identify them to Professional Write, so it knows which fonts are available:

1. Choose *Select cartridge 1* or *Select cartridge* from the Setup menu (which of these messages appears will depend on the printer you are setting up). When the Select Cartridge menu appears (Figure A.7):
2. Select the cartridge from the list:
   - Scroll through the list until the cartridge name appears;
   - Highlight the name, using the ↓ and ↑ keys;
   - Press ↵ to select the cartridge.

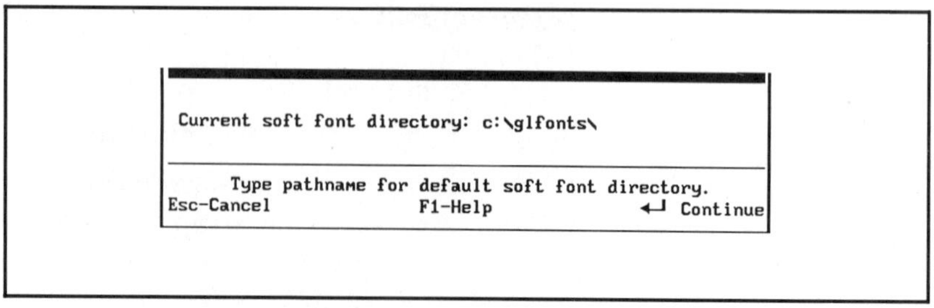

Figure A.6: Enter the name of the soft font directory here

If you are using two cartridges with your printer, choose *Select cartridge 2* from the Setup menu and then select the second cartridge using the above steps.

If, for some reason, you decide to stop using cartridges with your printer, enter this part of the Setup program and then select *No cartridge* from the Select Cartridge menu. This informs Professional Write that the fonts in that cartridge are no longer available.

Selecting the Regular Font

For any printer that can output in several different fonts, you must select the *regular font*, which is the default that will be selected by Professional Write for output. For HP Printers and compatibles, choose

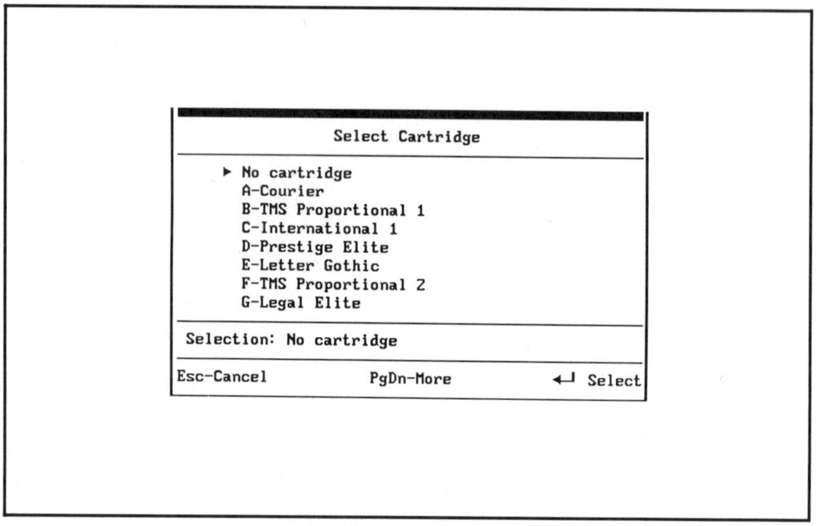

Figure A.7: Select your cartridge from this list

Select regular font from the Setup menu. For other printers, the Regular Font menu will automatically appear after you select your printer.

The Regular Font menu (similar to that shown in Figure A.8) lists all of the fonts currently available to your printer. For dot-matrix printers, these are the built-in fonts. For laser printers, these are the built-in fonts and also the fonts in the font family and cartridge(s) you selected.

To select the regular font:

1. Scroll through the menu until you see the font you want to select.
2. Highlight that font name and then press ↵.

Selecting an Unlisted Printer

Professional Write will be able to use only those styles for which you fill in the corresponding codes.

If you selected *Unlisted Printer* above, Professional Write has no information about which codes to send to the printer for special styles, such as boldface or italics. If your printer manual is available, you can find what these codes are and enter them on the Control Codes display that appears (Figure A.9) after you select *Unlisted Printer*.

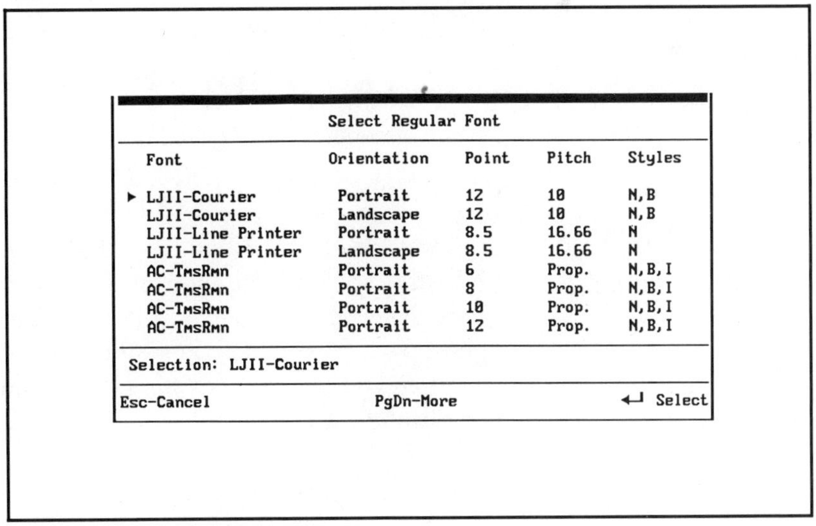

Select Regular Font

Font	Orientation	Point	Pitch	Styles
▸ LJII-Courier	Portrait	12	10	N,B
LJII-Courier	Landscape	12	10	N,B
LJII-Line Printer	Portrait	8.5	16.66	N
LJII-Line Printer	Landscape	8.5	16.66	N
AC-TmsRmn	Portrait	6	Prop.	N,B,I
AC-TmsRmn	Portrait	8	Prop.	N,B,I
AC-TmsRmn	Portrait	10	Prop.	N,B,I
AC-TmsRmn	Portrait	12	Prop.	N,B,I

Selection: LJII-Courier

Esc-Cancel   PgDn-More   ↵ Select

Figure A.8: Select the regular font from this menu

```
                  Control Codes for Unlisted Printer
 ____________________________________________________________________

 Boldface on       :
 Boldface off      :
 Underline on      :
 Underline off     :
 Italics on        :
 Italics off       :
 Superscript on    :
 Superscript off   :
 Subscript on      :
 Subscript off     :
 Compressed on     :
 Compressed off    :
 Letter-quality on:
 Draft mode on     :

 ____________________________________________________________________
                     Type printer control codes.
 Esc-Cancel                   F1-Help                       ↵ Continue
```

Figure A.9: Enter the control codes for an unlisted printer on this screen

To make an entry in this display, move the cursor to that line by using the Tab and Shift-Tab keys and then enter the code for that entry. Each entry must be entered as a *decimal* ASCII code, which is one or more two-digit numbers separated by commas. For example, suppose that your printer manual indicates that the code for *Turn on italics* is any of the following:

ASCII:	ESC 4
Decimal:	27 52
Hexadecimal:	1B 34

You would enter **27,52** on the line marked *Italics on*.

If you can't find the code for a particular style, just leave it blank. If you later select this style while working with a document, it will be ignored when the document is printed.

When you are finished filling in your entries, press ↵ to return to the Setup menu.

Customizing for a Serial Printer

If you selected a serial port (either AUX, COM1, or COM2) for your printer during the printer selection above, then the Serial Port

Settings dialog box (Figure A.10) will appear after you have made any other necessary selections for your printer.

If you don't know what the settings should be for your printer, leave the entries that appear in this box; they are the ones most commonly used. However, if the printer then fails to work properly, you'll need to consult the manuals for your printer and computer to determine the correct values to use here.

To enter a new value on a line in this dialog box:

1. Move the cursor to the line, using the Tab and Shift-Tab keys.
2. Enter the new value on the line. Make sure you completely erase the old value.

When you are finished entering the new values, press ↵ and the Setup menu will reappear (Figure A.2).

SETTING UP FOR SPECIAL PRINTER CODES

If you want to send special codes to the printer before and after each page and document, you can do so by selecting *Specify printer control codes* from the Setup menu and then filling in the display that

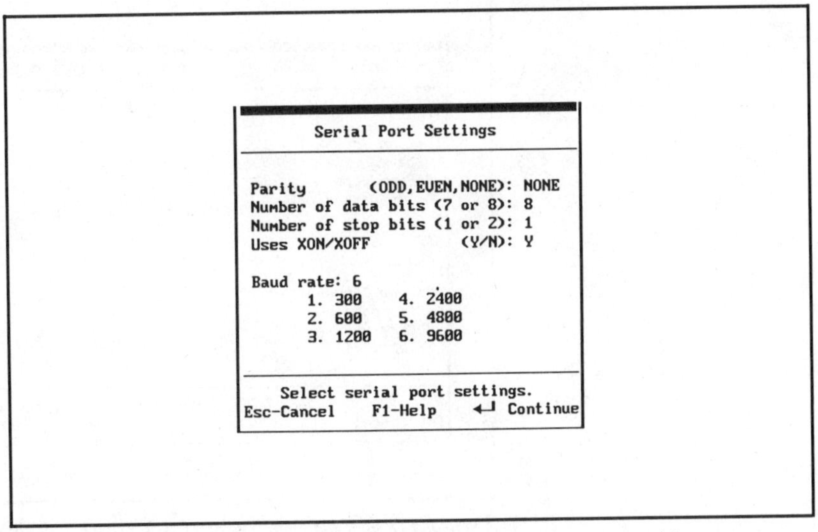

Figure A.10: Enter the information about your serial port on this screen

appears (Figure A.11). Although this option was created specifically for use with sheet and bin feeders, you may find it useful for other applications as well.

To make an entry, move the cursor to that line by using the Tab and Shift-Tab keys and then enter the code for that entry. Each entry must be entered as a *decimal* ASCII code, which is one or more two-digit numbers separated by commas. If you want to enter several codes for a particular entry, separate the codes by commas as well.

When you are finished filling in your entries, press ↵ to return to the Setup menu.

SELECTING A DEFAULT DATA DIRECTORY

If you are using a hard-disk computer, you can have Professional Write automatically select a particular directory each time you read and write documents. This handy feature can save you a lot of keystrokes during the course of a session with Professional Write.

To establish a default directory:

1. Select *Change data directory* from the Setup menu. When the dialog box shown in Figure A.12 appears:

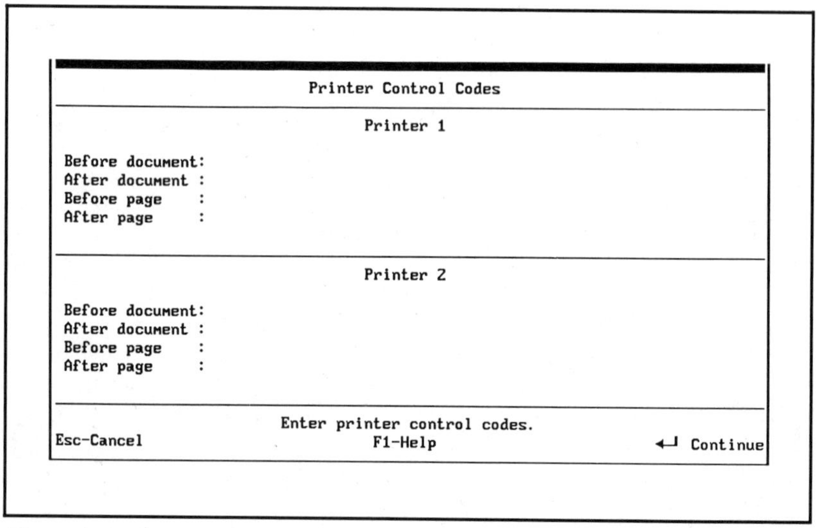

Figure A.11: Enter special printer control codes on this screen

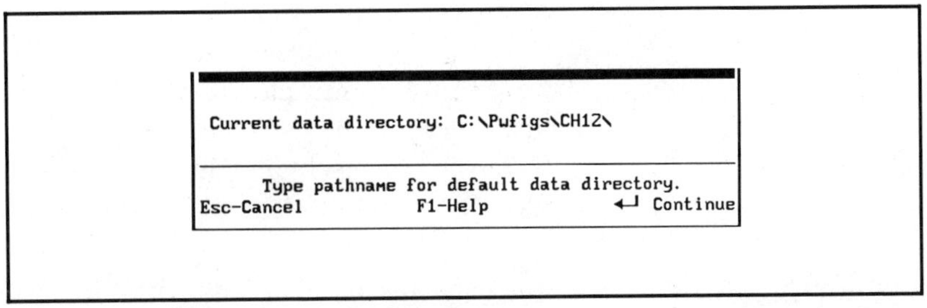

Figure A.12: Enter the name of the default data directory in this dialog box

Make sure to blank out the entire previous entry.

2. Enter the name of the disk drive and/or directory name. Make sure to include the complete path name of the directory. For instance, to use the directory \MYDATA on drive C, enter **C:\MYDATA**.

3. When you are finished, press ↵ to return to the Setup menu.

As you work with different groups of files, you may frequently want to change the default data directory. Because using Setup is so easy, you can change the default in a few seconds: Exit back to the Main menu from whatever you're doing with Professional Write, select *Setup*, and then follow the above steps.

Here are some other things to note about using a default data directory:

- If you are using a floppy-disk computer, you can specify **B:** as the default directory. Professional Write will then automatically access drive B whenever you retrieve or save documents.
- Specifying a default directory doesn't restrict you from using other directories as well; you can always specify any directory you wish for storing and retrieving files.
- When you select a default directory, it doesn't necessarily have to exist at that time. Just make sure you create it before you attempt to save or retrieve a document with Professional Write.

SELECTING A WORK DRIVE

For certain housekeeping chores, such as sorting files and converting one file format to another, Professional Write needs to make use of temporary files, which are created on the *current work drive*. Initially, this is set to C by Professional Write, but you may want (or have) to change it. For example, if you don't have a hard-disk computer, you should change the work drive to B.

Here's how to change the work drive:

1. Select *Change work drive* from the Setup menu.
2. Enter the name of the disk drive to be used for storing temporary Professional Write files and then press ↵ to return to the Setup menu.

SELECTING THE DISPLAY COLORS

If you are using a color monitor, you can select from three different color combinations used by Professional Write for displaying screens. To find the one you prefer, you'll have to experiment with each of them.

To select a color combination:

1. Select *Change screen colors* from the Setup menu.
2. Select the color combination you want to try by pressing the appropriate menu number. That color combination is established, and the Setup menu reappears.

With some computers, your screen may be unreadable when you start up Professional Write because the color combination that's currently set is wrong for the computer. If this is the case for your computer, you can "blindly" select *Monochrome* from the Setup program, which should make Professional Write's display appear normally. Here's how to do this:

1. Start with the DOS prompt displayed on your screen.
2. Start up Professional Write:

   Hard-disk computers: Enter the name of the directory containing Professional Write and then enter **PW**.

   Floppy-disk computers: Put the disk labeled *Start Up* in drive A and then enter **PW**.

3. Wait for the disk drives to stop moving.
4. Enter the following keystrokes, *exactly as shown*: **2, 6, 4.**

The Professional Write display should now appear normally, and you can proceed with the Setup program.

SELECTING THE SCREEN UPDATE SPEED

Professional Write can update your screen displays at two different speed rates: *fast* and *slow*. Normally, *fast* is preferable unless there are some noticeable unpleasantries on your Professional Write screen displays, such as bright flashes or other garbage.

When you first install Professional Write, it automatically detects what type of monitor you are using. If it's a color display, the *slow* screen update speed is automatically chosen.

Try changing this to *fast* and then see if your display appears all right. If it doesn't, return to Setup and change the update speed back to *slow*.

To change the update speed:

1. Select *Change screen update speed* from the Setup menu.
2. To select the *fast* speed, enter **Y** and then press ↵.
3. To select the *slow* speed, enter **N** and then press ↵.

SELECTING THE DEFAULT EDIT MODE

You can edit a document in one of two edit modes: *Insert* or *Overwrite*. Either of these can be chosen as the default setting, which is then automatically selected whenever you begin a Professional Write session. You can easily switch from one edit mode to the other within Professional Write with a single keystroke. Initially, Professional Write comes with *Insert* as the default setting.

To select either edit mode:

1. Select *Set default to insert/replace* from the Setup menu.
2. Enter either **I** for *Insert* or **R** for *Overwrite* (called *replace* by Professional Write) and then press ↵ to return to the Setup menu.

B COMMONLY OCCURRING PROBLEMS

This appendix lists some of the more difficult to understand problems that occur from time to time with Professional Write.

Problem: When a word is deleted from the beginning of a line, the *new* first word on that line may fit on the previous line, but Professional Write doesn't notice this and doesn't reformat the paragraph.

Solution: This is a basic flaw with Professional Write. You'll have to reformat the paragraph yourself: Position the cursor at the beginning of the word that should be moved up and then press the ⟵ key until the word jumps up to the previous line. If the word won't fit, nothing will happen.

This problem also occurs when you delete an entire line and the first word of the following line should be moved up.

Problem: Some lines in a table wrap around to the following line when printed.

Solution: Each line that incorrectly wraps around may be missing a hard return at its end. To add a hard return at the end of a line: Make sure that the Overwrite mode is on (cursor is a blinking line), position the cursor anywhere on the line, press End, and then press ↵.

Problem: A line in the middle of a paragraph ends abruptly, or it doesn't justify correctly.

Solution: There's a hard return where the line ends. To eliminate this hard return: Place the cursor on the offending line, press End, and then press Del.

Problem: How to keep two words together on the same line (that is, preventing the two words from splitting across two adjacent lines).

Solution: Delete the space between the two words, then enter a hard space (Ctrl-Spacebar). Professional Write interprets this as a single word and won't break it up at the end of a line.

Problem: When a document is viewed in the Preview mode, the page breaks don't appear in the same place as when the document is printed.

Solution: There are several possible explanations for this, most of which can't be fixed. The most likely cause is the existence in the document of a *JOIN* command. If you are joining another document to the one in the working copy, the joined document doesn't appear in Preview. This throws off the position of the page breaks as shown in Preview.

Another possible reason for incorrect page break positions is the existence of a *PRINTER* command in the document. Some *PRINTER* commands reposition the printer, and Preview can't know about this.

Problem: A line doesn't center or right-justify correctly.

Solution: The reason may have to do with the existence of proportionally spaced fonts in the document and the use of the Font Format print style. Insert either a *CENTER* or *RIGHT* command on a blank line (depending on what you want to do) immediately before the offending line. The *CENTER* (or *RIGHT*) command forces the following line to be centered, regardless of any other circumstances. Only the line immediately after the command is affected.

Problem: (1) Columns on a page don't line up properly when printed; or (2) when automatic indenting is used, the text doesn't line up correctly when printed.

Solution: The reason is probably that you are using a proportional font. To fix the problem, assign new tab positions to all of the problem lines. Each tab should correspond to the beginning of a column or an indented line. Then, make sure that the Font

Format print style is selected in the Print Options dialog box (for details, see ''Working with Columns'' in Chapter 9 and ''How to use Tabs'' in Chapter 5).

INDEX

E

F

J

K

L

M

N

O

P

T

TO JOIN THE SYBEX MAILING LIST OR ORDER BOOKS
PLEASE COMPLETE THIS FORM

NAME ______________________ COMPANY ______________________

STREET ______________________ CITY ______________________

STATE ______________________ ZIP ______________________

☐ PLEASE MAIL ME MORE INFORMATION ABOUT **SYBEX** TITLES

ORDER FORM (There is no obligation to order)

PLEASE SEND ME THE FOLLOWING:

TITLE	QTY	PRICE
______________	____	____
______________	____	____
______________	____	____
______________	____	____
TOTAL BOOK ORDER	____	$____

SHIPPING AND HANDLING PLEASE ADD $2.00 PER BOOK VIA UPS ______

FOR OVERSEAS SURFACE ADD $5.25 PER BOOK PLUS $4.40 REGISTRATION FEE ______

FOR OVERSEAS AIRMAIL ADD $18.25 PER BOOK PLUS $4.40 REGISTRATION FEE ______

CALIFORNIA RESIDENTS PLEASE ADD APPLICABLE SALES TAX ______

TOTAL AMOUNT PAYABLE ______

☐ CHECK ENCLOSED ☐ VISA
☐ MASTERCARD ☐ AMERICAN EXPRESS

ACCOUNT NUMBER ______________________

EXPIR. DATE ________ DAYTIME PHONE ______________

CUSTOMER SIGNATURE ______________________________________

CHECK AREA OF COMPUTER INTEREST:

☐ BUSINESS SOFTWARE

☐ TECHNICAL PROGRAMMING

☐ OTHER: ______________________

THE FACTOR THAT WAS MOST IMPORTANT IN YOUR SELECTION:

☐ THE SYBEX NAME

☐ QUALITY

☐ PRICE

☐ EXTRA FEATURES

☐ COMPREHENSIVENESS

☐ CLEAR WRITING

☐ OTHER ______________________

OTHER COMPUTER TITLES YOU WOULD LIKE TO SEE IN PRINT:

____

____

OCCUPATION

☐ PROGRAMMER

☐ SENIOR EXECUTIVE

☐ COMPUTER CONSULTANT

☐ SUPERVISOR

☐ MIDDLE MANAGEMENT

☐ ENGINEER/TECHNICAL

☐ CLERICAL/SERVICE

☐ BUSINESS OWNER/SELF EMPLOYED

☐ TEACHER

☐ HOMEMAKER

☐ RETIRED

☐ STUDENT

☐ OTHER: ______________

CHECK YOUR LEVEL OF COMPUTER USE

- ☐ NEW TO COMPUTERS
- ☐ INFREQUENT COMPUTER USER
- ☐ FREQUENT USER OF ONE SOFTWARE PACKAGE:
  NAME ____________________
- ☐ FREQUENT USER OF MANY SOFTWARE PACKAGES
- ☐ PROFESSIONAL PROGRAMMER

OTHER COMMENTS:

____
____
____
____
____
____
____

PLEASE FOLD, SEAL, AND MAIL TO SYBEX

SYBEX, INC.
2021 CHALLENGER DR. #100
ALAMEDA, CALIFORNIA USA
94501

SEAL

Special Keys

Esc	Stop current operation or exit from a menu or screen
↵	Continue current operation or start new paragraph
F1	Help
Ins	Switch between Insert and Overwrite edit modes
Del	Delete character at cursor
←	Delete character to left of cursor